Daily Surviva
Divorced Men

Surviving & Thriving
Beyond Your Divorce

Days 1-91

Dale J. Brown, Ph.D.

Beat Dog Press
2019

Praise for
A Daily Survival Guide for Divorced Men

I get two to four requests a day for a book endorsement and I must refuse most of them, but everywhere I open this book there is wisdom—and hard won wisdom—plus the need is so urgent and so widespread! So I want to go on record in support of Dale Brown's fine book. I know its truth from years of working with men.

– **Fr. Richard Rohr**, author of
Falling Upward: A Spirituality for the Two Halves of Life

In *Daily Survival Guide for Divorced Men* Dale Brown has written a book that challenges, inspires, and comforts men who have experienced divorce—and other losses—and are confronting the pain of it. As a hospice chaplain, Brown is acquainted with loss. Even more, he has experienced the deep pain of divorce himself and he writes out of the wellspring of experience. God is for us. Jesus is the healer. The Holy Spirit is the comforter, helper, and one who comes alongside. This devotional speaks directly to wounded men and walks with them on a daily journey to healing, wholeness, and forgiveness.

– **Dr. Everett L. Worthington**, Jr., author of
Forgiving and Reconciling: Bridges to Wholeness and Hope
Professor of Psychology, Virginia Commonwealth University

There is no better teacher than experience. Dale has walked through the pain of divorce which allows him to not only relate, but provide relevant help to other men walking through divorce themselves. This workbook helps other men with practical, powerful principles Dale has learned and applied first-hand. I recommend this material without reservation and can't wait to see how God will use this in the lives of men who need to know that a valley in life is not a dead-end road but simply a pathway to a life of joy and fulfillment.

– **Dr. Micah Davidson**, Lead Pastor, Real Life Church, Austin, Texas

Dr. Dale Brown has created one of the finest resources I have ever seen for men wandering through the pain and grief of divorce. He writes with a depth borne of his own experience that proves to be both therapeutic and inspirational. He invites you to join him on a journey of recovery and hope!

– **Dr. Dowell Loftis**, Director of the Connections Team
Baptist General Convention of Texas

I'm thrilled Dale Brown has used the universal language of initiation to tie together modern divorce dynamics for men with his devotional flavor. Modern men have had a handful of generations without any positive, culturally accepted initiation into healthy manhood, which correlates with the historical rise in divorce through the 20th century. In my experience, the two dynamics are inextricably linked. Ironically, in my 30 years of working mostly with boys of single mothers, I've come to see how so many men struggle to be successful husbands and fathers without some useful cultural guidance.

Divorce often makes us guys feel like failures as men (mine happened after 31 years of marriage). I'm lucky I had thousands of wild boys to push my buttons, make me find what would make them better and happier men, and listen to countless men question the very existence of their elusive "manhood." Brown's Daily Guide is useful whether you're creationist or evolutionist. He offers a steady, daily guide for his readers with a nice blend of ideas and approaches to help men find a healthier and happier way to reframe life after divorce.

— **Bret Stephenson,** author of *From Boys to Men: Spiritual Rites of Passage in an Indulgent Age*, founder of The Adolescent Mind
Founder and Executive Director of Labyrinth Center

Dale Brown is uniquely qualified to write this book for divorced men. He knows firsthand the devastation of rejection and yet has plotted a biblical and realistic course toward wholeness. Dale is a gifted communicator who presents bite-sized thoughts in a hopeful and memorable fashion. I highly recommend this book!

— **Dr. Jim Meyer**, author of *Church Coup* and
Founder of Restoring Kingdom Builders, Menifee, California

I have never been divorced but I know what it is like to lose what is most important in one's life. From my own journey out of despair and hopelessness I am convinced that in losing a spouse to suicide, one goes through a unique grieving process very different from losing a mate from physical illness. Dale Brown's extraordinary book has provided many pearls of wisdom for those who have walked in my shoes. That that was not his intention is a fine testament to the poignancy and words of universal wisdom that he has penned. I only wish I had had his guide twenty-five years ago as it would have provided great comfort and counsel to me when I needed it most.

— **Dick Collins,** Engineer, Phillips

All scripture quotations, unless otherwise indicated, are taken from the *Holy Bible, New International Version®*, NIV®. Copyright © 1973, 1978, 1984, 2011 by Biblica, Inc.™ Used by permission of Zondervan. All rights reserved worldwide. www.zondervan.com. The "NIV" And "New International Version" are trademarks registered in the United States Patent and Trademark office by Biblica, Inc.™

Other Scripture quotations are from the following sources:

Scripture quotations marked (MSG) are from *The Message*. Copyright © by Eugene H. Peterson 1993, 1994, 1995, 1996, 2000, 2001, 2002. Used by permission of Tyndale House Publishers, Inc.

Scripture quotations marked (ESV) are from *The Holy Bible, English Standard Version®* (ESV®), copyright © 2001 by Crossway, a publishing ministry of Good News Publishers. Used by permission. All rights reserved.

Scripture quotations marked (NLT) are taken from the *Holy Bible, New Living Translation*, copyright © 1996, 2004, 2007, 2013 by Tyndale House Foundation. Used by permission of Tyndale House Publishers, Inc., Carol Stream, Illinois 60188. All rights reserved.

Scripture quotations marked (AMP) are taken from *The Amplified® Bible*, Copyright © 1954, 1958, 1962, 1964, 1965, 1987, by the Lockman Foundation. Used by permission. (www.Lockman.org.) All rights reserved.

All books cited are from the Kindle Edition of the book unless otherwise noted.

Cover by ________________

The ebook contains information about divorce and dissolution of marriage. The information is not advice, and should not be treated as such. You must not rely on the information in the ebook as an alternative to legal, medical or financial advice from an appropriately qualified professional. If you have any specific questions about any legal, medical or financial matters you should consult an appropriately qualified professional. You should never delay seeking legal advice, disregard legal advice, or commence or discontinue any legal action because of information in the ebook.

Although the author and publisher have made every effort to ensure that the information in this book was correct at press time, the author and publisher do not assume and hereby disclaim any liability to any party for any loss, damage, or disruption caused by errors or omissions, whether such errors or omissions result from negligence, accident, or any other cause.

I have tried to recreate events, locales and conversations from my memories of them. In order to maintain their anonymity in some instances I have changed the names of individuals and places, I may have changed some identifying characteristics and details such as physical properties, occupations and places of residence.

Daily Survival Guide for Divorced Men: Surviving and Thriving Beyond Your Divorce Days 1-91

Copyright © 2019 by Dale J Brown

Library of Congress Cataloging-in-Publication Data

Brown, Dale J., 1961–

The Daily Survival Guide for Divorced Men: *Surviving & Thriving Beyond Your Divorce* Days 1-91 / Dale Brown.

p. cm.

ISBN 978-1-73231-940-0 (Soft cover)

1. Devotional calendars. 2. Devotional literature, English. I. Title.

BV4811. A535 1993

242.'2–dc20 93-18858

All rights reserved. No part of this publication may be reproduced, stored in a retrieval system, or transmitted in any form or by any means—electronic, mechanical, digital, photocopy, recording, or any other—except for brief quotations in printed reviews, without the prior permission of the publisher.

Printed in the United States of America

10 11 12 13 14 15 16 / ##-SK / 10 9 8 7 6 5 4 3 2 1

Copyright © 2019 Dale J. Brown

All rights reserved.

ISBN 978-1-7266-9433-9

To

Kelly
Sarah
Ken
Francisco
Mary Martha
Rex
Pat
Richard
Lindsey
Davis
&
Aaron

Without you I would not still be here.

Acknowledgements

WE STAND ON THE SHOULDERS—hopefully not the backs—of those who go before us and speak most deeply into our lives. I am most grateful for those who helped me stand when I wanted to fall, to rise up when I felt beaten down, to keep going when I wanted to stop.

My three children—Lindsey, Davis and Aaron---are strong, compassionate, smart, resilient people who have overcome much and stood by me. I am privileged to be their earthly dad and grateful for their love.

My parents, both now in heaven, were spirited innovative people who kept going. I get my grit and many other things from them.

When things fell apart at my New England church, I was surprised at who stood by me, who came against me and who didn't seem to care. Richard Collins, Matt Pierce, Bill Pillsbury, Donna Borges, Jim Grant, Ken LaCerte and many others come to mind of those who stood strong with me. The members of Celebrate Recovery met me at the bottom—they know what it's like to lose and they welcomed this 'loser' into their fold. I found Jesus among them.

Many of the members at Immanuel Baptist Church hung in there with me—Rex and Mary Martha Wiegand, Pat Biddle, Carl Trim, Jennifer Guajardo and others.

I am most grateful to Kelly. She has listened to my heart cries, steadied me when I stumbled, spoken for me when I stuttered and, most of all, kept believing in me.

A special thank you to Richard Collins who carefully read this manuscript.

The Sycamore

In the place that is my own place, whose earth
I am shaped in and must bear, there is an old tree growing,
a great sycamore that is a wondrous healer of itself.
Fences have been tied to it, nails driven into it,
hacks and whittles cut in it, the lightning has burned it.
There is no year it has flourished in
that has not harmed it. There is a hollow in it
that is its death, though its living brims whitely
at the lip of the darkness and flows outward.
Over all its scars has come the seamless white
of the bark. It bears the gnarls of its history
healed over. It has risen to a strange perfection
in the warp and bending of its long growth.
It has gathered all accidents into its purpose.
It has become the intention and radiance of its dark fate.
It is a fact, sublime, mystical and unassailable.
In all the country there is no other like it.
I recognize in it a principle, an indwelling
the same as itself, and greater, that I would be ruled by.
I see that it stands in its place and feeds upon it,
and is fed upon, and is native, and maker.[1]

~ Wendell Berry ~

[1]Copyright © 1998 by Wendell Berry. Reprinted with permission of Counterpoint Press.

Contents

Acknowledgements ix
The Sycamore xi
Where to Find Topic Series xvii
Introduction 1
Critical Things 13
How to Use This Guide 17
A Few Notes on What to Expect 19
Sources for Immediate Help 21
Day 1: You Will Get Through This Because God is For You 23
Day 2: Pain and What to Do with It 26
Day 3: Transformed or Transmitted? 29
Day 4: Giving Your Pain Away 32
Day 5: Your Soul is Like a Tire 36
Day 6: The Stages of Divorce 40
Day 7: The Stages of Divorce — (1) Shock 43
Day 8: The Stages of Divorce — (2) Raw Pain 47
Day 9: The Stages of Divorce — (3) Anger & Bargaining . . 51
Day 10: The Stages of Divorce — (4) Isolation / Loneliness / Depression 56
Day 11: The Stages of Divorce — (5) Turning the Corner . 60
Day 12: The Stages of Divorce — (6) Reconstruction 64
Day 13: The Stages of Divorce — (7) Acceptance & Hope . 68
Day 14: Moving Through These Stages 72
Day 16: Mission—Survive 77
Day 17: Mission—Thrive 81
Day 18: Mission—Resilient 84
Day 19: Mission—Strong 87

Day 20: Mission—Wise 89
Day 21: Losses—Concrete and Abstract 92
Day 22: Expectations of Yourself 96
Day 23: Expectations of Others 99
Day 24: Expectations of Your Children 102
Day 25: Expectations of God 107
Day 26: Rage 111
Day 27: Don't Make Stupid Choices 114
Day 28: Play Your Position 117
Day 29: Shadows 120
Day 30: Sleep is the Great Reset Button 123
Day 31: Get Moving 126
Day 32: When You Hurt Your World Shrinks 129
Day 33: When You Hurt You Become Super Sensitive . . . 132
Day 34: When You Hurt You May Lash Out 135
Day 35: When You Hurt You May Be Willing to do Anything to Get Out of the Pain 139
Day 36: When You Hurt You May Question Everything . 143
Day 37: When You Hurt You Don't Care 146
Day 38: The Four P's of Identity 149
Day 39: God is Your Anchor 152
Day 40: Suicide: Stay 155
Day 41: Suicide—Assessing Your Risk 160
Day 42: Suicide—Getting help 163
Day 43: Homicide 167
Day 44: Larger Than Life 170
Day 45: What Does a Win Look Like? 173
Day 46: The Win—Clarity 176
Day 47: The Win—Passion 179
Day 48: The Win—Solidarity with Others 182
Day 49: The Win—Solid Decisions 185
Day 50: The Win—Integrity 188
Day 51: Fail Forward . . . But Not Flat on Your Face! . . . 190
Day 52: Fail Forward (2) 193
Day 53: Fail Forward (3) 196
Day 54: Fail Forward (4) 199
Day 55: Fail Forward (5) 203

Day 56: Fail Forward (6) 206
Day 57: Fail Forward (7) 209
Day 58: Accepted by God (1) 212
Day 59: Accepted by God (2) 215
Day 60: Accepted by God (3) 218
Day 61: Accepted by God (4) 222
Day 62: Accepted by God (5) 225
Day 63: Accepted by God (6) 228
Day 64: Walden Pond or the North Atlantic? 230
Day 65: Go With the Flow 233
Day 66: Flow With the Go 236
Day 67: It's a War 239
Day 68: God Wins 242
Day 69: Thinking About Forgiveness 245
Day 70: Between Surviving & Thriving 247
Day 71: What You Hear is Important 250
Day 72: What You Say is Important 254
Day 73: You Aren't as Brilliant as You Think 257
Day 74: Between Fear and Hope 260
Day 75: Ultimate Hope 263
Day 76: Thin Skin, Hard Heart Or... 265
Day 77: Weak Enough, Strong Enough 268
Day 78: God Restores 271
Day 79: Regaining Your Footing 275
Day 80: Regaining Your Hope 278
Day 81: Regaining Your Strength 282
Day 82: Regaining Your Financial Health 286
Day 83: Regaining Your Standing with Your Kids 290
Day 84: Regaining Your Manhood 294
Day 85: Regaining Pride—The Right Kind! 297
Day 86: Regaining Your Courage 301
Day 87: Occupation or Vocation? 304
Day 88: Finishing Well 308
Day 89: Steady Strum 311
Day 90: Moving into the New Normal 314
Day 91: The Next Right Thing 317
Next Steps 323

Appendix A: Suicide Risk Assessment 325
Appendix B: Homicide Risk Assessment 337
Appendix C: Understanding Differences in People's Reaction to Death and Divorce 341
Appendix D: Balancing Fault and Responsibility 349
Appendix E: For Men Who Are Primarily Responsible for the Divorce 357
Appendix F: You Need Jesus 367
Works Cited 378
About the Author 384

Where to Find Topic Series

Topic:	Days:
Stages of Divorce	6-14
Mission of Men's Divorce Recovery	15-20
Expectations	20-25
When You Hurt...	32-37
Suicide and Homicide Risk and Assessment	40-43
What Does a Win Look Like?	45-50
Fail Forward	51-57
Accepted by God	58-63
Getting Your Life Back (*Regaining...*)	78-86

Introduction

In the day when I cried out,
You answered me, and
made me bold
with strength
in my soul.
Psalm 138.3

Note: If you need to begin the devotional now, skip to Day 1.

If you need immediate help, go to page 21.

I STAND WHERE A HOUSE has been just a few weeks before. Along with thousands of houses on the beach and for miles inland, a 27-foot storm surge had wiped the slab clean. Hurricane Katrina had made landfall just two months before right where I stood. Concrete foundations were all that was left of this community in Mississippi. There wasn't much debris—most of the houses and the stuff in them had been swept into the Gulf of Mexico.

I wasn't from Mississippi. I was a Texas boy transplanted to Massachusetts to be Senior Pastor of a church of about 500. When TV images of Katrina's destruction reached a diligent and godly member of my church named Caroline, God told her that our church would have a big part in helping a church and its surrounding community come back to life. God hooked us up with Pastor Don Elbourne of Lakeshore Baptist Church, and so began a long relationship that would send dozens of Yankees to the Deep South some twenty times in the coming years.

Our first trip was a reconnoiter mission consisting of Caroline, my wife and myself. And so, on that afternoon in early November in Lakeshore, Mississippi, I stood in the midst of what could only be described as utter destruction. Katrina made landfall on August 29, 2005 with winds of 135 mph and a 27-foot storm surge that raced inland six to twelve miles. The superintendent of Hancock County later told me that of the 10,000 buildings in his county, he could count on both hands those that were still standing. Unimaginably powerful winds and enormous waves took the lives of 300 people and destroyed nearly everything.

As I stood in a state of shock in the yard of one of the destroyed homes, I looked down and saw something any man would recognize: the plastic emblem from a Craftsman toolbox. Here is a picture of that very emblem:

I reached down and picked it up. Though scratched, it still proudly bore the name we all know so well: *Craftsman.*

How did this 6" × 1" lightweight chunk of plastic manage to stay in the yard of its owner with 135 mph winds screaming over it and 27 feet of water rushing overhead? I was bewildered. But I was also proud. I was proud of this little hunk of toughness. It had survived! I put it in my pocket that day. It has found a place on my desk ever since.

Through the years, my desktop plastic 'Craftsman' faithfully bore witness to pure survival as I counseled dozens of people through every crisis known to humanity. Sadly, far too many of the people who sat in my office were living through the storm of divorce. Hurricanes are not preventable. Divorces are. Yet men and women sat before me crushed at what their spouse had done to them through divorce. A few sat in my office burdened by guilt at what they had done to their wife or husband that led to divorce.

As I journeyed with these bruised and bleeding people, two thoughts ran through my mind. First, I was thankful that I was not in their situation—and I was strongly confident that I would never be in their situation. I was a pastor after all! I loved my wife and worked hard to keep her happy. My second thought was how glad I was that I did not have to get into the dating scene at my age!

Little did I know how all that would change. My downward spiral began on December 16, 2013. That evening I attended a regular monthly meeting of the Leadership Council (elders) of the church I had pastored for twelve years. I knew these men and women intimately. I had served them and served with them for over a decade. We traveled on mission trips, worked side-by-side ministering to people and we had sweat out the tough decisions together. When their businesses failed I was there. When one was falsely accused of child abuse, I was there. When babies were born and parents died, I walked beside them. I had no reason to believe they had questions about my leadership or any other aspect of my job as Senior Pastor. In fact, just a few months earlier they had delivered their annual review to me with the usual, "You are doing a great job but working too hard."

But by the time this December meeting was over, the faith I had vested in them vanished. As I sat in the meeting and fielded their questions which seemed odd and out of place, it slowly dawned on me that they had been meeting behind my back, I could not trust them or my staff, and I couldn't go to anyone in the church for help. I felt utterly betrayed by the people I had loved and trusted, served and served with for over a decade. Not only did I feel betrayed, I actually had been. The pain I would experience over the next six months was unspeakably deep.

This group kept me in suspense for the next five months, never directly accusing me of anything but also never transparently working toward a solution to whatever problem they thought we had. It was as if I had committed some unspeakable sin that even I didn't know about. In the end, they forced my termination. June 29, 2014 was my last Sunday. For the first time in decades, I was unemployed.[2]

The church in America today is not a growth industry. Pharmaceuticals? Now there is a growth industry! People will pay anything for their physical health but don't seem to care much about their spiritual health. The few churches looking for pastors or staff want young energetic bucks who, in their minds, can attract young families, the supposed *sine qua non* of successful churches. Youthful energy doesn't come through on resumes quickly perused by search teams. The job market for terminated 52-year-old pastors is slim. Six months of working my network, combing job websites and sending resumes yielded nothing.

So in December 2014 we moved back to Austin, our hometown. I remember sitting in a Starbucks searching and sending via their Wi-Fi. I thought to myself, *So far there are no bites on ministry jobs. I will apply to Starbucks!* So I did. They never called me.

But God came through as he always does. In April I landed a part time job as a Hospice Chaplain. Meanwhile, a small rural Baptist church of German heritage was interested in us. The church was located in Kyle, just south of Austin. Grateful for the opportunity to serve again as a pastor and convinced this was exactly where God wanted me, I was happy to go from pastoring a church of 500 on the North Shore of Boston to being the new pastor of a church of 50 out in a cotton field! Life finally seemed to be getting back on track. Little did I know that this was to be the shortest pastorate of my life.

My wife of 32 years was the founder and director of a non-profit organization that rescues children in Tanzania and Kenya. We had served together teaching in Tanzania for nearly a year in the mid-

---

[2]Our society rightly honors those who serve with sacrifice such as firefighters, police, teachers, military personnel, etc. Pastors are left out of this group but they shouldn't be. Most pastors are brilliant people who could have invested themselves in lucrative careers. Instead, they give themselves to the sacrificial and usual brutal service of humanity for low salaries and minimal benefits. Your pastor is an unsung hero. Tell him or her you appreciate them. And if you really want to help, get on the finance team of your church and make sure your pastor has good health insurance and a comparable retirement program. If you don't do it, I can assure you no one else will.

1990s and through the intervening years God had called her to rescue children in East Africa as the AIDS epidemic decimated the middle generation of adults, leaving millions of kids without parents. I was fully supportive of her work and did all I could to help her fulfill God's call on her life.

Her ministry involved her traveling to Africa about three times a year. Just as I began the new pastorate in Kyle, she left for an extended trip to Tanzania. My 14-year-old son and I moved into the parsonage while she was gone. After she returned in mid-September, I left on a two-week teaching trip to Kenya and Tanzania where I would be teaching pastors and their churches about leadership and (ironically) family life. Care of our son usually prevented us from traveling together.

On October 22, 2015, I began the 38-hour trip from Tanzania to home. At 5:15 pm on October 23, 2015, I pulled into the carport at the parsonage in Kyle. My wife and I had many common friends in East Africa and I was excited to share news of them and the rest of my trip with her.

As I entered the carport that evening, my wife stepped from the back door of the parsonage with her mother in tow. I thought this was a bit strange but reasoned that perhaps they were greeting me after the long trip. I was in for the shock of my life. She met me in front of her car and told me that she was leaving me, and had, in fact, moved out of the church parsonage into an apartment while I was gone, taking our son with her.

Numb with shock, I mumbled something, then went into the parsonage, immediately noticing how empty it was. On the kitchen counter was a manila envelope. Inside were legal documents, one of which stated that if I did not get a certain document signed and notarized by a certain date, the county constable would come to the parsonage and serve me papers. The thought of a constable coming to the parsonage of the church I pastored to serve me papers as if I were some kind of criminal horrified me.

As I pushed those papers aside I entered a surreal world in which everything I held dear was drifting away. It dawned on me that, try as I might, those things would never come back. I would lose my church, my chance at ever being a pastor again, my children, my hard-earned reputation, and the fulfillment of the dream and goal of growing old with the same person. I would now be a statistic—I would now be classified as 'divorced.'

All these things flooded into my mind and heart as I sat in a sparsely furnished house, alone. I walked into my son's room, now nearly empty. My heart was crushed. But I was exhausted—two weeks of intense teaching and the long journey home left me empty. I determined to go to bed.

The next morning I crashed. The weight of being unjustly terminated from the church I loved and now being abandoned by my wife of 32 years came crashing down. A hospice chaplain describes better than I can what that moment feels like: *All meaning seems to have evaporated leaving behind in its wake an empty sinking hollowness filled with darkness.*[3]

It was Saturday morning and I would be preaching to my new church in less than 24 hours. What did the future hold for these dear people who had embraced my family and who my wife had pretended to embrace in kind? What would I tell the church and when? Would it be possible to continue being pastor of these people I had just come to know but whom I already dearly loved? I wasn't a dentist who could separate my personal life from professional life. A pastor's professional life is integrally bound up in who he/she is personally. Whatever happened with my job would be directly related to my now shattered personal life. The thought of losing another church was unbearable.

It was ALL unbearable. My body wracked with grief as the weight of the disaster came crashing down. I sobbed and yelled and cursed the world. I shouted out my hatred of the leaders of the church who had terminated me and of my wife who had made life so difficult and now seemingly impossible. My mind (and heart and soul) overflowed with thoughts, including suicide.

In that moment on that Saturday morning I reached out to Ken,

---

[3]Mark LaRocca-Pitts, "Four FACTs Spiritual Assessment Tool," *Journal of Health Care Chaplaincy*, 21:2 (2015): 51-59, accessed January 3, 2017, DOI: 10.1080/08854726.2015.1015303.

my good friend and fellow traveler. It helped that he is a brilliant psychotherapist.[4] He immediately understood where I was psychologically. He gently talked me off the ledge and made sure I had someone I could be with in this intense agony (Ken was 2,000 miles away in Massachusetts). Ken instantly recognized that my soul was crushed and could break at any moment. His heart opened up to my extreme distress and he absorbed some of my pain. He calmly and quietly listened, and when he spoke it was clear he understood my state of mind and the condition of my soul. He knew exactly what I needed to hear. Saturday morning, October 24, 2015 was a critical moment for me. Things could have gone in several directions. Ken's availability, his compassionate, understanding heart, and his gentle instructions kept me on a track that would lead to healing and recovery.

When I look back on those first days and then the weeks and months that follow, I ask myself:

- What would have happened if I had chosen self-destruction rather than reconstruction?

- What was saved in my life then, now, and in my future by the compassionate and courageous help given to me by those closest to me?

- How many men are in this very place at this very moment—dying a million deaths from crushed dreams, destroyed reputations, families lost?

- How many kids are silently suffering through their parents' divorce, and how could their dads be helped to rescue them from needless guilt and wasted opportunities?

God used these and many other questions through the past three years to lead me to begin a ministry to divorced men. When I was facing the black hole of divorce, three people stepped in to build a

[4]Ken is a Licensed Mental Health Counselor in the state of Massachusetts.

bridge across the gaping chasm looming in front of me. God has called me to do for other men what these three people did for me. God called me to be here for you in your pain and agony. That's what the *Daily Survival Guide for Divorced Men* is all about. In my fractured state I rediscovered that time with God each morning and the wisdom offered by others through daily readings were the superglue that slowly put my fragmented soul back together.

Right now you are in pain and looking for relief. Know this: Our God who created a world of immense variety has many tools to get back on your feet and back in the game. And he will do it! You will get through this! But right now you are face down on the turf wondering if your playing days are over. They're not. You are God's son, and he doesn't leave his kids on the field alone and bleeding. His specialty, in fact, is taking wounded warriors and rehabilitating them into magnificent men who give back to the very world that beat them to the ground.

Through this process you will be transformed in remarkable ways. You may be thinking: *I've been hammered with everyone telling me to change! I'm sick of it! I don't have the desire or energy to change!*

Maybe some things in you really do need to change—patterns of thinking and behaviors that contributed to your divorce. Addiction to pornography (or the real thing), working too much, being a grump at home come to mind. Or maybe you've been picked apart from head to toe for inconsequential things and you are sick of being criticized. The last thing you want to hear from me is that you need to change!

I get that. That's why I used the word *transform* instead of *change.* What I don't mean by the word "transform" is to make you feel guilty or ashamed or afraid. When people change out of guilt, shame or fear, it doesn't last. And that kind of 'transformation' is not what is really needed or wanted. What I mean by transformed is the changing of your inward soul through a love relationship with God that is soul-nourishing and soul-building. Transformation is about God's good and powerful grace reshaping your mind, heart, soul and emotions for his glory and for your good. That's a good thing. It's good for God, good for you, and good for the world.

In fact, if you ride this kayak all the way to the ocean, you will actually be thankful for the pain you are in right now because you will recognize that what you have gained in really knowing and being known by God is far better than the challenging circumstances and the heartache the world can throw at you and anything good the world can entice you with.

Weird huh? That God can take something so terrible as your divorce and bring something spectacular out of it? But that's our God! He can take the crucifixion of his Son on Friday and turn it into a glorious resurrection on Sunday.

Just to be clear as to where we are headed with all this: God doesn't want to squeeze you from the outside until you fit some kind of mold that is acceptable to the people around you who have been squeezing you ever since you can remember. God wants to move in your life in a way you have never experienced, and through his powerful and amazing love, shift your heart and life in a direction that you will find deeply satisfying and fantastically rewarding. As God does this work inside you, all the external stuff that everyone has been griping about will naturally change. Some people will like what they see you becoming. Others will not. Oh well! We want to please God first.

Now is your chance to grow into the man God intended you to be. You will discover that the man he wants you to be is that man you really wanted to be all along. You will experience a confidence and peace that seems to 'fit' you and your particular universe. You will experience a solid grip that holds firm through the storms that try to uproot you and send you out to sea.

For you engineer types, you know that *work = energy*. God's work is his energy operating in the unseen depths of your soul (yes, engineer, you do have a soul!). God is not a drill sergeant who wants to erase who you are inside so you conform to some external standard. God's energy in you is motivated by his persistent love which relentlessly pursues you—his beloved son—so he can lavish his love on you and so you can really know him as your dad, perhaps the dad you never had.

Are you ready to experience God's love this way? Maybe all this seems daunting to you, perhaps overwhelming right now. As I look back on those first months following October 23, 2015, I remember that all I wanted was (1) relief from the pain and (2) hope for the future. Surviving through each day was about as much as my soul could grasp.

I also remember that taking a few minutes each morning to spend time with God *saved my life from suicide, gave me comfort knowing that I was loved beyond imagination, and kept alive a tiny ember of hope that this terrible time in my life would not last forever.*

You may be down, but brother, you are not out. You may be crushed, but my friend, you are not dead. You may be face down on the turf, but you will get up, take a deep breath, and get back in the game. No life has failed if God moves in, transforms, and transmits his grace, love and power to, in and through you.

Now a word regarding blame. Some of you reading this see yourself as the victim. You feel as if you have been on the receiving end of a raw deal. Others of you are perpetrators. You did something that was really wrong, like cheating on your wife. There are two sides (or more) to every story. When a couple divorces, both are at fault. But it is also true that usually one is more responsible for the dissolution of the marriage than the other. The bottom line: whether you see yourself as the victim or the perpetrator, this daily guide is for you. The reality is that all of us are both vics and perps. We have all fallen short of the glory of God, of the ideal husband, of the perfect father.

But there is tremendous hope. By his power and through his grace, God can repair the damage done to you. By his power and through his grace, God can forgive the damage you have done to others, including your ex-wife and your family. We are damaged and we cause damage. We are messed up and we mess up others. A significant piece of the healing journey is to understand this simple concept—we all need to be repaired and we all need to be forgiven.

When we enter this process something amazing happens: As we experience God's gracious healing and gentle conviction he begins to use us to clean up our messes and help repair others. I know this all sounds daunting right now but it is doable by (1) taking one day at a time, (2) seeking God's grace and strength, and (3) holding on to hope in this moment and for the future.

Sitting next to my computer in front of me is that 6" $\times$ 1" chunk of toughness, that Craftsman emblem that began its journey attached to a brand new shiny toolbox bought by some guy in Lakeshore, Mississippi. Little did it know that it would end up on the desk of a newly single ex-pastor living in a one-bedroom apartment in Kyle, Texas. But it did and here we are—survivors! That emblem has made it so far and so have I!

But friend, I want to do more than survive. I want to thrive. Hence this daily guide to help you survive and thrive. If a non-descript hunk of plastic can ride out Hurricane Katrina and give inspiration to you and me, who knows what God has in store for you! My scratched-up Craftsman emblem still bears witness to survival and inspires me to keep going. I want you to keep going too. God has a bright future for you.

Nulla tenaci invia est via . . .
For the tenacious, no road is impassable.

How to Use This Guide

Choose a time . . . morning, lunch, evening. Mornings are best because you can usually control when you get up. Everything in your mind and body will tell you that getting up 30 minutes earlier than normal is not normal! Trust God to make up the energy you lose from a little lost sleep, and he will do it. I promise.

Find a quiet place . . . free from distractions.

Settle your mind. Ask God to quiet your thoughts. Don't worry if your brain is still cluttered. God is just glad we show up.

Ask God to give you peace. Take a deep breath and rest in his care. For guys this is tough because we want to be in control. Surprise! – you are not in control and in the end, that's a good thing. Recognize this reality by giving yourself into God's care. Imagine him giving you a huge bear hug.

Listen to, play or sing along with some **worship songs** if this is helpful.

Read this Daily Guide beginning with the first day. The readings are designed to carry you along a journey of healing. Note that some days will involve more reading than others. Hang in there and read each day completely. Nothing is more important than your recovery, so giving yourself time to the process of recovery is a worthy investment.

Take time to pray. Prayer is not complicated. Just tell God what you want to say him. If you are new to this, this will be a one-way conversation–you will talk and God will listen. With time and patience, however, you will begin to hear the voice of the Shepherd.

It may even be that a time comes when you listen to God more than you talk to him.

If writing stuff down (**journaling**) helps, do it. For decades I've heard how wonderful journaling is. Frankly, I've been too busy to journal. But if it helps to put your thoughts down, do it. You may write out what is going on in your life or perhaps write out a prayer to God. Writing out your feelings can help get them out of your mind and in a place you can go back to if needed. This is especially helpful in dealing with anger.

When you are in a bad spot emotionally—say you are in a rage—use the table of contents to find the daily readings that relate to any topic (*anger* for example). Just the act of slowing down, finding this book, looking up the topic and reading a helpful word will dispel your rage in amazing ways, and relieve other negative emotions as well.

A Few Notes on What to Expect

Some of the quotes (*Thought for the Day*) will not be expressions of what I believe to be true. They are meant to get you to think. Take them as they are and consider whether they express truth or not.

Many of the readings are designed to be in a short series. In other words, we will explore one topic over a series of several days. Each day will give you something to think about and push you along this road to recovery. But some days may not be wrapped up neatly. Keep reading, keep thinking, keep praying! A table with the series titles and places they show up is found on page xvii.

I will not cover dating in this devotional. The only advice I will give is that if you are newly divorced, it is generally recommended not to date until you get your feet on the ground and experience significant personal growth. The general rule is to wait two years. If you are an addict, you need to get healed before you date. This is a must and will save you and your future partner untold heartache and hardship.

The journey you are on is hard. Remember that you will get through this. ***You will Survive and Thrive beyond your divorce.***

What you are experiencing now doesn't define you and will not last forever. Healing and hope are ahead of you. Believe it because it is true. I know. I've been there.

Sources for Immediate Help

If you think you may do harm to yourself or someone else or to property you are in an immediate crisis that needs attention now. Call one of the numbers below or go to their website now (services with only a website do not have a crisis phone line).

For direct and immediate help, **Dial 911**. First Responders help people in all situations. If you are in crisis they will know what to do to help you.

National Suicide Prevention Lifeline: 800-273-8255
www.suicidepreventionlifeline.org

Find a local counselor or therapist. These people are trained to help people like you who are in crisis. Just as you would not try to handle a heart attack on your own you should not expect to navigate the trauma of divorce without the help of wise and experienced professionals.

Men's Divorce Recovery phone number and website: **978-204-0480.**
www.mensdivorcerecovery.org;

Homicide Prevention Hotline & website: 800-273-8255 (same as the National Suicide Prevention Hotline) *www.savingcain.org*

Alcoholics Anonymous: *www.aa.org*

Celebrate Recovery (A Christian-based recovery program for all addictions meeting in local churches): *www.celebraterecovery.com*

Divorce Recovery: 800-489-7778 *www.divorcecare.org*

Help with **Pornography**:

- Be Broken Ministries, Jonathan Daugherty, *www.2.bebroken.com*
- Faithful & True Ministries, Mark Laaser *www.faithfulandtrue.com*
- Pure Desire Ministries, Ted Roberts, *www.puredesire.org*

Day 1: You Will Get Through This Because God is For You

The Word

In the day when I cried out, you answered me,
and made me bold with strength in my soul.
— Psalm 138.3

Thought for the Day

You start with a darkness to move through,
but sometimes the darkness moves through you.
~ Dean Young

The Most Important Question on my mind growing up was, "Am I good enough?" The answers from my dad and others were conflicted. On one hand, I was told I was special and nothing could stop me. I would be spectacular. On the other hand, if I was anything less than spectacular, it was my fault. Given the deluge of criticism I received, it seemed that though I was special, I never seemed to measure up to my specialness!

Not to kick a dead horse till its teeth fall out, but most of us men grew up with this double message from our parents, our teachers, our peers. To be accepted we had to jump through hoops that were just out of reach. The message we received was, *you can do it . . . but you probably won't.*

Implicit in this message was that people were both *for me* and *against me*, both my friend and my enemy, my companion and my challenger. People were as likely to push me down as they were to help me up.

God is not like that. *Did you get that?* God is not a super-sized human being who acts like the people who raise us and cast us off into adulthood. God is *for* you. He is *with* you. He is *on your side.* He wants you to *win*, to *succeed*, to have *peace.* He is not capricious, he does not change his ways or his thoughts. He is not human. He is God.

So what about this God? Whose side is he on? Romans 8.31 says, *"If God is for us, who can be against us?"* God IS for you!

This is the truth you need to let sink deep in your soul: God **IS** for you, and because he is for you, ***you will get through this.***

The Apostle Paul goes on to say in verse 32, *He who did not spare his own Son, but gave him up for us all—how will he not also, along with him, graciously give us all things?*

Perhaps you cheated on your wife and the bed you now lie in is the bed you made. Maybe you came home from work to find your stuff on the curb with a note attached, *"Get out!"* Perhaps you came home to find your wife and kids gone, the house empty. Maybe you and your wife had a terrible argument and one of you stormed out. It could even be that you hit your wife and you now face criminal charges.

There are perps and vics, and the reality is that we are all some of each. Whatever your situation, whoever you think are, God is *for* you. He wants you to know him and experience his presence and his power to sustain you through this time and transform you into the man he made you to be. Just start with this simple reality: **God is FOR you.**

If you don't believe that right now, give God time and space to work. Ask him to show himself to you. He will do it, I guarantee it!

In the day when I cried out, you answered me, and made me bold with strength in my soul.

Psalm 138.3

Think About It . . .

- Who do you imagine God to be?
- If you were face-to-face with God, what would he look like? What would he say? What would he do?
- Where do you think your images of God came from?

Life Commitment:

I choose to believe God is for me and that he is on my side. I choose to believe that despite what circumstances may say about my life, God has my best interests in mind and I can trust him with my present and with my future.

Day 2: Pain and What to Do with It

The Word

What I feared has come upon me; what I dreaded has happened to me. I have no peace, no quietness; I have no rest, but only turmoil.

— Job 3.25–26

Thought for the Day

All meaning seems to have evaporated leaving behind in its wake an empty sinking hollowness filled with darkness.[5]

~ Mark LaRocca-Pitts

Wikipedia defines pain as *a distressing feeling often caused by intense or damaging stimuli.*

Pain defined with words and pain experienced in real time are two very different things. The moment I knew I was being divorced, my soul was transported to a place it had never been before. The pain I experienced cannot be explained, only experienced. Millions of men experience this pain, but it goes unspoken and unaddressed because our culture says that men cannot feel that way. But I did.

After about six months of spiraling black thoughts, emotions tumbling all over the place and living through the sheer agony of what I was going through, I wondered what would happen if I just started posting *all* my thoughts on Facebook. What if I posted raw, unfiltered comments on what I thought, what I felt, and what I considered doing?

---

[5] Mark LaRocca-Pitts, Four FACTs Spiritual Assessment Tool, *Journal of Health Care Chaplaincy*, 21:2, 2015, 51-59.

The few times I revealed my thoughts and feelings on Facebook, the pushback was swift and trite—the theme of the message being, *"God will take care of you, suck it up, have faith. Get over it."*[6]

In other words, "We don't really want to hear about your problems, and we certainly don't want to listen to you whine about them."

But I was dying inside. My heart was crushed, my soul disintegrating within me. Then I found this passage in the biblical book of Job: *What I feared has come upon me; what I dreaded has happened to me. I have no peace, no quietness; I have no rest, but only turmoil.*[7]

Job was a manly man. He was super successful and seemed to be a genuinely good and humble man, but strong as well. But when his world came crashing down, he told it like it was: *What I feared has come upon me; what I dreaded has happened to me. I have no peace, no quietness; I have no rest, but only turmoil.*

If you think you are not in pain, check again. If you think you cannot feel your pain, step back and observe what you are feeling. If you think it is unmanly to name your pain and try to offload it, then consider Job. Job hurt and he said how much he hurt.

Here is a great truth largely ignored by our society: ***Wounds to the soul are just as painful and damaging as wounds to the body.*** People clearly have no grasp of this profound yet unrecognized reality. In our society men are not expected to experience any soul pain and we should not expect any comfort or consolation when we do.[8] For a more thorough examination of this phenomenon go to

---

[6]For more insight, see Andrew Root, *There's No Crying on Social Media!* accessed March 24, 2017, http://www.christianitytoday.com/ct/2017/march/theres-no-crying-on-social-media.html?utm_source=ctweeklyhtml&utm_medium=Newsletter&utm_term=14285049&utm_content=502739904&utm_campaign=email.

[7]The story of Job (pronounced like it rhymes with 'robe') is found in the 18th 'book' (or chapter) in the Old Testament of the Bible. Job was a righteous, prosperous man who loved God. But Job lost everything—his family, his wealth, his health—very quickly to various disasters.

[8]Miriam Greenspan writes: *As a nation, we seem to believe that, with the right effort, we can completely eradicate emotional suffering. In either case, whether it's control or catharsis we seek, we regard negative emotions as a dangerous hindrance to the good life. The focus is on dispelling such feelings, not learning from them.... In the throes of grief, fear, or despair, we generally believe that giving feelings like these too much*

Appendix D.

Here's the thing: *God did not cause your pain but he knows about it.* And he knows that he can do something with your pain—like ease it up over time and even transform it. God doesn't waste pain. Let this truth sink in: *God does not waste pain.* God will absorb and transform your pain if you let him.

One of my favorite thinkers states, *You will be wounded. Your work is to find God and grace inside the wounds.*[9]

You're in pain—deep pain. The world may not want to hear about it or even care, but God does. Tell him about your pain. Then ask him to do something with it. If you keep your heart open, you will find God and grace inside the wounds. That's what this journey is about. Hang in here with me.

Think About It . . .

Think back to a time when someone caused you pain. What did you feel? Anger? Sadness? Resignation? Hopelessness? Helplessness?

What did you do? Rage? Retreat? Learn something new?

What do you feel right now?

Life Reality Check:

I acknowledge my pain. It hurts and it hurts deep in my soul.

---

space in our psyches is a sign of emotional weakness or breakdown. We turn away, not toward them. Miriam Greenspan, *Healing through the Dark Emotions: the Wisdom of Grief, Fear, and Despair* (Boston: Shambhala, 2011), 31, 27.

[9] Richard Rohr, Joseph Durepos, and Tom McGrath, *On the Threshold of Transformation: Daily Meditations for Men* (Chicago: Loyola Press, 2010), p. 255.

Day 3: Transformed or Transmitted?[10]

The Word

A bruised reed he will not break, and a smoldering wick he will not snuff out. In faithfulness he will bring forth justice; he will not falter or be discouraged till he establishes justice on earth.

— Isaiah 42.3–4

Thought for the Day

We can choose to throw stones, to stumble on them, to climb over them, or to build with them.

~ William Arthur Ward

Pain comes to all living creatures, but the unique pain of divorce comes to only some of us. Whatever the source, the question before you is, *What will I do with my pain?* This is an extraordinarily hard question to answer and however you answer it now will be challenged in the days, weeks and months ahead. You will be asking this question of yourself many times and will have to struggle with the answer each time.

When others have answered this question poorly, untold misery has been visited upon our world. That's because of a fundamental law of the universe: *Pain that is not transformed is transmitted.*[11]

---

[10]This phrase comes from Richard Rohr whose wisdom and ability to turn a phrase I greatly admire. I can't think of a better way to say this so with humility I shamelessly borrow from Fr. Rohr. I am grateful that he gave me permission to share his wisdom.

[11]"Richard Rohr Quote." A-Z Quotes, accessed December 28, 2016, http://www.azquotes.com/quote/814475.

Untransformed pain turned *outward* becomes violence against others. Pain turned *inward* turns to violence against oneself. Neither is a healthy option.

Untransformed pain lashes out at others and self. Untransformed pain only multiplies because the victims of our untransformed pain must decide what to do with the pain we have inflicted on them. And so the cycle that began in the Garden continues ravaging the world today.[12] Untransformed pain is like spilling oil on a pond—it keeps spreading and is impossible to put back into the jar.

We lash out at others because we think that if we unload our pain we will be rid of it. But hurting others only increases our pain, it never diminishes it. If we turn our pain against ourselves, we somehow believe that we can kill our pain with pain. That's like trying to sober up by drinking more whiskey! To think we can use pain against others or ourselves to lessen our own pain doesn't make sense. But it is what most of us do.

You hurt. Like Job you *have no rest, only turmoil.* What to do with your hurt? There is a better way. Today, would you commit to continuing the journey to find that better way?

Think About It . . .

- As you begin your journey toward recovery, think about what you are doing with your pain . . .

- In what ways are you offloading your pain onto *others*?

    __ I lash out at others.

    __ My mind is dominated by thoughts of revenge.

[12]The 'Garden' to which I refer is the Garden of Eden. The story of humanity's creation, fall and redemption starts in this remarkable story found in Genesis, the first book of the Bible, the first four chapters (Genesis 1-4). I recommend reading these chapters. It explains a lot of how we got here, what went wrong, and God's purpose in bringing us back. For a different (but I believe to be thorough and true) view of these chapters, see John H. Walton, *The Lost World of Genesis One: Ancient Cosmology and The Origins Debate* (Downers Grove, IL: IVP Academic, 2009) and John H. Walton, *The Lost World of Adam And Eve: Genesis 2-3 and the Human Origins Debate* (Downers Grove, IL: IVP Academic, 2015).

__ I am seeking ways to hurt those who have hurt me.

- In what ways are you turning your pain inward onto *yourself*?

  __ I have serious thoughts of suicide. (If so, call the Suicide Prevention Hotline: 800-273-8255 and go to Appendix A for help.)

  __ I am depressed.

  __ I am engaging risky behaviors, not caring what happens to me.

  __ I am medicating myself with alcohol and/or drugs.

- Is your strategy working?

  __ Yes, I feel better and believe that lashing out is a productive strategy for dealing with my pain.

  __ No, though it seems that transmitting my pain would get rid of it, I still feel the pain.

  __ I'm not sure . . . still thinking about it.

  __ No, I need a better way to handle my pain.

Life Commitment:

I have a choice as to what to do with my pain. Though at this moment I don't fully understand what this means, I choose to let God transform my pain. I choose not to transmit it.

Day 4: Giving Your Pain Away

The Word

Therefore, since we are surrounded by such a great cloud of witnesses, let us throw off everything that hinders and the sin that so easily entangles, and let us run with perseverance the race marked out for us.

Let us fix our eyes on Jesus, the author and perfecter of our faith, who for the joy set before him endured the cross, scorning its shame, and sat down at the right hand of the throne of God.

Consider him who endured such opposition from sinful men, so that you will not grow weary and lose heart.

— Hebrews 12.1–3

Thought for the Day

Even if the whole world refuses to understand or validate the anguish one is experiencing, yet Jesus Christ never changes. He always understands and remains willing to help and bring healing to every throbbing emotion.[13]

~ Keturah Martin

It was the last run of the day. The sun was setting, the slopes beginning to clear of skiers. I pushed off the mountain and fairly screamed down the course. All was well until the bottom of the run. My ski caught the top of a stump protruding through the snow. I

[13] Keturah C. Martin, *Jesus Never Wastes Pain but Can Bring Eternal Gain* (Bloomington: Xlibris, 2014), 392.

tumbled end-over-end, the skis whirling around me. Blood gushed down my face when I sat up. Damage assessment revealed a deep gash on my head.

An hour later a doctor used needle and thread to sew my head back together. It hurt. How did I endure this painful experience? I got through it by focusing on something else: the amazing story I had to tell back in school!

When we hurt from divorce, there is no glory in the pain, only the pain. This frustrating and intensifying dynamic of the pain of divorce can tempt us to transmit our pain to the ones who have caused it, including ourselves. And rare is the man (including myself) who has not transmitted his pain in some way—or a lot of ways.

There is another way, a third component that can lift us out of the cycle of experiencing pain then transmitting it, only to get slammed again, and transmitting it again. Our pain can be *transformed* instead of *transmitted.* The catalyst (and source) of this transformation is Jesus himself.

Let us fix our eyes on Jesus . . .

When I was sitting in the doctor's office my pain was transformed by fixing my eyes on myself and the glory the story would bring to myself.

When you are sitting alone with the horrendous pain of divorce, you may fix your eyes on yourself out of pity or guilt, or you may fix your eyes on your ex out of anger. There's no glory in that.

Instead, look to Christ and consider what he did with his pain. Jesus was perfectly innocent—he had never sinned. Yet he suffered the worst injustice and the most painful consequence: death on a Roman cross. What did he do with his pain?

Jesus knew God was transforming his pain into glory for God and for our good. Through the amazing story of Jesus' sacrifice for us, God would be the hero of the greatest love story ever told, and the object of his suffering (us), would be saved from an eternity in hell and, instead, spend eternity in heaven.

Jesus didn't focus on the people who nailed him to the cross. Jesus lifted his eyes to God. God's glory came first, not personal revenge.

To Jesus our salvation was a higher priority than his personal comfort. Jesus could sit with his pain knowing that enduring his pain would glorify God and save us from hell.

You are in pain. There is no personal glory in this pain, no great story to tell your friends when you get back to school. Your pain is embarrassing, frustrating, maddening. But your pain is not beyond transformation and redemption. Take your eyes off yourself and *Consider him who endured such opposition from sinful men, so that you will not grow weary and lose heart.*

Reality check: I know this may be nearly impossible to read much less think about actually putting into practice. In fact, you may be about to throw this book through the window! Hang in there with me. God will do a work in you. It will take time.

By looking to Jesus you are taking your eyes off yourself and those who caused your pain. In the days ahead we will explore the dynamics of how to focus on Jesus, but for now, commit to looking to Christ rather than focusing on yourself or your ex.

Think About It . . .

- Who is Jesus to you? Was he weak or strong? Was he a man or a wimp?

- What do you think Jesus thought when he was being nailed to the cross? If you were Jesus, what would you have been thinking?

- noindent What would have happened if Jesus had chosen revenge while hanging on the cross, sending death angels to eliminate those who had unjustly nailed him on those wooden beams?

Life Commitment:

Though I don't understand all that this means right now, I choose to let God transform my pain by fixing my eyes on Jesus. I deliberately choose to trust that Jesus can transform my pain for God's glory and my good.

Day 5: Your Soul is Like a Tire

The Word

For this reason, since the day we heard about you, we have not stopped praying for you and asking God to fill you with the knowledge of his will through all spiritual wisdom and understanding. And we pray this in order that you may live a life worthy of the Lord and may please him in every way: bearing fruit in every good work, growing in the knowledge of God, being strengthened with all power according to his glorious might so that you may have great endurance and patience, and joyfully giving thanks to the Father, who has qualified you to share in the inheritance of the saints in the kingdom of light.

— Colossians 1.9–12

Thought for the Day

Spiritual Disciplines are instruments of God's grace which, through the Spirit, transform us daily into people who reflect Jesus' love, obedience, humility, and connection to God.[14]

Your soul is like a tire. No, I didn't say your soul is tired, though your soul may *feel* very tired. Let me suggest a different way to view your soul. Your soul is not *tired*, it is *flat*.

Ever since I can remember I have lived on my bike. Back in the day we rode our bikes without helmets and common sense. There was nothing like flying my banana seat bike off a homemade plywood

[14] *Spiritual Disciplines*, (Peabody, MA: Rose Publishing, July 7, 2014).

ramp and onto that ever-so-unforgiving asphalt! Now I ride 25 miles dodging cars, rocks and the heat.

If you are a cyclist *you know that your tires leak.* In fact, *every time I get ready for a ride I pump a little air in my tires.* Low tires translate into a slow and sluggish bike. Slow and sluggish is not me. I want to ride high and clean, fast and efficient.

Your soul is like a bike tire. It leaks. All kinds of things steal the air out of your soul—people poking at you, financial worries, expectations of others that go unmet. Most of our 'leakage' comes from within—*what we tell ourselves about ourselves.*

From the beginning we as boys are asking ourselves, *Am I good enough?* And if truth be told, our constant answer to ourselves is, *Not even close.* If you keep telling that to yourself long enough, you will have a flat soul. As in an all-the-way-to-the-ground flat soul.

Now you've been through a divorce. Divorce is a knife plunged into your soul—it takes you right to the ground.

When I arrived home on October 23, 2015 after 38 hours of travel from Tanzania only to be met in my garage by my wife telling me she had left me, that was a knife plunge straight to the soul. I went straight to the ground. With my soul flat on the ground I knew I wasn't going anywhere for a while.

Every time I ride my bike I must put a little air in the tires. Every day you and I must put a little air back into our souls. If you don't, you will be flat. Tired, flat souls need air. Whether your soul is flat all the way to the ground or just a little low, what do you use to put the air back in?

In 'Christian speak,' the means by which we put air back into our souls are called *Spiritual Disciplines.*

There are many spiritual disciplines but for you right here, right now, I want to recommend the following:

- **Solitude**—Spending time alone to be with God and to read and to think.

- **Prayer**—Honest conversation with your True Father.

- **Fellowship**—Being with other Christians who nourish your soul through understanding, challenge and encouragement.[15]
- **Guidance**—Positioning yourself to follow God's best path for his glory, your good and the good of those around you.[16]
- **Study**—Reading and really thinking about what God is saying to you through his Word, the Bible and through the wisdom of others.
- **Worship**—Giving back to God the worth he is due.
- **Confession**—Talking openly and honestly about your life with a trusted circle of friends.
- **Submission**—Humbling yourself before God, trusting that in God's economy (which is the only 'economy' that ultimately matters), the way up is down.
- **Service**—Learning to live with an open hand.

I've ridden my bike hundreds of miles without a flat. But in one ride I had two! Life is like that. Whether cruising fast and efficient or stuck by the side of the road, you need air. Let God pump up your soul through the means listed above. You may not be doing all of the things listed above. That's OK. Pick one or two that will be most helpful to you *now.*

Think About It . . .

- Are you taking time to let God put air back in your soul?
- Of the spiritual disciplines listed, which do you think would be most helpful to engage in first?
- Which is the least appealing?

---

[15]Bill Donahue, *Leading Life-Changing Small Groups: Groups that Grow,* (Grand Rapids: Zondervan, 2012), Kindle Locations 782-783.
[16]Richard J. Foster, *Celebration of Discipline* (New York: Harper Collins, 2009), 175.

Life Commitment:

My soul needs air. God can pump me back up, but only if I let his air in. I commit to using these tools God has given me to get me back on the road again.

Day 6: The Stages of Divorce[17]

The Word

The Lord himself goes before you and will be with you; he will never leave you nor forsake you. Do not be afraid; do not be discouraged.

— Deuteronomy 31.8

Thought for the Day

If you're going through hell, keep going.

~ Winston Churchill

THE GOOD NEWS IS THAT THERE are stages of divorce. That is, there are certain thoughts, emotions and events you are experiencing right now that most people also experienced when they traveled this painful journey. These stages usually loosely follow a sequence or progression. It helps to know others have walked this painful road before you and have emerged on the other side intact. Many emerged even better than they were before. That's our goal.

It also helps to know that what you are experiencing is normal. It's common to feel raw pain, anger, depression and many other emotions. When you begin to feel better you will know that it is OK to be getting better and that, for most people, the trajectory is toward recovery, not years of pain, isolation, loneliness and depression. You really will get through this. The hard part is that this is a journey and journeys are made only one step at a time.

[17] I found this basic outline of the stages of divorce in several places online but with no attribution despite attempts to track down the original author.

I'm a hiker and my favorite places to hike are the mountains. I have planned many hikes for many groups of people. The scene is always the same as we gather at the bottom of the mountain—everyone is excited but also nervous. We are eager to get to the top but we also know that the way to the top is up a really steep path just beyond the trailhead sign.

The first mile is difficult—your legs protest this sudden change from sitting comfortably in a car to pushing your body (plus a pack) up the mountain.

Then the body kicks in and things rock until about midway up the trail. At that point your mind knows there is no turning back but you also know you're only halfway up the mountain. A rest stop with a nice view helps renew strength and the view gives encouragement when you see how far you've come.

The last hard part is just before the summit. Your legs are exhausted, the summit seems further than possible, but you also know you're almost there. Sometimes the mind has to tell the legs to move, and they do. By pushing on you break through the last trees to reach a granite peak with stunning views all around. The group is all smiles and mutual congratulations—you made it!

Divorce is a tough mountain to climb. Like a hike, you start at the bottom and put one foot in front the other. With enough steps over enough time, you get to the top.

As you move through these stages of divorce it's good to know you really are making progress. There's not much you can do to speed up the process but you *can* slow it down. Determine now to being open to experiencing each of these stages as they come and seeking the right help and doing the right things to keep moving.

Divorce is a hard journey. You will think and feel things you have never thought or felt before. Allow yourself permission and space to get through this. And remember, *Don't make things worse.* You will get through this.

Think About It . . .

- Think back to a time when you suffered a loss. What did you think and feel when you first understood the scope of the loss?
- What was the process you went through to get to a point of accepting the loss and being able to move on? The way you processed that loss is probably the way you will process this loss.
- A chart outlining these stages can be found at https://bit.ly/2oXIEqo.[18]

Life Commitment:

My thoughts and emotions are all over the place right now. Despite this, I am committed to pressing on through this journey. Though I'm at the bottom of the mountain with a heavy pack, I know if I put one foot in front of the other, I will summit.

[18]https://storage.googleapis.com/wzukusers/user-25216852/documents/5b5dc76fd12feKZ2eTlI/The\%20Stages\%20of\%20Divorce\%20Chart\%20DSGFMB1\%20Legal.pdf.

Day 7: The Stages of Divorce — (1) Shock

The Word

After this, Job opened his mouth and cursed the day of his birth.
— Job 3.1

Thought for the Day

The wound that unifies all men is the wound of their disposability.
~ Warren Farrell

When I stood in the nearly empty house after my wife left me, I was in total shock. I couldn't believe what I just heard. My mind raced in a million directions. Raw unmitigated pain poked it's black and fiery head into my brain and the fire singed my heart. But just for a moment. My brain's shock-absorbers kept most of the pain away, giving me time to think and feel through the entire terrible state of things.

When bad news is received the brain quickly scans the information. When it realizes the catastrophic nature of the event, the brain slows serious thinking. The region of the brain known as the Inferior Frontal Gyrus (IFG) has been shown to interfere with the ability of the brain to process bad news in its totality, thus protecting the soul from extreme trauma.[19] God designed us to be able to receive only small

[19] https://www.ncbi.nlm.nih.gov/pmc/articles/PMC2845804/, accessed June 6, 2018.

doses of catastrophic news. This is so we are not overwhelmed to the point of radical but ill-considered actions like suicide or homicide.

Though the brain filters the bad news, some bad news gets through. What follows is a flood of horrifically negative emotions.

Sean Witwer describes his own emotions when he was served with divorce papers:

> *I'm not sure how many negative emotions can flood a body at once, but this is one of those rare instances in life that can never be described sufficiently by mere words. Unless you have ever experienced it, you can't understand the mix of disbelief, rejection, grief, sadness, brokenness, and shock that hits. My heart was in a blender and my wife turned it to 'high.' My body was hit by a numbing, sick, empty feeling and I trembled inside.*[20]

What you might feel and experience at this stage:

- Rage which may be expressed in shouting, crying, throwing or damaging objects and/or the desire to hurt someone, including oneself.
- Numbness, a sense of disbelief. *I can't believe this is happening.* A sense that time has slowed down.
- Anxiety and perhaps panic when you project into the future what this moment means in the long-term.
- Guilt at what happened that led to this moment.
- Emptiness, a feeling that usually comes when you've gone through the above emotions.
- A strange sense of being detached from reality. You may experience a sense of loss of reality, of being in a hazy, unreal world. You observe the environment as though watching a

[20] Sean Witwer, *Divorce Recovery 101: A Step by Step Guide to Reinvent Yourself in 30 Days* (Amazon Digital Services, 2016), Kindle Locations 393-402.

movie, remote and detached from the events happening around you. You are unable to wake up from this dream into the real world.[21]

- Thoughts of wanting to end your life. Suicidal thoughts are common after any extreme loss. If you are experiencing thoughts of taking your life, go to Appendix A to assess your risk and get help. The National Suicide Hotline is **800-273-8255.**

- Emotional fluctuation, that is, switching between thoughts of the positives of the pending divorce and the extreme negatives. The brain is wired to try to find the good in every negative circumstance, so it is natural that we would think of something positive in the midst of the bad news. Extreme mood swings are common at this stage.

- Many people lose their appetite and they struggle to sleep. Some experience a tightness in their throat. Sighing is also common.

- Relief—some may feel a sense of relief, especially if you saw it coming or were the initiator. But given that 80% of divorces are filed by wives and that only 20% of divorced people experience divorce as a significantly positive event, most men will not feel relief. Those who do feel an initial sense of liberation often later experience these stages of negative emotions.

Your goal at this point is to simply survive without making decisions that will cause lasting harm.

Survival Strategies:

Reach out for help to God and two or three wise friends, a counselor and a pastor. *Talk it out or you will take it out.* As you talk it out, don't be surprised if you repeat the story of what happened many times. Repeating the story is how our brain is wrestling with accepting this new reality.

---

[21]Bruce Fisher and Robert Alberti, *Rebuilding: When Your Relationship Ends*, 4th Ed., (Oakland: New Harbinger Publications, 2016), Kindle Locations 2064-2066.

Don't believe everything you're telling yourself about yourself or the situation. Don't project into the future what could happen. Just live in and through this moment.

Duration: Numbness and shock last a few hours to a few days. If you are stuck in shock for several weeks, seek help immediately. Being stuck is measured by intensity of emotions and functionality. If you can't go to work or do normal daily tasks, intervention is called for. Reach out to a counselor for help.

Success: You know you are moving through shock when you are able to acknowledge the reality of the situation enough to begin to deal with it.

Identity issue: The question you will be asking yourself at this stage is, *"What happened?"*

Think About It . . .

- If you feel you are still in shock, get help.

Life Commitment:

Though the earth gives way and falls into the heart of the sea, God will get me through this (Psalm 46). I commit my present and my future to his care. And I call upon him for comfort, knowing he wants to comfort me in my pain and eventually heal me.

Day 8: The Stages of Divorce — (2) Raw Pain

The Word

How long must I wrestle with my thoughts and every day have sorrow in my heart? How long will my enemy triumph over me?

— Psalm 13.2

Thought for the Day

The biblical way to deal with suffering is to transform what is individual into something corporate. Most cultures show a spontaneous comprehension of this. The suffering person is joined by friends who join their tears and prayers in a communal lament. They do not hush up the sound of weeping but augment it.

If others weep with me, there must be more to the suffering than my own petty weakness or selfish sense of loss. The community votes with its tears that there is suffering that is worth weeping over.

~ Eugene Peterson

Most of us have experienced excruciating physical pain. One time my stomach was cramping so badly I went to the ER. I was willing to do whatever it took to get out of the pain. When I arrived at the ER a team quickly mobilized to attend to me with the shared goals of diagnosis, pain relief and healing.

Everyone has experienced emotional pain as well. Though our society treats emotional pain and physical pain differently, emotional pain is just as real and damaging as physical pain. It's important for you to realize this and give yourself permission to feel your heartbreak and expect help and relief.

We experience pain when we feel a loss of any kind. Divorce introduces layers of losses that touch multiple areas of life.

This stage is described well here:

> *As the shock wears off, the pain begins. This is a time of emotional upheaval.... You will experience overwhelming and excruciating pain—pain so palpable as to even feel it physically. Physical symptoms may include loss of appetite and weight loss or gain, chest pain, insomnia and extreme fatigue. Emotional symptoms of sadness, anger, guilt, anxiety, restlessness, and agitation will most likely occur. The hallmarks of this phase are rapid mood swings, intense emotions and the feeling of lost control over your life. You may even feel like you are losing your sanity.*[22]

What you might feel and experience at this stage:

Hurt, pain, anguish, sorrow. I'm not sure any language has the words to capture what the deeply wounded soul feels like.

Sadness—a heaviness, a shadow, a darkness. *Outside were sun and billowing clouds, people going about their normal lives. But how could that be? How could things be so blissfully routine and ordinary out there when you're feeling so much darkness and despair in here?*[23] Our English word 'sad' has its roots in the Germanic languages that meant 'full.' Sadness is a heaviness, a weightiness that overshadows and underlies everything in a person's life and thoughts. It 'fills' your soul with gray.

---

[22] Author unknown, *The New Grief Stages: Finding Your Way Through the Tasks of Mourning*, accessed March 23, 2018, https://www.recover-from-grief.com/new-grief-stages.html.

[23] H. Norman Wright, *Experiencing Divorce*, (Nashville: B&H Books, 2017), Kindle Locations 399-401.

Fear of how you will do life now, what you will tell others and what they will think of you, how you will make it financially.

Rage which may be may be expressed in shouting, crying, throwing or damaging objects and/or the desire to hurt someone, including oneself. Like a hurt animal, hurt humans may lash out at self or others. (See Day 34)

Regret at things said or done or not said or not done.

Trouble catching your breath and frequent sighing.

What is unique to divorce at this stage?

Your experience of pain at this stage will depend on your relationship to your spouse before the divorce and if you are the Leaver or the Left.

If you were in love with your spouse and enjoyed her company, you will experience the pain of separation. You will miss being with her. Like death, then, the separation caused by divorce will create separation pain in your life.

If you were unhappy with your wife and didn't like being around her, you won't experience the pain of separation as much. But you *will* experience the lost dream of being a family and all the things attendant to that. In my experience as a pastor helping men through divorce, I observed that before a wife left her husband, he was often unhappy and desired to be away from her. Then when she actually left him, he longed to be back in the family. He didn't know what he missed until it was gone.

Even if you were unhappy in the marriage and wanted out, men often long for what they now miss—the routine of family life, being a part of his children's lives, even doing life together as a married couple.

Unique to divorce is the pain of the ripping apart of an emotional bond. Divorce is the deliberate intentional severing of a bond by one partner, a bond that was to last until death. No one gets married planning to divorce later. At some point you were in love with your spouse. Divorce involves both the radical separation from someone you presumably loved at one time, *and* the rejection of that person.

In some ways death is easier. If my wife had died I would presume she loved me. I would miss her but I would not experience the added pain of rejection. Divorce introduces the heartbreak of rejection into the already heavy burden of separation. (See Appendix D for a comparison of the death of a spouse to separation because of divorce.)

The major **survival strategy** is to ride it out. Don't do anything violent or permanent. Don't believe what you are telling yourself about you. Believe what God says about you. Connect with a good friend who can hear your anguish without trying to smooth your pain over with easy fixes. Find a counselor and/or pastor to sit with you in the agony.

Duration: Raw pain comes and goes for days, weeks or even months.

Success: Success looks like surviving intact without damaging yourself or others. Success is experiencing God's comforting presence. Successfully navigating through this stage doesn't mean that you will never feel the raw pain again. Success is experienced when the intensity and the frequency of the pain diminish over time.

Identity issue: The question you will be asking yourself at this stage is, *"Why me?"*

Think About It . . .

Think back on a time when you experienced raw pain as a kid, teenager or adult. What did you do then? Do you regret any actions you took back then? What can you do differently now?

Life Commitment:

I commit to riding this pain out, trusting that it won't last forever and God will get me through it.

Day 9: The Stages of Divorce — (3) Anger & Bargaining

The Word

For man's anger does not bring about the righteous life that God desires.
— James 1.20

Thought for the Day

Broken hearts are very vulnerable; they must be guarded carefully. When your heart has been broken, it can either become more soft and pliable to the work of God, or it can become hardened toward God and the things of God. And it is a strong temptation to harden our hearts toward God when he has disappointed us and when it feels like he has deserted us. If your heart is broken, are you willing to allow this hurt to serve as a softening agent that makes you more aware of God, more alive to his purposes, more sensitive to his Spirit at work on you and in you? Or will you let your heart become hardened so that you no longer hear his word, accept his rebuke, experience his mercy?

~ Nancy Guthrie

Divorce rips apart what God put together. Ripped things hurt and hurt people rage. Anger is a dominant emotion among the divorced, especially in the one who is left. Many divorcees are caught off guard by the intensity of their anger—so much so that experts have labeled this 'divorce anger.'

Anger is a dominant emotion among men. For many men nearly every negative emotion is processed and expressed as anger. Sadness may come out as anger. Grief may come out as anger.

Given that divorce causes much anger and men are, by nature, angry, we should not be surprised that divorced men experience anger intensely and for a long time. Genevieve Clapp notes that *Anger and divorce go together about the same as do love and marriage.*[24] As we come together in love, we split apart in rage. In one study, one third of men were intensely angry ten years after their divorce was final. This is stunning.[25]

Anger may flair up at certain flashpoints: (1) when you are told or somehow discover she is leaving, (2) when the property is divided, and (3) when decisions are made regarding custody of the children. It's at these points where the losses are particularly felt.

For better or worse, anger serves several purposes: it releases negative energy, it may get people to change or take action, it makes us feel powerful. When it comes to divorce, we may resort to anger to try to hang onto our ex or to punish her for her decision to leave. We may use anger to defend our case in the court of public opinion, even if that 'court' is just a few friends.

For these and many other reasons, divorce and anger go together like a hand in a glove, or maybe we should say, like a fist into a boxing glove.

At the same time, you may desperately want your wife back. It is in this phase that bargaining kicks in. I remember sending two texts to my soon-to-be ex-wife agreeing with two of her complaints against me, complaints with which I totally disagreed! I was trying to get her back, but I was also furious. This is a hard line to walk: to be angry and yet try not to express anger in a way that will drive her away.

Not only do we try to bargain with our ex to get her back but we might also try bargaining with God: *I will go to church if you will get*

[24]Genevieve Clapp, *Divorce and New Beginnings: A Complete Guide to Recovery, Solo Parenting, Co-Parenting, and Stepfamilies*, 2nd edition (Hoboken, NJ: Wiley, 2000), Kindle Location 742.

[25]Ibid., Kindle Location 747.

her back for me. I will give my tax refund to help orphans if you will send her back to me.

When it becomes clear that our bargaining has failed, anger may explode in newly destructive ways. It's important to *think through every proposed action stemming from anger for its potential to harm others or yourself.*

What you might feel and experience at this stage:

- Pure anger, fury, hatred. The thoughts in your head may produce strong enough emotions that they want to be expressed outwardly in destructive ways such as physical harm to yourself or to others or to property.
- Feelings of affection for your wife that will drive you to attempt to bargain with her, God or others to get her back.
- Emotional fluctuations, swinging between anger and affection.
- Cognitive dissonance: your mind is filled with reasons to be angry at her but also thoughts on how to get her back.
- If you're the perpetrator, strong feelings of guilt.

Unique to divorce at this stage is the emotional struggle to balance fury at what has been lost with trying to retain enough emotional control to convince her to come back. This dynamic leads to strong emotional fluctuations between anger and hope, hope and despair. Your goal at this stage is not to harm others, yourself or property.

The strategies to achieve this goal include finding constructive ways to express your anger. On a practical level, intense physical activity is a lifesaver. Sweat it out at the gym, on the road, in the ring.

Another key to successfully navigating this stage is to express your thoughts and emotions to your trusted friend and to allow your counselor, therapist or pastor guide your decision-making. Decisions made in anger can have lasting consequences. It's best to *Write it out, Shout it out, Talk it out,* not *take it out.*

Duration: Bargaining should not last more than six months. Depending on your personality type, the circumstances of the divorce and the help you pursue in processing your anger, intense anger can last from six months to years.[26] The shorter the better. If anger is driving your thoughts and behavior years after the divorce, you are stuck and need help.

Success: At some point you will either reconcile, in which case you would not be reading this book. Since you are reading this book this means that she didn't come back to you. Success at this stages means you accept she is not coming back. You accept the loss. Success looks like moving forward, not letting anger bind you to the past. Success is finding hope in the future, having non-combative relations with your ex, and not spilling your anger onto your children.[27]

Identity issue: The question you will be asking yourself at this stage is either, *"Why did she reject me?"* Or *"Why was I so stupid?"*

Think About It . . .

- How has anger been useful in your life in the past?
- How have you usually expressed anger? Violence? Shouting? Passive aggressiveness?

[26]Judith Wallerstein, Julia Lewis, and Sandra Blakeslee, *The Unexpected Legacy of Divorce: A 25 Year Landmark Study* (New York: Hachette Books, 2000), Kindle Location 586.

[27]Clapp notes this hopeful aspect of anger: *Your anger may have a useful aspect. It can make it easier to distance yourself from your former spouse so you can get on with your life, but only under one condition: that you do get beyond your anger and let it go. As long as you hold onto your anger, you will be bound to your ex as surely as if you were still in love; the only difference is that the bonds will be negative rather than positive. For your own sake, you need to eliminate both the positive and negative bonds with your former partner. You have the potential to create a future in which your former spouse will no longer have power over you and will no longer trigger an emotional reaction within you.* Clapp, *Divorce and New Beginnings*, Kindle Locations 758-760.

Life Commitment:

What has happened has left me devastated, hurt and angry. I commit to expressing my anger constructively. I can be angry without being an angry man.

Day 10: The Stages of Divorce — (4) Isolation / Loneliness / Depression

The Word

I will not leave you as orphans; I will come to you. Before long, the world will not see me anymore, but you will see me. Because I live, you also will live.

— John 14.18-19

Thought for the Day

During my years caring for patients, the most common pathology I saw was not heart disease or diabetes; it was loneliness.

~ Dr. Vivek H. Murthy,
Surgeon General of the United States

Stage 3—*Anger and Bargaining*—is a reaction to the events precipitating your divorce. Anger and bargaining feel like you're doing something about this incredible pain in your life. You hope rage will somehow change the situation. You bargain, hoping to get your life back where it was before she decided to leave you.

Stage 4 begins when you recognize that anger and bargaining haven't worked. Anger and bargaining feel like action that will produce results, namely getting out of the intense pain and reconciling with your ex. When this doesn't work your soul goes on the defense, which is to huddle, turtle, withdraw, and slink away to nurse your wounds. Men like to fix things. When our efforts to fix our marriage don't work, we slither away in defeat.

What you might feel and experience at this stage:

- Exhaustion, loss of energy and enthusiasm. Anger is exhausting. Bargaining takes huge investments of emotional energy. You are spent and simply don't care anymore.
- Worthlessness. Self-pity. Your best efforts have failed. She rejected you and won't have you back. You are not lovable or likeable anymore, or so it seems that way.
- Sadness, grief, misery. Negative thoughts dominate.
- Everything is gray.
- You may experience feelings of intense isolation, loneliness, emptiness.
- Activities you enjoyed seem pointless.
- Food may lose its taste.
- Isolating yourself and engaging in passive activities such as watching TV or sleeping are appealing.
- The thought of starting anything new will be met with a sigh and desire to take a nap.
- Other signs of depression are fatigue, irritability, messiness, physical pain, numbness, trouble concentrating and suicidal thoughts.

What is unique to divorce at this stage?

The combination of severe losses brought on by the divorce and the added pain of rejection make loneliness and depression compounding problems in recovering from divorce. At this point in the process your friends may be tired of walking this journey with you and may abandon you or at least pull back. This adds to our isolation and gives us one more reason to turtle up.

The major **survival strategy** at this stage is to balance your need to invest less energy in life with your need for remaining connected to people and activities that will give life again. Say *yes* to activities and invitations even though everything in you wants to say *no.*

It is here that you may experience God's unique presence. Lettie Burd Cowman was an American Christian writer and missionary in the early twentieth century. I have found her devotional *Streams in the Desert* amazingly timely and helpful. She writes regarding the Bible verse *"What I tell you in the dark, speak in the daylight; what is whispered in your ear, proclaim from the roofs"* (Matthew 10: 27):

> *Our Lord is constantly taking us into the dark in order to tell us something. It may be the darkness of a home where bereavement has drawn the blinds; the darkness of a lonely and desolate life, in which some illness has cut us off from the light and the activity of life; or the darkness of some crushing sorrow and disappointment. It is there He tells us His secrets—great and wonderful, eternal and infinite. He causes our eyes, blinded by the glare of things on earth, to behold the heavenly constellations. And our ears suddenly detect even the whisper of His voice, which has been so often drowned out by the turmoil of earth's loud cries.*[28]

Expect God to find you in your dark place and give you comfort, encouragement and, eventually, a new calling for the next stage of your life.

In addition to staying connected to God, you must stay connected to your counselor. You must *not* believe everything you are telling yourself. For years I have told depressed people, *Don't believe everything you are telling yourself right now. Your thinking is distorted. Instead, listen to what wise and trusted friends are saying to you.*[29]

Cling to hope: how you are *thinking* now will change. You will have more positive thoughts as time goes by. How you are *feeling*

---

[28]L. B. Cowman, *Streams in the Desert: 366 Daily Devotional Readings* (Grand Rapids: Zondervan, 2008), 150.

[29]For more information about depression, go to https://www.webmd.com/depression/guide/detecting-depression\#1.

now will change. You will feel better in time.

If you're stuck in a pattern of negative, cynical thinking, you may be depressed. If you know you have some reasons to be positive but your mind can't go there despite your best efforts, see a counselor/therapist and your medical doctor. Living with depression is nasty, and counseling, along with medication (if needed) can literally save your life. There is no shame in getting the help you need.

Duration: Clinical depression is defined as having experiencing the above signs and symptoms for most of the day, nearly every day, for at least two weeks. If this is you, you need help. Help will include conversations with a counselor, therapist, psychiatrist and/or pastor. Treatment recommendations may include medication. This stage may last for weeks or months. The more you push back by remaining engaged with the world, the shorter this stage will be.

Success: You will know you are getting through depression when you wake up one day realizing that you have had more good days than bad days and when you begin to want to do things again.

Identity issue: The question you will be asking yourself at this stage at this stage is, *"Who am I?"*

Think About It . . .

- When you experienced rejection in the past, what did you do?
- How strong is the pull in you to withdraw from the world?
- What is one thing you can do today to push against the urge to turtle?

Life Commitment:

Though I feel a strong pull toward isolation, I will not give in. I will say 'yes' to any invitations that come my way to engage in life again, and I will take steps to be a part of the world again.

Day 11: The Stages of Divorce — (5) Turning the Corner

The Word

There is surely a future hope for you, and your hope will not be cut off.

— Proverbs 23.18

Thought for the Day

Discouragement focuses more on the broken glories of creation than it does on the restoring glories of God's character, presence, and promises.

~ Paul David Trip

At some point you will realize that you are having more good moments than bad, and when the bad moments come they are less intense. Gradually life doesn't seem so hard and traumatic. Your energy slowly returns. Your sleep improves and you begin to think more clearly.

A terrible thing happened, and you won't forget this terrible thing. But in a healthy recovery process, the terrible thing doesn't dominate your brain space like it did when the event first occurred. Healthy recovery is evidenced when the pain of divorce and remembrances of the events surrounding it diminish in size. They are there, but not prevailing over all your thinking.

As life begins to return, determine to thrive beyond your divorce by working on your own issues that contributed to your divorce.

Don't use these glimmers of new energy to go back to old habits that may have put you in this situation in the first place. Take this opportunity to envision a new future for you, your kids and a potential mate.

A caution: Some people may experience a return to depression at this stage. Just when you are beginning to feel better, triggers can send you back to the Raw Pain stage. Don't let setbacks keep you down. Remember how far you have come and the bright possibilities for the future.

What you might feel and experience at this stage:

- Less pain, more hope.
- More energy.
- Better sleep.
- More desire to live life.
- Triggers that may set you back momentarily or for hours or even a few days.

What is unique to divorce at this stage?

The challenge divorce brings to turning the corner compared to other traumas such as the death of a loved one is that the tragedy is less defined in time. You must find ways to move past an event that keeps rolling out before you because your ex is still part of your life. Put another way, if your wife had died, it would probably be easier to accept her loss and move on. Divorce presents challenges because something died (your marriage) but a big part of that something keeps living (your ex). Envisioning life without your wife is more difficult because she still lives.

Survival strategies include staying connected to God, family, friends, your counselor and pastor. Determine to begin the road to building a new life with healthy habits. Take on habits that will support your mission to fulfill God's calling on the rest of your life (more on this later). Turning the corner after a great tragedy is an opportunity to remake your identity. Resolve to reject old destructive ways of living and, instead, take on habits that will make a new and better you.[30]

Duration: Turning the corner feels like a slow pivot. This is rarely a 'light bulb' moment. Light begins to dawn gradually as you begin to see hope for your future.

Success: As you begin to have glimmers of hope that you will survive this, you launch an identity separate from your spouse. You see yourself as father to each of your children, not the 'dad half' of the father/mother team. You make plans that are tailored to you without consideration of what your ex-wife will think. You think about her less often and with less emotion.

Identity: The question you will be asking yourself at this stage is, "What could be in my future?"

Think About It . . .

- Have you experienced glimmers of hope?
- Do you have more energy?
- Are you sleeping better?
- If not, don't despair. Hang on—things will get better!

[30] If you want to date again and possibly remarry, it is crucial that you start doing *now* what women want. Bluntly, women today want a man who is godly, honest, clean, neat, hard working, reliable, compassionate, humble and yet strong. They want a man who can take care of himself but is not too proud to receive a woman's love.

Life Commitment:

When I begin to feel better and see a future for myself, I determine I will use this blank slate to let God build a better me.

Day 12: The Stages of Divorce — (6) Reconstruction

The Word

No eye has seen, no ear has heard, no mind has conceived what God has prepared for those who love him.
— 1 Corinthians 2.9

Thought for the Day

The land of God's promises is open before us, and it is His will for us to possess it. We must measure off the territory with the feet of obedient faith and faithful obedience, thereby claiming and appropriating it as our own.
~ L. B. Cowman

My hunch is that if you have reached this stage you would not be reading this book. If you still have the reconstruction stage ahead of you, know that *you will get through these stages of divorce.* There is hope for your future. Nothing in your heart or head may be believing this right now, but be confident: ***you will survive divorce***. My job is to help you move beyond mere surviving into truly thriving.

As you consider your future, you have much to look forward to in this stage. At Stage 6 you make critical choices as to what kind of future you will have. Ask God who he wants you to be and what he wants you to do. Bounce ideas off trusted friends. Make sure the new things you try are healthy, not self-destructive. Build habits that are life-giving to you and to others.

At this stage it's common to try on new 'identities.' In my own case, I felt my ex-wife had suppressed elements of my identity partly because she didn't like to do many of the things I liked to do, most of which are outdoors. So in my reconstruction phase I hiked, backpacked, skydived and cycled like a wild man!

But all is not easy at this stage. Psychologist Corine Scholtz notes that:

> *In many ways, this is the most psychologically stressful aspect of the divorcing process. Being married is a primary source of self-identity. Two individuals enter a relationship with two separate identities and then co-construct a couple identity about who they are and where and how they fit into the world. When their relationship ends, they may feel confused and fearful, as though they no longer have a script telling them how to behave.*
> *At this time the divorcing person faces a major change in self-perception. Often during this time period, they may try on different identities, attempting to find one that is comfortable for them. Sometimes during this period adults go through a second adolescence. Similar to their first adolescence, people may become very concerned about how they look, how they sound. They may buy new clothes or a new car. Many of the struggles an adult experienced as a teenager may reappear.*[31]

[31] Corine Scholtz, Stages of Divorce: *What Do Individuals Really Go Through?*, accessed April 11, 2018, https://www.marriage.com/advice/divorce/stages-of-divorce-what-do-individuals-really-go-through/. Clapp writes: *An identity crisis almost always accompanies divorce. Over the years of married life, spouses inevitably relinquish some of their individuality and pursuits in the interest of the marriage. And because of their shared years, children, home, commitments, and activities, their lives become interdependent, as if the two are woven into a single fabric. With divorce, couples must disentangle the threads of their lives, and the process may leave each with a shaky identity, in need of reworking before it can stand on its own. There are other contributors to the post-divorce identity crisis. Most people lose many of the material possessions that have become part of "who they are." Most have to assume new tasks that are out of character for them. Many feel as if they are no longer part of society's mainstream. People commonly feel they have been left adrift without an anchor. Questions believed to be settled long ago now resurface: Who am I? What do I want out of life? Where do I go from here? Your job now is to forge an identity*

Reconstruction can be tumultuous as you regain energy to move forward. You may have many ideas of what your future could be. At the same time, rebuilding is a daunting task.

What you might feel and experience at this stage:

- Fluctuating emotions as you engage the task of rebuilding your identity.
- Excitement that a new life is waiting for you.
- Conflicting desires about who you want to be.
- Desire to build your identity by trying on various experiences. If you never skydived or learned how to dance, you just might find yourself jumping out of an airplane at 14,000 fee or learning swing!
- Swinging between confidence and fear, initiative and withdrawal.

What is unique to divorce at this stage?

All trauma causes a foundational dis-integration of identity and the challenge of re-integrating yourself to accommodate the changes that come from loss. Divorce carries with it the burden of shame and a sense of failure. Getting the energy to rebuild your life from a more diminished position is a challenge.

Survival strategies include remaining connected to a counselor/therapist who can help guide you to make wise choices through the reconstruction of your identity. It is here that walking closely with God

---

separate from that of your former partner and from your marriage. You no longer have to be the person your spouse expected you to be. You can create a lifestyle of your own design, speak with your own voice, and pursue your own interests. But it will take time, and until you decide who you are, what you like, what you want to do, and where you are going, you will be between "selves," in a sense, and this may be uncomfortable for you. Clapp, *Divorce and New Beginnings*, Kindle Locations 2133-42.

is critical, as he desires to call you into the second half of your life with a clear and strong purpose (see Days 87 and 88). Being part of a local Christian men's group will help you discover how other men have navigated the challenges of life to emerge stronger and better.

Duration: Reconstruction can take months as your mind and soul slowly work through the process of identity formation and re-formation.

Success: As you picture what successfully navigating this stage looks like, ask yourself what you want people saying about you at your funeral. Success starts with deliberately choosing habits that will build a lifestyle of God's design, passionately pursuing his mission for your life.

Identity: The question you will be asking yourself at this stage is, *"Who is God and what does he desire from me and for me?"*

Think About It . . .

- What stage do you think you are in right now?
- What aspects of your identity have been diminished or destroyed because of the divorce?
- What habits in your old life need to go?
- What new habits will you choose to build a better you?
- Have you heard God's call on your life as to what he wants you to do and be for the rest of your life, or at least the next few years?

Life Commitment:

God can and does use suffering to strip me down and rebuild me into the man he wants me to be. I submit to his loving hand of guidance and strong call upon my life so that I will finish well.

Day 13: The Stages of Divorce — (7) Acceptance & Hope

The Word

This poor man called, and the Lord heard him; he saved him out of all his troubles.
— Psalm 34:6-7

Thought for the Day

Optimism and hope are radically different attitudes. Optimism is the expectation that things—the weather, human relationships, the economy, the political situation, and so on—will get better. Hope is the trust that God will fulfill God's promises to us in a way that leads us to true freedom. The optimist speaks about concrete changes in the future. The person of hope lives in the moment with the knowledge and trust that all of life is in good hands.
~ Henri J. M. Nouwen

British Entrepreneur and motivational speaker Rasheed Ogunlaru says, *Sometimes in life there's no problem and sometimes there is no solution. In this space—between these apparent poles—life flows.* [32]

[32] Rasheed Ogunlaru, *azquotes*, accessed June 7, 2018, http://www.azquotes.com/quote/673473. Our Western mindset makes acceptance of hard events more difficult. John Reich and colleagues note that Western and Eastern philosophies... *offer contrasting views on the nature of conscious experience most likely to sustain well-being. Western views focus on choice and mastery over the environment, whereas Eastern philosophies emphasize full awareness and acceptance of experience, however*

In the last stage of divorce recovery you come to accept that you are divorced and it can't be undone. The process of divorce was (and still remains) painful, but the best way forward is forward. You accept what happened and choose to move on.

Clapp notes that:

> *Those who successfully complete this stage have learned to accept the end of their marriages and the role they played in the breakup. They have disentangled their lives from those of their former spouses and created separate identities. They have achieved detachment from their former partners, so there is no longer a need for either hostility or dependence. And they have clarified their priorities, set realistic goals, and found a satisfying lifestyle.*[33]

The key marker of success at this stage is that your ex and the events surrounding your divorce don't dominate your head space. Perfect acceptance would be that you seldom think of your ex and when you do, you don't have strong feelings of anger/resentment nor do you have strong feelings of lingering desire/attachment. Your ex becomes one of millions of other people.

That's the perfect scenario. The reality is that you and I will always have emotions—sometimes strong emotions—when we think of our ex and the marriage we had. How influential are those thoughts over our lives? Is lingering pain still being transmitted to others around us or has God transformed our pain into energy to forge into the future he has for us? Recovery will be characterized by the latter.

Another critical and difficult issue is forgiveness. Perfect recovery would mean complete forgiveness of ourselves and our ex and any people involved in the demise of our marriage. This is a long and

---

painful, to gain an enlightened and "joyous" view of the world. John Reich, *et al*, *Handbook of Adult Resilience* (New York: Guilford Publications, 2012), 8. Timothy Keller writes that *Sociologists and anthropologists have analyzed and compared the various ways that cultures train its members for grief, pain, and loss. And when this comparison is done, it is often noted that our own contemporary secular, Western culture is one of the weakest and worst in history at doing so.* Timothy Keller, *Walking with God through Pain and Suffering* (New York: Penguin, 2013), 20.

[33] Clapp, *Divorce and New Beginnings*, Kindle Locations 274-76.

hard road which I address in the second book in this series, *Daily Survival Guide for Divorced Men Book 2: Days 92-180.*

When in the acceptance stage, you will agree that

> *Resilience transforms. It transforms hardship into challenge, failure into success, helplessness into power. Resilience turns victims into survivors and allows survivors to thrive. Resilient people are loath to allow even major setbacks to push them from their life course.*[34]

What is unique to divorce at this stage?

The fact that your ex still lives and may be engaged in a new relationship makes acceptance more challenging for divorced men. The fact that 80% of divorces are filed by women means that many men are the ones who are the 'left.' Being the one left makes acceptance difficult. The leaver has clearly weighed her options, made a decision acceptable to her and followed through. She worked through the acceptance part of the divorce *before* she divorced. The one left has to work through these stages of divorce from a stance of surprise rather than calculated decision.

The major **challenge** at this stage is to stay connected to God, your dream, other people. When you feel you are slipping back, talk it out. Don't let the past rob you of your future!

Duration: This stage usually begins around two years after the Date of Separation (DOS) and can take years to complete.

Success: You know you're in this stage when thoughts of your ex don't elicit strong positive or negative emotions, you're engaged in living your new identity with energy and enthusiasm, and you have a separate and growing relationship with your kids.

[34] Karen Reivich, *The Resilience Factor: Seven Essential Skills For Overcoming Life's Inevitable Obstacles* (New York: Random House, 2003), Kindle Locations 114-116.

Identity: The question you will be asking yourself at this stage is, *"How far will God take me?"*

Think About It . . .

- When you think of your ex, what emotions do you experience?
- Has God given you a mission and purpose for your future? If not, ask him to, and then be patient while waiting for the response.

Life Commitment:

Though a terrible thing happened to me I know God has a plan and a future for me. I am eager to know his plan for me but also willing to be patient for him to work in my life, preparing me for his future.

Day 14: Moving Through These Stages

The Word

Brothers and sisters, I do not consider myself yet to have taken hold of it. But one thing I do: Forgetting what is behind and straining toward what is ahead, I press on toward the goal to win the prize for which God has called me heavenward in Christ Jesus.

— Philippians 3:13-14

Thought for the Day

Good management of bad experiences leads to great growth.

~ John Maxwell

The Greek word in the scripture above that is translated with the English phrase *straining toward* is **epekteinomai**. The root of this word means *to stretch*. Interestingly this word has two prefixes attached to it, *epi* and *ek*. Without getting too technical, these two prefixes greatly intensify the meaning of the root word. In other words, Paul is saying that though he has much in his past that could haunt him, he is really stretching toward the future, pressing in on God's purpose for his life.

How long does it take to get through these stages of divorce, and do you just go right through them or is it more circular or more back and forth? It depends and maybe and yes.

We are unique humans with many factors involved in our divorces. Each of us will go through these stages at different rates. And 'going through them' doesn't usually mean a straight linear progression (sorry about that you engineers!). You may be in the middle of Stage 5—'Turning the Corner'— and see your ex at the grocery store, sending you back to Stage 1 for a moment.

The key here is to see yourself making progress despite brief setbacks.

Another key is to measure your progress in terms of how you are functioning and how you are feeling. If the divorce happened four years ago and you are barely able to crawl out of bed, there's a problem that needs professional help. If you are expressing your pain in destructive habits such as drinking, drugging, porning or anything else that is less than God's best, you will be slow in progressing toward Stage 7 (and you will continue doing damage to yourself and others).

How are you doing? The best way to answer that question is to have honest conversations with your counselor/therapist and a couple of good friends who love you enough to accept you as you are but not leave you where you are.

Think About It . . .

- A chart outlining these stages of divorce can be found at https://bit.ly/2oXIEqo. Go there now and determine where you are in this process.

- Now ask your friends and counselor where *they* think you are.

Life Commitment:

I do not consider myself yet to have taken hold of it. But one thing I do: Forgetting what is behind and straining toward what is ahead, I press on toward the goal to win the prize for which God has called me heavenward in Christ Jesus.

Day 15: Mission—Empower

The Word

In the day when I cried out, you answered me,
and made me bold with strength in my soul.
– Psalm 138.3

Thought for the Day

Men's Divorce Recovery exists to ***Empower*** *Divorced Men through Support, Knowledge and Encouragement to Survive and Thrive beyond their divorce to become Resilient, Strong and Wise men in their world.*
~ Mission Statement, Men's Divorce Recovery

Several months after my divorce was final, God spoke to me. He clearly invited/commanded me to start a ministry to men like myself who had experienced the shock and pain of divorce.

The call God has placed upon me came in the way he usually speaks to me—words come into my mind I know are not from me. I have experienced his call several times in my lifetime—the call to go into ministry, the call to spend a year teaching in Tanzania, the call to pastor each of the churches I have been privileged to serve. But this call to Men's Divorce Recovery was different. In each of my previous calls, God's voice was mixed with my own unhealthy (but probably unavoidable) dose of personal ambition.

I was a 'career pastor.' I had worked hard on my Ph.D. to have all the external qualifications I could acquire to lead churches to new-found greatness. I was bound up in the throes of the first half of a man's spiritual journey—building up the 'kingdom of me.' Don't get me wrong. I served these churches and cared for them from the very depths of my heart. As a pastor/leader, I duly shared the credit and took the blame. I enthusiastically worked to fulfill God's call upon my life to pastor each church diligently and faithfully. But the pressure to take the church to the 'next level,' to grow ever bigger and brighter, to bring back the 'glory days' was unrelenting.

At the time of this writing I am 56 years old. Despite my best efforts, I have lost a wife and two churches in eighteen months, surely some sort of record. Personal losses have multiplied—my hard-earned reputation, my career as a pastor and teacher, hundreds of thousands of dollars in lost wages. My losses look different than yours, but *they are all losses and loss hurts.*

But I am not despairing because God has called me from the midst of what the world may perceive as a failed life to reach other men hammered by divorce and/or personal failure.

The mission statement of Men's Divorce Recovery (above) reflects my own personal desires regarding the goals, the means to reach the goals, and the desired outcomes of Men's Divorce Recovery. Let's spend a few days unpacking the important truths in MDR's mission statement.

FIRST, Men's Divorce Recovery exists to **Empower** Divorced Men. The last thing a divorced man feels is empowered. Quite the opposite in fact. We feel *neutered.*

Yet we know that the amazing grace of God finds its home in the midst of devastation and desolation. What emerges from the combination of a yielded heart and God's grace is a man humbly empowered to fulfill his purpose with courage and conviction.

So far you have been living on your own power. Though you may have thought you were powerful, you weren't. Divorce and other life blows reveal how little power we really have.

But God *is* powerful—fantastically more powerful than we can imagine (and we have amazingly powerful imaginations). The journey through the pain and loss of divorce can lead you away from reliance upon your own power to tapping into God's incredible power. Though you have been drained of power in so many ways, *don't despair.* God is ready to take up the slack where you lack.

Time after time God says to me, *Hold on, I've got you, I am sustaining you, I will see you through this, you will get through this!*

I let God take my pain, heartache and worries. When I let go and relax into him, I am relinquishing dependence on my own power and letting him handle things in his power. My mind clears, my tight chest relaxes, and I am off the ledge once again.

The key is hearing God's invitation to take the load and then consciously allowing him to have it.[35]

Think About It . . .

- What or who is the source of the power for your life?
- What or who makes you powerless (or less powerful)?
- How do you feel when you are powerless (or less powerful)?
- What do you do when you are powerless (or less powerful)?

Life Commitment:

I give up. I give up trying to be strong, powerful, mighty and important based on who I believe myself to be. God is bigger and better. He is stronger and wiser. I defer to him. I give him control over my life. I let him be my power source.

---

[35]Dallas Willard writes, *God wants to be wanted, to be wanted enough that we are ready, predisposed, to find him present with us. And if, by contrast, we are ready and set to find ways of explaining away his gentle overtures, he will rarely respond with fire from heaven. More likely, he will simply leave us alone; and we shall have the satisfaction of thinking ourselves not to be gullible.* Dallas Willard, *Hearing God: Developing A Conversational Relationship with God* (Downers Grove: InterVarsity Press, 1999), 273.

Day 16: Mission—Survive

The Word

This poor man called, and the Lord heard him; he saved him out of all his troubles.

The angel of the Lord encamps around those who fear him, and he delivers them.[36]
— Psalm 34:6-7

Thought for the Day

You see, if you quit, you lose. But so long as you stick it out, you're still in with a chance.
~ Bear Grylls

This poor man called . . . When I read this verse I hear the cry of a guy who has had to deal with so much he just hangs his head and sings, *"Nobody knows the trouble I've seen, nobody knows but Jesus."* Brother, I've been that poor man!

[36]To fear God in the Bible means to have a reverential awe of him. Part of that awe is to literally fear him—he is the most powerful being in the universe and is rightly feared (Matthew 10.28). At the same time, to be in awe of God is to be amazed by him and his handiwork in creation and beyond. William Eisenhower says, *As I walk with the Lord, I discover that God poses an ominous threat to my ego, but not to me. He rescues me from my delusions, so he may reveal the truth that sets me free. He casts me down, only to lift me up again. He sits in judgment of my sin, but forgives me nevertheless. Fear of the Lord is the beginning of wisdom, but love from the Lord is its completion.* William Eisenhower, "Fearing God," *Christianity Today*, March 1986.

Men's Divorce Recovery exists to Empower Divorced Men through Support, Knowledge and Encouragement to ***Survive*** *. . .*

Divorce is a body blow that takes you to the mat. Our first priority is to survive this take down and eventually get back on our feet to fight another day.

I have never been in armed combat, but I understand that when a soldier goes down, several things happen. First, the wounded man cries for help. Next, his buddies respond by immediately coming to his aid. Third, they protect their fallen comrade from further harm. Fourth, they stabilize the wounded man and, lastly, they get him out.

Divorce is not the same as an RPG going off in your Humvee, but the impact of divorce on the soul is a slashing wound which cuts through the heart. In the midst of your pain, call on God. When you call on the Lord, he sets into motion the same process that happens on the battlefield.

Look back again at Psalm 34:6-7:

He ***Hears***. God hears all our prayers, but when he hears the cry of a desperate man, he bends his ear in a way that gives special attention to the one crying out. God hears that cry whether the pain is of the body or of the soul. Like a mother who instantly recognizes the wail of her baby amidst ten other screeching babies, your cry to God is instantly heard and given special attention.

He ***Encamps***. When a soldier goes down, his buddies immediately surround him with weapons facing outward to protect the wounded warrior from further harm. In the same way, God surrounds you. He is a refuge, a place of safety. The attacks may continue but the impact of those attacks on your soul are shared by God who is beside you and all around you and in you. He's got your back (and your front).

He ***Saves***. The Hebrew word used here means *victory*. The poor man is surrounded by God's mighty protecting angels and help is immediately given to heal and restore. Just as treatment of the wounded soldier begins on the battlefield, so does God begin to stop the bleeding in your soul *right now.*

He ***Delivers***. The Hebrew word basically means *he gets you out of there!* Just as powerful forces are marshaled to get a wounded soldier off the battlefield and into a field hospital, so too God gets us out of the painful place we are in. It will take a while, but to know you will not always be in pain is a ray of hope giving you resolve to hang on.

Survival begins with calling out to God. As proud men who are defined by our ability to go it alone and live a self-sufficient life, this is a hard and humble place to be. But the smart poor man is going to do one simple thing: *Call on the Lord.* God is coming to your aid right now.

One other thing: If you are in survival mode, ***set realistic expectations***. No one expects a wounded soldier to function at the same level he was before he was shot. In the same way, when you are in the middle of divorce, your ability to function will be diminished. Learn to be OK with that (see **Day 22**).

When things were really hard, I had less energy or motivation to do things. I wanted to sleep more and things looked gloomy, even good things. I lost a big chunk of that *oomph* that I relied on to get through the day. To cope, I cut things in my daily schedule that weren't necessary. But I kept doing the things that I knew gave me life—my morning time with God, eating right and exercising, and fulfilling my commitments to work. This is a good survival strategy.

Think About It . . .

- Where are you in the journey? Have you just been 'hit' and are lying on the battlefield with serious wounds? If so, have you called out to God for help? Have you reached out to others?

- How have you experienced God's rescue before?

Life Commitment:

I am calling on the Lord for help right now. Just as there is no shame for the wounded soldier to admit he is hit and needs immediate help, I declare that there is no shame for me to call on God (and others) to save, deliver and heal me. God, help me!

Day 17: Mission—Thrive

The Word

He is like a tree planted by streams of water, which yields its fruit in season and whose leaf does not wither. Whatever he does prospers.

— Psalm 1:3

Thought for the Day

Success is the ability to go from one failure to another with no loss of enthusiasm.

~ Winston Churchill

For the first months after I was body-slammed by divorce, survival was my goal. I could not look beyond getting through that day. Whereas before I had been full of energy and fire, now I was a dull ember just trying to keep a little glow going. Before I was hit with the divorce my mind was happily jumbled with all kinds of new ideas and ways of doing things. Now my brain was struggling to just wrap itself around this new reality of unwanted events. During those days, I counted surviving each single day a huge victory.

But there came a day when I realized that just surviving was not going to do it for me. I was meant for more than just muddling through the day, collapsing into bed at night for sleep's sweet escape once again. I am made to fulfill a larger purpose. I am part of a grander design.

Most people survive major crises. The power of a human being to keep going is truly remarkable. But we are made for more than surviving. We're meant to *thrive.*

That's why thriving is a huge part of our mission statement: *Men's Divorce Recovery exists to Empower Divorced Men through Support, Knowledge and Encouragement to* ***Survive and Thrive beyond their divorce...***

MDR exists to 'catch' you in your pain with the initial aim of rescuing you from disastrous decisions often made when one is in extreme misery. Beyond *survival,* however, we embrace the amazing reality that God never wastes pain but turns it on the enemy for Kingdom good. The goal is to help you move beyond surviving to thriving. True thriving is to live out the purpose for which you were made.

Business consultant Paul Stoltz says that for you to first survive and then thrive through setbacks you must *"Identify your mountain, your purpose in life, so that the work you do is meaningful."*[37]

Stoltz goes on to write,

> *I've discovered that people seem to share a core human drive to ascend, to move forward and up along one's mountain or purpose in one's life. But it's tough. If defining—let alone staying true to a worthy aspiration for one's life—were easy, more people would make it happen. The vast majority stop short or bail out.*[38]

If you're in survival mode right now, so be it. Set your expectations accordingly. But expect that God has more for you than merely getting through the next day. God has a plan to use this intense pain for his glory and for your good. It may seem inconceivable right now, but it's true. I've seen it over and over again with men who have been hammered by divorce—God has a plan and a future for you—and it's good!

---

[37]John Maxwell, *The Maxwell Daily Reader: 365 Days of Insight to Develop the Leader Within You and Influence Those Around You* (Nashville: Thomas Nelson, 2007), 379.

[38]Paul Gordon Stoltz, *Grit: The New Science of What It Takes to Persevere, Flourish, Succeed* (Climb Strong Press, 2014), Kindle Location 1106.

Think About It . . .

- Think back on a time when you were thriving. What energized you? What fulfilled you?
- Where are you now? Surviving? Ready to Thrive? Just making it through the day? Feeling a little renewed energy?

Life Commitment:

Though I find it hard to see right now, I am choosing to trust God not to waste my pain. I commit to being receptive to his greater call on my life and I look forward to hearing his call and fulfilling his greater purpose in my life.

Day 18: Mission—Resilient

The Word

I am able to do all things through Him who strengthens me.
– Philippians 4:13

Thought for the Day

The special characteristic of a great person is to triumph over the disasters and panics of human life.
~ Seneca

To put it simply, resilience is the ability to bounce back. Technically, the definition goes like this: *Resilience is the capability of a strained body to recover its size and shape after deformation caused especially by compressive stress.* The Latin base of resilient is *salire,* a verb meaning "to leap."

Resilience is the ability of the football player who has been 'shaken up' to shake it off and stand up to play again. It's the ability of the runner to push through the last mile of the race.

I love the White Mountains of New Hampshire. One of my favorite hikes is up Mt. Lafayette. Combined with Mt. Lincoln and Little Haystack, it's a grueling nine miles with 3,860 feet of elevation.

One particular trip I was leading a group from my church. One of the men, Mike, slipped off a wet rock and twisted his knee. He grimaced in pain as we assessed what to do. Nearly halfway through the hike, Mike determined to keep going.

As happens with the wounded, Mike lagged. As we began our descent I was with two of Mike's kids further along the trail. The kids and I stopped for a breather. Mike eventually caught up to us. As Mike approached, one of his kids said, *Hey look, Dad's alive!* Mike *was* alive, and still in the game, though moving slower than the rest of us. Mike was resilient![39]

Men's Divorce Recovery exists to *Empower Divorced Men through Support, Knowledge and Encouragement to Survive and Thrive beyond their divorce to become* ***Resilient****, Strong and Wise men in their world.*

Quitters are remembered for, well, quitting! And then they are quickly forgotten. But those who persevere are remembered not for what put them down but how they managed to get back up.

How will you get through this? Where does your resilience come from?

The only enduring answer is that our ability to bounce back comes from God. When we *reach the end of our strength,* smart men *reach out to God.* If my survival is up to me, my strength is limited which means I will give up which means I will not be resilient.

Not so God. His strength is unlimited as is his unswerving commitment to you. For his **glory** he wants you to endure. For your **good** he wants you to bounce back. He is invested in your success, and your success depends on you getting back up. Getting back up depends on God.

When Paul wrote *I am able to do all things through Him who strengthens me,* he was not talking about leaping over tall buildings or building a wildly successful corporation. He was talking about resilience. *Through Christ* I can get back up and keep going. Tell God right now that you need him to pick you back up. Tell him that you need his strength to get through this day. Then take a deep breath. You are in good hands.

[39]In case you are wondering, we didn't abandon Mike on the trail! My team took turns walking with him.

Think About It . . .

- When have you been down and then gotten back up? How did it feel to get back in the game?
- When have you walked away from the challenge? Do you regret the decision to quit?
- What does getting back up look like right now?
- What does relying on God for your strength look like?

Life Commitment:

The easiest thing to do when down is to stay down and then slink off unnoticed. I will not do the easy thing. With God's strength, I will get up and get back in the game.

Day 19: Mission—Strong

The Word

God is our refuge and strength, an ever-present help in trouble. Therefore we will not fear, though the earth give way and the mountains fall into the heart of the sea, though its waters roar and foam and the mountains quake with their surging.

— Psalm 46:1–3

Thought for the Day

How do you become an adult in a society that doesn't ask for sacrifice?
How do you become a man in a world that doesn't require courage?

~ Sebastian Junger

It was the darkest day in human history. The very best man who offered the best shot at justice and reform was—just like all the rebels before him— nailed to cross timbers and left to die a slow and agonizing death. The message the government wanted to send was simple: *We are strong, you are not. Obey us or you will be bones on a cross.*

But death was not to hold him. Three days later the Rebel came back to life. But the Rebel had to die before he could legitimately say he had conquered death. To beat the power of Rome and the power of sin and Satan, Jesus had to restrain himself. He had to stay on the cross. And staying on the cross took all the strength he had.

Ironically, to be powerless enough to accomplish our salvation, Jesus had to reach deep within himself for incredible strength to tap another kind of power, the power to overcome without leaving footprints on the backs of those before him. This was a new kind of strength. It's the kind of power and strength God calls men to.

Men's Divorce Recovery exists to *Empower Divorced Men through Support, Knowledge and Encouragement to Survive and Thrive beyond their divorce to become Resilient, **Strong** and Wise men in their world.*

Being strong does **not** mean ***wielding power over others***. Being strong means ***yielding power to God*** and following him and his way. His way is distinguished by a quiet, humble power that nothing can shake.

That's why the writer of Hebrews lifts up Jesus as our hero:

> *Let us fix our eyes on Jesus, the author and perfecter of our faith, who for the joy set before him endured the cross, scorning its shame, and sat down at the right hand of the throne of God. Consider him who endured such opposition from sinful men, so that you will not grow weary and lose heart.* (Hebrews 12.1–3)

In a world weakened by so much dissension, dissolution and anemic leadership, MDR exists to guide men into their true role as men of God. Godly men are strong in a humble yet unyielding way.

Think About It . . .

- When do you feel most powerful?
- When have you powered over another through sheer strength? What was the outcome?
- When have you restrained yourself? What was the outcome?

Life Commitment:

The next time I want to use power to lash out someone I will restrain myself. I will know that this is true strength.

Day 20: Mission—Wise

The Word

Get wisdom, get understanding; do not forget my words or swerve from them. Do not forsake wisdom, and she will protect you; love her, and she will watch over you. Wisdom is supreme; therefore get wisdom. Though it cost all you have, get understanding. Esteem her, and she will exalt you; embrace her, and she will honor you.

— Proverbs 4:5–9

Thought for the Day

Talent is God given. Be humble.
Fame is man-given. Be grateful.
Conceit is self-given. Be careful.

~ John Wooden

A distinct memory I have of my first days at the University of Texas was that I was sure all the other incoming freshmen had it figured out and I was the only one who was still trying to. Much to my surprise, I learned that everyone else was still trying to figure it out too!

Thirty-five years later as a hospice chaplain I sit with the old to the extremely old. I have learned that they are still trying to figure it out as well. Even the 99-year-old retired pastor had his moments of wondering. Somehow that is both comforting and disturbing.

Wisdom is of two elements: *seeing clearly* and *deciding correctly.* To make wise decisions takes clarity of vision. Clarity is one of our 'wins' (**See Day 46**).

When your life has been turned upside down by divorce, you need clarity. But just because you have clarity doesn't mean you will make winning decisions. Wisdom means more than just seeing the world clearly. Wisdom entails making decisions based on the correct information and the right motivation.

It is critical during this time of upheaval that you make wise choices. You need to think with a clear head and decide with a pure heart.

To do this requires that you look outside yourself for wisdom. You must relocate the source of your wisdom from yourself to God. The source of all wisdom is God, and God showed himself most clearly to us in his Son, Jesus Christ. If you want to know how to live wisely in this world, listen to everything Jesus said and watch what he did.[40]

One of the goals of MDR is that you *Survive and Thrive beyond your divorce to become a Resilient, Strong and* ***Wise*** *man in your world.*

Will you relocate the source of your wisdom from yourself to God? Will you follow Jesus in finding clarity and courage to make wise decisions? If so, you can take some steps right now to make that happen:

- **Ask God for wisdom**. Expect him to give it.[41]
- **Read the Bible**. A good place to learn about Jesus is to begin reading the book of John. Read a few verses each day asking yourself *"What did Jesus say and what did he do?"*

---

[40]Dallas Willard writes, *[Jesus] is not just nice, he is brilliant. He is the smartest man who ever lived. He is now supervising the entire course of world history (Rev. 1:5) while simultaneously preparing the rest of the universe for our future role in it (John 14:2). He always has the best information on everything and certainly also on the things that matter most in human life. Let us now hear his teachings on who has the good life, on who is among the truly blessed.* Dallas Willard, *The Divine Conspiracy: Rediscovering Our Hidden Life in God* (San Francisco: HarperSanFrancisco, 1998), 96.

[41]*If any of you lacks wisdom, he should ask God, who gives generously to all without finding fault, and it will be given to him. But when he asks, he must believe and not doubt, because he who doubts is like a wave of the sea, blown and tossed by the wind. That man should not think he will receive anything from the Lord; he is a double-minded man, unstable in all he does.* (James 1.5–8)

- **Find a church** that follows Jesus. Go and listen. Ask questions.
- **Find some other guys** who are following Jesus. Get together to bounce your ideas off them. Allow God to use other godly men to help you gain clarity of mind purity of heart.

Think About It . . .

- *First we make our choices, then our choices make us.* Consider the past year. What choices did you make and what were the consequences?
- If you made poor choices, determine now to make better choices from this moment on (beginning with following the steps above for gaining wisdom!)

Life Commitment:

I can choose my source of wisdom. I choose to follow Jesus. He's a lot smarter than me! Choosing Jesus is my first good choice!

Day 21: Losses—Concrete and Abstract

The Word

Though the fig tree does not bud and there are no grapes on the vines, though the olive crop fails and the fields produce no food, though there are no sheep in the pen and no cattle in the stalls, yet I will rejoice in the Lord, I will be joyful in God my Savior. The Sovereign Lord is my strength; he makes my feet like the feet of a deer, he enables me to go on the heights.

— Habakkuk 3.17–19

Thought for the Day

Heartbreak knocks the wind out of you, and the feelings of loss and longing can make getting out of bed a monumental task. Learning to trust and lean in to love again can feel impossible . . .. In those moments when disappointment is washing over us and we're desperately trying to get our heads and hearts around what is or is not going to be, the death of our expectations can be painful beyond measure.

~ Brené Brown

As young men we work hard to acquire, to gain, to gather. We get an education, we get a reputation. We get a job, we get money. We get a wife, we get kids. We get a house. We get friends. We get status and standing. The first half of life is about getting, gathering, collecting.

Midlife is the pinnacle of our gathering. We have a house that is almost paid for. Our career is at its zenith. We are well respected and well paid. We have kids who are getting married and having grandkids for us to enjoy. We have growing 401k's and a hopeful future filled with happy grandkids, financial security, rest and fun.

At least that's the dream. The reality is that while the first half of life is about getting, the second half of life is about losing. All that is gained in the first half of life is lost as we grow older, until, finally, we lose our bodies and leave the world and everything we accumulated behind.

Divorce accelerates the losses of the second half of life and, because divorce often happens at midlife—at the supposed pinnacle of all we have worked so hard to acquire—the losses seem doubly painful.

I have felt deeply—*really deeply*—the losses caused by divorce. I ache in the places where words cannot go. I lost my family, my career, my reputation, my income. These losses hurt so much because they are real. I have felt angry, lonely, exhausted, shamed, embarrassed and sad. I count my losses and alternate between intense anger, despair and sadness.

The journey to healing encompasses and embraces the realities of these losses. You cannot gloss over them, cover them up, numb them away with drugs or forget about them with a new hobby, girlfriend, job or career.

The reality is that we are all on a pathway of loss. As a hospice chaplain I see people at the end of their lives. Most of these folks are old, some are very old. Some are very wealthy and live in mansions. Some are super poor and live in shacks (literally). Some are white, many are Hispanic, a few are black. Some have had amazing careers. Others have spent much of their adult lives in prison. In the end, death takes away all they have ever been. Death leaves behind all they worked for. Every person on the planet is on a pathway of the loss of all they have acquired on earth.

While divorce accelerates this journey, it is a journey we must all face. How can you and I navigate this journey with grace? How can we finish well?

Trust in God. You will lose every material thing that you own right now, including your body. Without God, what do you have? The journey through the pain and loss of divorce can lead you away from reliance upon your own power to the wisdom of relying completely on God's amazing presence and power. This is a journey we all must eventually take *so why not start this journey now?*

Give it to God. Let God take your pain, heartache and worries. When you let go and relax into him, you are relinquishing dependence on your own power and letting him handle things in his power. Your mind clears, your tight chest loosens, and you are off the ledge once again. Time after time I have heard God say to me, *Hold on, I've got you, I am sustaining you, I will see you through this, you will get through this!* And he has. That's the cool thing–he has done it! So I can trust him to keep doing it, and you can too.

Know everything that is lost will be restored, now or later. Read Hebrews 11. The writer tells tales of mighty men and women of faith who, through their amazing commitment to God, made huge differences on earth. But keep reading. The last part of Hebrews 11 tells of anonymous men and women who suffered terribly for their faith. Lost, alone, forgotten to the world, they were not forgotten by God. Hebrews 11:40 says, *God had planned something better for us so that only together with us would they be made perfect.* God has something better planned for you.

You will regain what you have lost. For some of us, our restoration will be like Job's, who received on earth double what he had lost (Job 42.10). Others of us will see our reward on the other side. Either way, it's good.

Choose happiness today. The losses are real, deep and they hurt. You may have lost nearly everything. But to choose to sit in the midst of the ruins of the tower you so carefully constructed *and remain there* does no one any good. If you choose to sit in the rubble, you will spend your days alone. You will deprive the world of what you have to offer for the years you have left. Instead, reframe the inner dialogue in your head and heart using the tools of gratitude and hope.

The Apostle Paul had it right when he wrote, *I consider my life worth nothing to me; my only aim is to finish the race and complete the task the Lord Jesus has given me—the task of testifying to the good news of God's grace.* (Acts 20.24)

Think About It . . .

- In this time of loss, what loss (your role as husband, role as father, your reputation, standard of living, money to settle your divorce and pay your lawyer, living arrangement, etc.) has hurt (or is hurting) the most? Why does that particular loss hurt so much?
- Is it possible for anyone to really know God without experiencing deep, soul-wrenching loss?
- What does trusting God and giving it to him look like to you?

Prayer . . .

Dear Heavenly Father, You created me for a specific purpose. I am Your masterpiece. You have plans to prosper me and to give me hope and a future. It is my heart's desire to accomplish what you created me to do. You know what would satisfy the deepest longings of my heart. And if I take delight in You, You will give me the desires of my heart. Even when adversity comes against me and keeps me from fulfilling my dreams and desires, You promise that my gifts and calling will never be withdrawn. Help me to trust in You with all my heart and not lean on my own understanding. As I seek Your will for my life, You promise to teach, guide and instruct me in which path and direction to take. Thank you, God. You restore my dreams and satisfy the desires of my heart.[42]

[42]Violet James, *God Restores: Prayers & Promises for Restoration* (Maximum Potential: 2017), 7.

Day 22: Expectations of Yourself

The Word

And we, who with unveiled faces all reflect the Lord's glory, are being transformed into his likeness with ever-increasing glory, which comes from the Lord, who is the Spirit.
— 2 Corinthians 3.18

Thought for the Day

Do I really dare to let God be to me all that he says he will be?
~ Oswald Chambers

As you move into the future, what can you expect of yourself? Of others? Of God? We will answer these questions the next several days.

What does your future look like to you right now? If you're in the middle of a divorce or just divorced, the future can look distressingly bleak. The losses are piling up and those losses have a way of snuffing out what tiny rays of hope that may remain.

Don't despair. Whatever is *now* will change. Whatever you feel *now* will *not last forever*, or even for very long. Whatever losses you have incurred can be restored with God's help and blessing.

What can or should you expect from yourself in this time? Expectations can be disappointing if we set them as standards by which we choose to measure ourselves. On the other hand, expectations can and should be aspirational—expectations can lift us up to think and do things that are good for us. Expectations can be targets to aim for. We know that without a target we lose focus and direction.

Without goals we are always successful . . . at nothing. Expectations help us set targets that pull us forward.

With these things in mind . . .

Expect yourself not to give up. Paul Meyer, founder of the Success Motivation Institute, says, *Ninety percent of those who fail are not actually defeated. They simply quit.*[43] Most people don't quit. Most people keep going. Be one of those people. Though it feels like it is almost too much to bear, at some point you will realize that it was *only* almost too much to bear. You will get through this.

Expect yourself to grow. Tell yourself that you will be a different person at the end of all this, and that you *want to* and *will be* a *better* person. You owe that to yourself, to your kids, and to the world at large.

Expect yourself to know God better. Like Jacob by the Jabbok River (Genesis 32.22-32), expect to wrestle with God. Like Jacob, expect God to both wound you and bless you. Expect God to take you down a bit and lift you up a lot.

Expect to feel better. The sting of grief and loss will lessen in frequency, intensity and duration.

But expect to hurt. There is no way to simply forget all this and not hurt anymore. As time goes by, the pain will be less intense and less frequent.

Expect yourself to be a contributor to the world. Expect God to invite you into a partnership with him that will bring him glory, bring you good and bring good through you to the world. Expect God to make this a win-win for everyone. Expect to feel good about living the second half of your life for someone other than yourself.

---

[43]Quoted in Maxwell, *The Maxwell Daily Reader*, 220.

I like the encouragement John Maxwell gives us:

> *You certainly can't control the length of your life—but you can control its width and depth.*
>
> *You can't control the contour of your face—but you can control its expression.*
>
> *You can't control the weather—but you can control the atmosphere of your mind.*
>
> *Why worry about things you can't control when you can keep yourself busy controlling the things that depend on you?*[44]

Think About It . . .

- On a scale of 0 to 10, how hopeful are you about your future, zero being completely unhopeful and 10 being completely confident of God's plan for you and your future healing?

  0—1—2—3—4—5—6—7—8—9—10

- Read through the expectations listed above. Which of these expectations do you see happening in your life right now? Which are on the radar? Which seem beyond reach?
- Ask God to move you toward each one of these expectations.

Life Commitment:

I hurt but I know it won't be forever. I am down but I know I will get back up. I have been wounded but I know someday I can forgive. I have sinned greatly, but I know I am forgiven and I can make amends. I am hopeful about what God will do in my future, and I expect both of us to make it together. The best is yet to be.

---

[44]Ibid, 193.

Day 23: Expectations of Others

The Word

Now while [Jesus] was in Jerusalem at the Passover Feast, many people saw the miraculous signs he was doing and believed in his name. But Jesus would not entrust himself to them, for he knew all men. He did not need man's testimony about man, for he knew what was in a man.

— John 2.23–25

Thought for the Day

Maybe ever'body in the whole damn world is scared of each other.

~ John Steinbeck, *Of Mice and Men*

We are all empty cups desperately wanting to be filled. Our problem is that we go to the wrong source for filling.

We mistakenly expect other people to be faucets of clean, clear, soul-quenching water. What we fail to realize is that *they* are empty cups as well and *they are seeking to be filled from us*! When our expectations of other people are not met, we are hurt, angry and disappointed. We blame the other for not meeting our expectations.

It is at this point that we might try to get our cups filled with *things*, rather than relationships. We call this *addiction*. The heart of addiction is that we establish a relationship with an object (drugs, alcohol, stuff, work, etc.) and make people objects.[45]

[45] Craig Nakken, *The Addictive Personality: Roots, Rituals, and Recovery.* (Center City, MN: Hazelden, 1988). Nakken writes, *Addiction is an emotional relationship with*

Paul David Tripp is right when he says, *Many people say they believe in God, but they shop horizontally for what can be found only vertically.*[46] Satisfaction, security, strength and fulfillment can only be found in a solid relationship with God. God certainly uses people in our lives to fulfill some of our needs, but the people are the gift, God is the Giver.

In the hands of God, people can become amazing sources of help to us and us to them. But they are the gift, God is the Giver. We trust God to place people in our lives to meet certain needs, and we trust God to place us where we can be of most help to others. But we understand that God is the source and that because of our sin, his tools (us) are flawed and temporary.

With this in mind, what can you expect of people? **We can expect them to meet some needs in our lives but not *every* need.** God uses people to meet some of our needs, but God is always the source.

Because all people are sinners (Romans 3.23) **we can expect people to fail us.** We remember the wisdom of John Gardner: *Most people are neither for you nor against you; they are thinking of themselves.*[47] We really want to believe people will be strong, loyal, honest and true to us. This simply will not be this side of heaven.

A Buddhist saying has helped me: *The glass is already broken.* In other words, at some point, the glass that holds my water will break. When it does, I am not surprised because I knew this moment

---

an object or event, through which addicts try to meet their needs for intimacy. When looked at in this way, the logic of addiction starts to become clear. When compulsive eaters feel sad, they eat to feel better. When alcoholics start to feel out of control with anger, they have a couple of drinks to get back in control.... Addiction is a pathological love and trust relationship with an object or event. Because addiction is an illness in which the addict's primary relationship is with objects or events and not with people, the addict's relationships with people change to reflect this. Normally, we manipulate objects for our own pleasure, to make life easier. Addicts slowly transfer this style of relating to objects to their interactions with people, treating them as one-dimensional objects to manipulate as well. Nakken, *The Addictive Personality*, 26.

[46] Paul David Tripp, *New Morning Mercies: A Daily Gospel Devotional* (Wheaton, IL: Crossway, 2014), Kindle Location 3701.

[47] *John Gardner's Writings*, accessed August 06, 2017, http://www.pbs.org/johngardner/sections/writings_speech_1.html.

would come. *People will disappoint.* If you expect this, you won't be as overwhelmed when it happens.

We can learn to walk the line between trust and cynicism. God calls us to love and trust one another. But he also knows that trust is earned and can be broken. Trust *first* in God, and when people disappoint, expect it and forgive. In doing this, we can walk the fine line between blind trust of people and the depressing pit of cynicism.

There is hope, but it begins with God and then moves to people as he places people in our lives. When people disappoint, God is there to catch us, renew us, and get us ready for our next encounters where we have the opportunity to be to people what they need, which is to say, we have the opportunity to represent our kind, benevolent awesome God to others.

Think About It . . .

- What are you expecting from others?
- How and when have people let you down?
- How can you learn to walk with realistic hope and expectations of others and stay out of the pit of cynicism?

Life Commitment:

My commitment is first to God then to others. I will get my soul filled from God and then let him use me to fill others and let him use others to fill me. I will remember that he is the Giver and people, including myself, are the gifts.

Day 24: Expectations of Your Children

The Word

Fathers, do not exasperate your children; instead, bring them up in the training and instruction of the Lord.

— Ephesians 6.4

Thought for the Day

Children ought not to be victims of the choices adults make for them.

~ Wade Horn

A young woman named Leslie writes:

> *One of the most painful and significant events in my life was my parents' divorce. It felt as if my family had died and my whole life as I knew it would change forever. For me, the divorce was sudden and unexpected.*
>
> *My father left the house one night and would never return as the Dad I grew up with. He had fallen in love with someone else, which shattered all my thoughts and feelings about what a happy marriage my parents had. They were supposed to be together forever... "until death do us part."*
>
> *My body literally went into shock, and I cannot recollect what I did for days or weeks after hearing the news about my parent's separation. I was about to graduate from high school, and the last few weeks of school were a daze.*

All I could think about was when would my dad return to my mother and this whole nightmare be over. I had my high school prom to go to, which I hated and did not want to attend. I don't even remember if any family member said good-bye to me as I embarked on what was supposed to be a night to remember.

I remember my father driving to the house for visits with my mother. My siblings and I would wait to see him, and sometimes he would leave the house without ever saying hello or good-bye. None of us could really be there for each other because we were all hurting over a relationship that was unique and special to each one.[48]

I have sat many times with couples wrestling with divorce. The common theme in these counseling sessions was *selfishness.* As I listened to the husband and wife take turns stabbing each other, all I could hear was a radical self-centeredness that left little room for concern for their children.

At some point I would ask, *So, how are the kids doing through all this?*

The typical response was, *They are doing OK.*
To which I would reply, *How do you know?*
To which they would say, *They seem to be handling it fine.*
To which I would reply, *How do you know?*
To which they say, *Well, they aren't saying much.*

Really? Mom and dad are the bedrock of every child's life. They are born completely dependent on you! You are the first people they know and trust. And yet you believe they are OK because they aren't saying anything even as the foundation of their lives crumbles before them?

---

[48]John W. James and Russell Friedman, *When Children Grieve: For Adults to Help Children Deal with Death, Divorce, Pet Loss, Moving, and Other Losses* (New York, NY: HarperCollins, 2001), 199-200. Emphasis mine.

Leslie's heartfelt re-telling of how she experienced her parent's divorce is revealing:

> *It felt as if my family had died and my whole life as I knew it would change forever.*
>
> *My body literally went into shock, and I cannot recollect what I did for days or weeks after hearing the news about my parent's separation.*
>
> *All I could think about was when would my dad return to my mother and this whole nightmare be over...*
>
> *None of us could really be there for each other because we were all hurting over a relationship that was unique and special to each one.*

If you think your child is not suffering through this time, you are badly mistaken. Your child is probably experiencing the very feelings Leslie experienced, but he/she doesn't know how to put his/her feelings into words. As adults we find putting appropriate words to our emotions challenging. How can we expect children to express themselves at all? Instead of trying, they clam up. We assume their silence means they are fine. Big mistake.

When I have counseled self-centered couples fighting with one another, more than once I have said, *You are expecting your children to act like adults while you act like children. It is time you act like adults and let your children be children!*

Whatever you are experiencing emotionally, no matter your level of pain, guilt, shame, embarrassment, anger, etc., ***you must be a dad to your children***. They are hurting more than you know. They deserve your love.

So the real question is not, *What can you expect from your children?* but *What can your children expect from you?*

Your children should be able to expect . . .

Your time and attention. You *must* make time for each child. This will be difficult but it must be a priority. When you are with your children they should expect your full attention. They are hungry for your attention but they may not know how to express it. Assume they desperately need you because they really do.

Your tenderness. This is not a time to be hard, tough or thick-skinned. This is a time for tenderness, compassion and an open heart. This is a time to acknowledge that things are hard. Say something like this: Name of your child, *this is a hard and terrible time for all of us. I am so sorry for what you are going through. I know it must be painful beyond words. I am happy to hear whatever words you have to say. I will always be here for you. This is not your fault. We will get through this together. Whatever happens we will take care of you.*

Access to counseling. Read Leslie's story again. She needs and deserves a safe place to pour out her heart. She wrote, *None of us could really be there for each other because we were all hurting over a relationship that was unique and special to each one.*

You can be there for your kids, and you should, but patients in the ER can't and don't help one another. Doctors and nurses do. Offer counseling for your kids and do whatever it takes to make it happen. Spend the money. Take the time to get them to the appointments.

Reassurances that they will be taken care of.

This is *not* a time to . . .

Rag on your ex. There will be a time for you to share your side of what happened, including personal confession where you have failed. Now is not the time. If you can't say anything nice about your ex, don't say anything at all.

Make false promises. We all want to reassure our children, but we must not make promises we can't keep. Don't say, *I think mom and I are going to get back together* if it is not true.

Compensate by spending lavishly on your kid. Kids see right through that. They want love, not things.

Think About It . . .

- One of the most important things you can do during this time is to put yourself in your child's place. If you were your child, what would you be thinking? If you were your child, what would you be feeling? What would you be afraid of? What would you need most from your dad?
- Now, with a heart of compassion, go love on your kids. They deserve the best you have to give to them.

Life Commitment:

My kids deserve my best and I will give it to them no matter what it takes.

Day 25: Expectations of God

The Word

In the day when I cried out, you answered me, and made me bold with strength in my soul.

— Psalm 138.3

Thought for the Day

The Lord will make a way for you where no foot has been before. That which, like a sea, threatens to drown you, shall be a highway for your escape.

~ Charles Spurgeon

On October 3, 2003 performer Roy Horn was attacked by a tiger while performing the famous Siegfried & Roy show in Las Vegas. Fortunately Roy survived. Many people blamed the tiger. But comedian Chris Rock nailed it when he said, *That tiger ain't go crazy; that tiger went tiger !*[49]

Tigers do tiger things. Guess what? *God does God things.*

And what God does is show up in the middle of our crises, traumas and disasters. The reality is that we don't usually come to God in good times. We come to God when our lives fall apart. It's just the way it is.

[49]Chris Rock, *Chris Rock Tiger Gone Crazy*, https://www.youtube.com/watch?v=kGEv5dC0lo4, accessed October 22, 2017.

When it all hits the fan, we get humble and needy. At that point the smart people cry out to God and God rescues us. These are the places where we can expect God, our Rescuer, to do his rescuer thing.

So what can you expect of God as you continue down this pathway?

Expect God to show up.

Every Christmas we celebrate that God showed up. Christmas is all about God's Son, *wrapped in flesh*, leaving heaven and inserting himself into the mess of humanity, not just to visit but to stay with us: *The Word became flesh and made his dwelling among us. We have seen his glory, the glory of the One and Only, who came from the Father, full of grace and truth.* (John 1.14)

Jesus didn't do a lot of explaining about why the darkness is dark. But he knew that light pushes out darkness. You may not know why your life is the way it is right now, but Jesus is light and he will show up with you to push back the darkness.

Expect God to comfort you.

Divorce hurts beyond words. Even the 'manliest' of men get hurt. When we are hurt we want comfort. Take King David, for example. There was no more manly man than King David. As a young shepherd boy, he took down a giant warrior over nine feet tall. He led men into battle many times. When it comes to manly men, David rates! Yet he wrote about God: *He heals the brokenhearted and binds up their wounds.* (Psalm 147:3) Yep, manly men hurt, and manly men need God to heal our manly, broken hearts. If you let God comfort you, you will have an experience like no other.

Eugene Peterson observes that *We don't have to wait until we get to the end of the road before we enjoy what is at the end of the road.*[50] Heaven is a pain-free place of comfort. You can enjoy heaven on earth *now*. God loves to comfort his people.

---

[50]Eugene H. Peterson, Dale Larsen, and Sandy Larsen, *A Long Obedience in The Same Direction: 6 Studies for Individuals or Groups, With Guidelines for Leaders & Study Notes* (Downers Grove, IL: InterVarsity Press, 1996), Kindle Location 1711.

Expect God to make a way.

The Israelites were up against the Red Sea on one side and a charging Egyptian army on the other. When all seemed lost, God made a way. He is doing this for you and will continue to do it for his Glory, for your good and for the good of the world. (See Exodus 14-15)

Expect God to call you into a new purpose.

God doesn't waste pain. Only you can waste your pain by not following God's mission for your life. Our world is a damaged and hurting place. God calls his people to be *wounded healers* to our dark world. God will take what has happened to you and call you to help others who only you can help:

> *Praise be to the God and Father of our Lord Jesus Christ, the Father of compassion and the God of all comfort, who comforts us in all our troubles, so that we can comfort those in any trouble with the comfort we ourselves have received from God. For just as the sufferings of Christ flow over into our lives, so also through Christ our comfort overflows.* (2 Corinthians 1.3–5)

Expect God to empower you.

If God calls you he will equip and empower you. He certainly did this for me. After my divorce I was physically, emotionally and spiritually exhausted. And yet I heard his clear call to write this book. He not only gave me the energy to get up at 4:30 every morning to write it, he woke me up to get on with it!

Tony Dungy writes:

> *When we focus on the obstacles in front of us, they seem to grow larger and larger until we give up. But if we focus on what God can do through us—and on His promise that if we delight in Him, He will give us the desires of our hearts—we become confident and able to achieve whatever we were designed to achieve. Start each day by focusing on what needs to occur that day. Set your mind on what you are attempting to achieve and where you want to go. If it's a God-honoring goal and you are following His leading, believe*

that He wants you to achieve it. And you will begin to see your heart's desires fulfilled.[51]

Think About It . . .

- How is God showing up in your life right now?
- If you don't see him at work in your life, find a trusted friend or pastor to help you see God's hand in your life. We live in a muddy, foggy world. God is at work but sometimes we need help seeing him do his God thing.
- Have you heard God's call on your life? If not, give him time. In his timing he will call you to a lifetime mission.

Prayer:

God, my life is in tatters. So much has been lost. So much damage has been done. But despite the hurt and pain, I believe that you not only will show up in my life, I believe that you want to show up. I open my life and heart to you. I desire your comfort. I know you will call me. I look forward to you rebuilding, renewing and restoring my life, for your Glory, for my good, and for the good of the world.

[51] Tony Dungy and Nathan Whitaker, *The One Year Uncommon Life Daily Challenge* (Carol Stream, IL: Tyndale House Publishers, 2011), Kindle Location 2468.

Day 26: Rage

The Word

My dear brothers, take note of this: Everyone should be quick to listen, slow to speak and slow to become angry, for man's anger does not bring about the righteous life that God desires.
— James 1.19–20

Thought for the Day

Anger is the fluid that love bleeds when you cut it.
~ C.S. Lewis

C.S. Lewis was an intellectual titan of the mid-20th century. He still reigns as one of the most brilliant cultural commentators of the modern era. I had the privilege of visiting his home in Oxford, England. As part of the tour we visited his grave at Holy Trinity Church in Headington Quarry where he is buried.

While standing beside the grave of this amazing and brilliant man who had (possibly) done more for the cause of Christianity than anyone since the Apostle Paul, we were told that the church almost didn't let Lewis be buried there. The reason? Late in life Lewis married a woman named Joy Davidman. Joy was divorced. Because Lewis had married a divorced woman, the church at first refused to allow his burial in the church yard.

I had to wonder how Lewis might have felt had he known of his church's initial refusal to bury him in their cemetery.

I think he would have been angry. But I think his anger would have moderated into a quiet, well-considered acceptance of the world as it is and things as they are.

Lewis wrote, *Anger [is] the anaesthetic of the mind.*[52] Indeed, it is. In the pain of divorce, anger feels good. It soothes the wounds and allows a way for us to process intellectually and emotionally what has just happened relationally.

Kristin Armstrong writes,

> *[Anger] is a valid reading on the spectrum of human emotion. It is our barometer of injustice. It is sometimes the impetus for great change. It can be the fuel of self-preservation. But we are instructed in Scripture to manage our anger, and this means our anger cannot manage us.*[53]

I have raged. I have yelled and screamed. I have thrown a few things. I have imagined a lot of things. I went to a self-defense class and beat the snot out of 'Century Bob,' the martial arts dummy that looks like a guy. I've gone to the gun range and imagined faces on the targets. Yep, even a pastor can be driven to thoughts like this through pain-induced anger!

I have also learned that in our culture for a man to express anger is strictly forbidden. If you say what's burning in your soul most people immediately cut you off, usually because they simply don't know what to say or do. They won't respond to you on Facebook or text or email. Things go dead once you let it fly (see Appendix D).

But the fact is that when you are angry, you *are* angry. Anger is a natural emotional response to pain. Lewis rightly said, *Anger is the fluid that love bleeds when you cut it.*[54]

---

[52] C. S. Lewis and Walter Hooper, *Poems* (San Diego: Harcourt Brace & Co., 1992), 125.

[53] Kristin Armstrong, *Happily Ever After: Walking with Peace and Courage Through a Year of Divorce* (New York: Faith Words, 2008), Kindle Location 2938.

[54] Wayne Martindale and Jerry Root, editors, *The Quotable Lewis* (Carol Stream, IL: Tyndale House Publishers, 1990), Kindle Location 1291.

The next few days we will look at ways to manage this real and powerful emotion. There is a difference between being a man who is angry and being someone who is defined by anger, that is, an angry man.

Let me leave you with this thought from C.S. Lewis: *To rail is the sad privilege of the loser.*[55] Maybe that's the heart of our anger. Divorce feels like a huge loss. And that really gets under our skin. But we don't have to end up angry men.

Think About It . . .

- Are you angry? Why?
- Think back on a time when you were furious. What did you do? What were the results?
- How can you be angry and yet not become an angry man?

Life Commitment:

I am a man who is angry but I don't want to end up being an angry man. God, help me manage this fire in me.

[55] C. S. Lewis and Walter Hooper, *Selected Literary Essays* (New York: Cambridge University Press, 2013), "Addison" (1945), para. 4, p. 156.

Day 27: Don't Make Stupid Choices

The Word

In your anger do not sin; Do not let the sun go down while you are still angry, and do not give the devil a foothold.
— Ephesians 4.25–27

Thought for the Day

First we make our choices, then our choices make us.
~ Anne Frank

I'm not about to tell you not to be angry. Nothing chaps my hide more than when people tell me not to be angry. I **AM** angry! I lost my family, my career, my reputation, my income. Loss hurts and when I am hurt I get mad.

But being angry and expressing it in non-destructive ways is a good choice that can save you and many others much pain and suffering.

In your anger do not sin. Anger is not a sin but it can lead to sin when it dominates your thoughts and plots.

Psychologist Robin Goldstein explains the dynamics of anger in a divorced man:

> *Sadness feels weak and men often experience humiliation when they feel weak. This makes it easy to become angry. Anger feels powerful. It can cause men to say or do things that hurt the person who rejected them. This tough guy stance may come out*

with friends and family who try to support the bereaved man, pushing them away. The message can be "I don't have a problem, I can handle this fine on my own." A high price is paid for that momentary sense of power; further isolation and often further despair. A greater toll is taken when the anger leads to a more complicated divorce or when children are exposed to the toxicity of a parent's hostility.[56]

What can you do with your anger that will not lead to more despair or drive others away? Poor choices include drinking yourself under the table, having sex with anyone and anything, isolating yourself from the world, binge watching Netflix, killing yourself or someone else. Those are just a few stupid things men do when they are angry. Don't do anything on this list.

Instead, **talk**. Talking is God's way of us working it out in our mind and soul. I can't explain why talking works, I just know it's true. You *must* find a trusted and wise friend, counselor, pastor, therapist . . . someone!

Get moving. Burn off anger. In six months I rode my mountain and road bikes over 3,000 miles. I channeled the anger in my head and heart through my legs into the pavement. Why not use anger to get in better shape?

Solve the problems you can solve. Abraham H. Maslow said, *I suppose it is tempting, if the only tool you have is a hammer, to treat everything as if it were a nail.*[57] Time to expand your toolbox. You will get energy from solving problems instead of raging against them.

These are just a few ways to deal with anger. We will look at these

---

[56] Robin Goldstein, *Divorce Recovery: Stages of Divorce Recovery for Men Article Series,* accessed February 16, 2017, http://robingoldstein.net/divorce/stages-of-divorce-recovery-for-men-article-series/.

[57] Abraham H. Maslow, *Toward a Psychology of Being Quotes by Abraham H. Maslow,* accessed February 17, 2017, http://www.goodreads.com/work/quotes/2216557-toward-a-psychology-of-being.

and other suggestions in more detail in the next several days. The main point is to not give in to what your anger is tempting you to do. Believe me, I *thought* about doing all kinds of things, many of them illegal! But thinking about doing something and actually doing it are two very different things. Though anger tempts us with the rationalization of justification, in the end, to choose the hard way of venting anger constructively makes you stronger, not weaker.

I like what Ben Horowitz says about the impact of our decisions: *Every time you make the hard, correct decision you become a bit more courageous, and every time you make the easy, wrong decision you become a bit more cowardly.*[58]

Determine that *a temporary state [will not become] a permanent trait.*[59]

Think About It . . .

- Why do I always feel right when I am angry?
- Is my anger a temporary state or is it becoming a permanent trait?

Life Commitment:

I am angry but I don't want to be known for my anger. I commit to actively seeking ways to express my anger appropriately.

[58] "Ben Horowitz Quotes," BrainyQuote, accessed February 17, 2017, https://www.brainyquote.com/quotes/quotes/b/benhorowit529646.html?src=t_wrong_decision.
[59] Armstrong, *Happily Ever After,* Kindle Location 2554.

Day 28: Play Your Position

The Word

In his heart a man plans his course, but the Lord determines his steps.

— Proverbs 16.9

Thought for the Day

No one ever healed from a blow to the head by hitting themselves there again.

~ Leslie Becker-Phelps

My favorite position in football is linebacker. The linebacker plays the rush and covers the pass. He's on the move, mentally covering the entire field, but singularly focused on where the football might be and being there when it is. Linebackers have to be smart, fast and tough.

Imagine being a quarterback looking across the line into those amazing eyes of Mike Singletary (Chicago Bears, 1981-92). Who would want to be a receiver about to receive the earth-shattering impact of Lawrence Taylor (New York Giants, 1981-93)?

Even though linebackers cover more of the football field than any other defensive player, *linebackers still have to play their position.* In fact, everyone does. Success in football requires that each player *knows* his position, *stays* in his position and *plays* his position to the best of his ability.

The quarterback calls a pass play in the huddle. Each guy immediately knows his position. Most important to the success of the play will be the determination of the receiver to know his route and then run it with precision. When the ball is snapped the quarterback drops back and—if the receiver is open—throws the ball to the pre-planned and much-practiced tiny spot on the 57,600 square-foot football field where the receiver will eventually be. Everyone on the team knows the route and believes in it. Each runs here and pushes there, trusting that if everyone plays his position, the plan will work.

But as Helmuth von Moltke famously said, *No battle plan survives contact with the enemy.*[60] That's why the coaches watch hours of the tapes of the other team's defense. The idea is to anticipate how the enemy will react, and adjust accordingly.

But what if the coaching staff had a video of the game they were *going to play*? Every move could be planned with precision! I know this is a bit *Back to the Future-ish*, but in a way, that's what God does for us. He has a position for us to play. But he knows how everything plays out. Though it seems we have been knocked *out of position*, God helps us recover and get back *in position.*

Divorce is like a quarterback blindsided by a wild-eyed Mike Singletary or hammered by Lawrence Taylor. Divorce knocks you out of position. But God is bigger than this giant blow in your life.

God gave us free will. He doesn't cause these body-blows—we cause them from our poor choices and/or they happen to us because of the terrible choices of others. The amazing thing is that God's grace is stronger than evil and his plan supersedes the chaos of life on earth.

Can you trust the plan? Can you play your position? Surrendering to God's plan is one of the best ways to handle your anger.

Despite all the chaos around you, know that God is not surprised by what has happened in your life. Trust him to take this pain and transform it into something better than you imagined. When you release control of your present and future to him, you will sense a relief that is far better than any of the other things you might have

[60]Helmuth von Moltke, *No Battle Plan Survives Contact with the Enemy*, accessed September 24, 2017, http://www.lexician.com/lexblog/2010/11/no-battle-plan-survives-contact-with-the-enemy/.

tried.

God is in the game and so are you. It's not over till it's over. Trust him to get you to victory.

Think About It . . .

- What position did you play before the divorce? Husband, dad, provider? How have those positions changed?
- Trust God to take you from where you are to where he wants you to be. Trust him that his plan is good and right. Commit your ways to his care, then follow his direction.

Life Commitment:

Though I am flat on the turf, I trust that God will get me back up and give me a new route.

Day 29: Shadows

The Word

What causes fights and quarrels among you? Don't they come from your desires that battle within you? You want something but don't get it. You kill and covet, but you cannot have what you want. You quarrel and fight. You do not have, because you do not ask God.

— James 4:1–2

Thought for the Day

Grief that is ignored turns into depression or hopelessness. Hurt turns into cynicism, lack of trust, or worse. Anger turns into bitterness and hatred.

~ Henry Cloud

I sat with a woman who had been repeatedly abused in unspeakable ways by male members of her family of origin. We were at once on a battleground and on holy ground as she reached deep into her crushed soul and drew the pain from the depths into her consciousness. Then, with incredible courage, she formed the words in her mind and then actually spoke out loud the trauma that had been done to her. That she had not taken her life years ago was a testimony to her strength and God's power and love.

Over the course of some weeks we learned something together. We learned that while this huge ugly *thing* remained in her, it kept growing and dominated her 'life space.' It defined her, even years later. But once we put the ugly thing out on the table, the light of the truth and God's healing power shrank the thing back to its proper size in her life.

It's not that talking about this thing eliminated it from her life or memory. The *thing* just finally shrank to its *right* size. Where before it dominated everything about her, now it was remembered as a terrible and ugly thing in her past, *but it was in her past.*

Here's the deal. We all have black and ugly things in our lives. We are all wounded and we carry the wounds of our parents and others with us. Much of our energy goes to keeping these shadows pushed down. As long as life is good, the shadow stays hidden. As Robert Bly says, *The naïve man who flies directly toward the sun will not be able to see his own shadow. It is far behind him.*[61]

But as John O'Donohue says, *We cannot seal off the eternal. Unexpectedly and disturbingly, it gazes in at us through the sudden apertures in our patterned lives.*[62]

Divorce knocks us off our course toward our sun and suddenly our shadow becomes glaringly visible. The holding tank we have constructed to contain the shadow cracks and starts to leak. This can be a terrifying moment as the shadow grows and the ugliness leaks out.

Don't be terrified by this. All of us have this stuff inside. Now is the time to recognize it for what it is but not be terrorized by it. The stakes are high: scared people become angry, destructive people.

Henry Cloud makes the point that *just as you do not want a tumor growing in your brain, you do not want one growing in your heart either. There are no benign tumors of the heart.*[63]

By recognizing that the good, the bad and the ugly are in all of us and that God knows this and will get us through it, the shadow becomes less frightening and we are able to deal with it. God is not surprised by what's in us. After all, he took all the terrible things in us and killed them on the cross. He knows more about your shadow

[61]Robert Bly, *Iron John: A Book About Men* (Boston: Da Capo Press, 2015), 126.

[62]John O'Donohue, *Anam Ċara: A Book of Celtic Wisdom* (New York: Harper Perennial, 2004), 42.

[63]Henry Cloud, *9 Things You Simply Must Do to Succeed in Love and Life: A Psychologist Probes The Mystery Of Why Some Lives Really Work And Others Don't* (Detroit: Gale, Cengage Learning, 2008), Kindle Location 333.

than you do, and because he has dealt with it, he has the power to give us healing.

Think About It . . .

- What lurks in your heart?
- What do you think will happen if you just keep pushing it down?
- What are the potential risks and rewards of bringing it out into the open and dealing with it?

Life Commitment:

I am strong and weak, good and bad, bright and dark. I can celebrate the good and deal realistically with the bad.

Day 30: Sleep is the Great Reset Button

The Word

On my bed I remember you; I think of you through the watches of the night. Because you are my help, I sing in the shadow of your wings. My soul clings to you; your right hand upholds me.

— Psalm 63.6–8

Thought for the Day

I love sleep. My life has the tendency to fall apart when I'm awake, you know?

~ Ernest Hemingway

Who needs sleep? Not busy, important people. Not people who want to succeed or climb the ladder. The only people who really need sleep is . . . *everyone.* Especially when you've been hammered by life.

Elijah was a mighty prophet. He risked everything for God in the face of an overwhelming enemy. You may recall the story—he went head-to-head with evil King Ahab and the priests of Baal. He challenged them to a cosmic dual between Baal and Yahweh. The scene was the top of Mt. Carmel. The priests of Baal built an altar for their god. Elijah built one to Yahweh. The god who burned up the offering would be the winner. The losers would be slaughtered.

The priests called upon Baal to rain down fire. Nothing happened. They cried out more, Elijah taunted, still nothing. Then Elijah called on Yahweh. Fire fell down consuming every part and parcel of the sacrifice. God and Elijah won!

But there was this woman named Jezebel. She was the queen and when she heard the news from Mt. Carmel she was furious. She sent word to Elijah: *I'm coming after you.* And what did this mighty man of God do in response? He ran like his pants were on fire! The Bible says it like this:

> *Jezebel sent a messenger to Elijah to say, "May the gods deal with me, be it ever so severely, if by this time tomorrow I do not make your life like that of one of them." Elijah was afraid and ran for his life.* (1 Kings 19:1–3)

Amazing how men can go toe-to-toe with each other but one woman can send us running!

Elijah ran for his life. And then, exhausted, he did what all of us should do when life turns upside down—he collapsed under a tree and slept. The next verses describe the tenderness of God: *All at once an angel touched him and said, "Get up and eat." [Elijah] looked around, and there by his head was a cake of bread baked over hot coals, and a jar of water. He ate and drank and then lay down again.* (1 Kings19:5–6)

Amanda Jameson hiked the 2,650-mile-long Pacific Crest Trail. When asked what she learned on that arduous journey, she said, *Sleep is the great reset button.*[64] I like that.

Despite extensive medical research, we still don't know much about sleep. It's thought that during sleep your brain runs a sort of garbage pickup routine. Your brain produces by-products as it works through the day. During sleep these by-products are literally picked up and carried off, performing a cleanup and reset function.[65]

---

[64] Amanda "Zuul" Jameson, *Advice From a Hiker Who Finished the Pacific Crest Trail*, Backpacker.com, February 14, 2017, accessed February 20, 2017, http://www.backpacker.com/trips/advice-from-a-hiker-who-finished-the-pacific-crest-trail.

[65] *"10 Fascinating Things That Happen While You're Sleeping," Prevention*, March 21, 2016, accessed February 20, 2017, http://www.prevention.com/health/what-happens-during-sleep/slide/9.

When life tumbles in, your brain is working overtime, hence more toxic by-products. You need more sleep to clean out your brain. John Steinbeck said that *it is a common experience that a problem difficult at night is resolved in the morning after the committee of sleep has worked on it.*[66]

Men who are **H**ungry, **A**ngry, **L**onely and **T**ired (HALT) make poor decisions. The fuse is short and the will is weak when we are tired. Give yourself a break . . . let your body, mind and soul mend through sleep.

Elijah didn't know all that was going on in his brain when he collapsed into sleep under the tree in the desert, but God did. The result was that through sleep and good food, Elijah was prepared to hear God and take the next step in his life.

Having trouble with anger? Sleep on it.

Think About It . . .

- How much sleep do you get?
- If you are having trouble sleeping ask God for help. Check with your doctor and/or therapist to see what they may be able to do to help you sleep.
- Check out this website from the https://goo.gl/gikwV6National Sleep Foundation for tips and tricks for getting and staying asleep.

Life Commitment:

Sleeping doesn't mean I am lazy, it means I'm human. Sleep is designed by God to reset and refresh me. If ever I need good sleep, it's now.

[66]"John Steinbeck Quotes," BrainyQuote, accessed September 24, 2017, https://www.brainyquote.com/quotes/quotes/j/johnsteinb103825.html.

Day 31: Get Moving

The Word

Do you not know that your body is a temple of the Holy Spirit, who is in you, whom you have received from God? You are not your own; you were bought at a price. Therefore honor God with your body.

— 1 Corinthians 6.19–20

Thought for the Day

Making excuses burns zero calories per hour.

~ Anonymous

Today's encouragement is short and simple. *Start doing something, anything, that gets your heart beating fast and makes you sweat.* You don't have to do it a long time. You don't have to pay anything to do this. No need for special clothes or shoes. The weather doesn't have to be perfect. You don't have to go anywhere special. All you have to do is *do it.* Do ***something*** that gets your heart beating and your body sweating.

Study after study can give you all the info you could ever want on why exercise is good for you. But the real problem is not *information*, it's *motivation.*

So here's the deal. If you can't do 50 pushups, do 10 today. Do 10 pushups a day for a week. Then next week do 15. Ten pushups today is better than zero. When you do 10 pushups a day this week and then 15 next week, you will see progress and you will be motivated.

If you can't walk 100 yards without your heart coming out of your chest, start with 50. Just do it. *Start today, right now.*

It won't be fun. Putting your heart and lungs into chaos can be exhilarating, but it is not *fun* in the traditional sense of the word. It actually feels more like *work.* Those people who tell you this will be easy and exciting set you up for unrealistic expectations.

I'm not going to tell you it is fun but I can tell you it really feels good. It feels good to drop weight. It feels good to know you can eventually handle that five-mile hike or run with your kids or get on a bike and travel on your own power 20 miles.

It feels good to not have sleep apnea, high blood pressure, acid reflux, chest pains and high blood sugar *simply because you consistently put your heart and lungs into chaos for 30 minutes a day.*

Is this fitness stuff really so complicated? If you eat more calories than you burn, you will get fat. The opposite is true. If you burn more than you eat, you will lose weight. Mean old Mr. Science! But that's the way it works. No matter what anyone tells you, there are no shortcuts or magic pills. Eat less, exercise more, that's it.

Now is the time to get off the couch and do *something. Something* is better than *nothing* and a bunch of *somethings* add up to *a lot of good things* for you.

If you need a few inspirational quotes, here they are:

Better sore than sorry.

Nothing tastes as good as skinny feels. (My personal favorite)

Sweat is just fat crying.

Get comfortable with being uncomfortable.

Pain is weakness leaving the body.

Three months from now you will thank yourself.

No pain. No Gain. Shut up and train.

Work hard. Stay humble.

Sore? Tired? Out of breath? Sweaty? Good . . . It's working.

Good things come to those who sweat.

Sore muscles are the new hangover.

Motivation is what gets you started. Habit keeps you going.

Your fitness is 100% mental. Your body won't go where your mind doesn't push it.

I guarantee you this: No matter how you feel when you start a workout, you will *not* feel worse after your workout. No matter how you feel when you begin a workout, you will not regret having worked out.

Try me on this one. Get moving. And you will want to check with your doctor before you do anything too strenuous.

Think About It . . .

- No . . . don't think about it. Just get up and do SOMETHING to get your heart beating and your body sweating!

Life Commitment:

I am getting up to do something that will get my heart beating and my body sweating.

Day 32: When You Hurt Your World Shrinks

The Word

Then Job took a piece of broken pottery and scraped himself with it as he sat among the ashes.

— Job 2.8

Thought for the Day

When we're in the middle of adversity, it feels all consuming. Faith flickers, hope falters, courage burns low. It sometimes seems as if the dark times will never end. And these are the hours when the enemy of our soul whispers his lies of discouragement and despair.

~ Joni Erickson Tada

The day before I preached a sermon about marriage and divorce I glued two pieces of plywood together flat lengthwise. During the sermon I illustrated the effects of divorce by ripping the boards apart. I said something like this: *The biblical word describing marriage is the word for 'glue.' When we divorce, we believe we can cleanly and neatly separate. But divorce is not neat or clean. It's like these two boards, glued together, then ripped apart.*

When I ripped the boards apart, they left a mess of splintered wood and globs of dried glue. It was ugly.

The people left church that day with one image in their minds: the boards being ripped apart and the mess they left behind. Divorce causes tremendous suffering. When we suffer we deeply experience the rips and tears in our lives.

Suffering causes things to happen to our perception. Suffering shrinks our world.

Time slows down to *this moment.* If we think about the *past* it hurts—either we deeply regret the mistakes that led to our divorce or we grieve the hard work we put in to avoid such a catastrophe, efforts which now seem wasted.

The *future* is so uncertain and painful, we can't think about it. Whatever we had planned for our future is now off the table. The pain of the past and the uncertainty of a frightening future compress time to the terrible *now.*

When we hurt, **space** also compresses. Forget my vacation trip to Colorado, forget my plans to remodel the kitchen, forget organizing my desk. Pain is the heat that shrinks our space around us.

This was driven home to me when I was asked by a family to visit their 32-year-old son who was dying of a rare form of cancer. I went to the hospital, introduced myself, and began to chat it up. He seemed disengaged from what I was saying. Then, without a word, he stood up, pulled up his hospital gown, and urinated into a plastic urinal as if I wasn't there.

For this 32-year-old man, time and space had shrunk to this brief moment and to his hospital bed. He didn't care about anything I said. He just needed to pee, so he did. Two days later he died.

When the Old Testament figure of Job had lost everything, his world shrank to an ash heap: Then Job took a piece of broken pottery and scraped himself with it as he sat among the ashes. (Job 2.8)

If this is the way you feel, then . . .

- Know that it's normal to feel like time and space have shrunk to this moment and this tiny space.

- When the terrible pain of divorce is upon you, you may feel the urge to shrink time to nothing and to exit the space. We call this option *suicide*, and it is a bad and terrible idea. It's OK to experience compressed time and space, just don't let the pain squeeze the life out of you. If you feel like this at this moment, read the next point . . .
- You will not always feel like this. The process of healing will re-expand time and enlarge your space. *I promise you that you will not always feel like this.* But if you are considering suicide as a viable option to your suffering, call the National Suicide Prevention Hotline now: 800-273-8255. You can call me as well.[67] Go to Appendix A to read more about suicide and how to assess your risk for it.

Think About It . . .

If you are new to divorce, have you experienced how pain can shrink your time and space?

If you are further down the road of recovery, are you experiencing an expansion of time and an enlarging of your space?

Life Commitment . . .

It is normal for pain to compress time and shrink my space. I commit to living through this moment, but I pray to God that he will deliver me from this pain, and I trust he will do it. I will hold on.

[67] My cell phone is 978.204.0480. Visit http://www.mensdivorcerecovery.org for more information and resources for help.

Day 33: When You Hurt You Become Super Sensitive

The Word

Why is life given to a man whose way is hidden, whom God has hedged in? For sighing comes to me instead of food; my groans pour out like water. What I feared has come upon me; what I dreaded has happened to me. I have no peace, no quietness; I have no rest, but only turmoil.

— Job 3.23–26

Thought for the Day

We rarely start with God. We start with the immediate data of our lives—a messy house, a balky car, a cranky spouse, a recalcitrant child.

~ Eugene Peterson

I HAVE WALKED WITH MANY MEN AND WOMEN through the heartbreak of divorce. One couple in particular comes to mind. Both were super-achievers. Each had tried to overcome tremendous adversity the world's way, and had ended up in more pain than when they started. They finally found Christ and things between them improved.

But staying together was not to be. For whatever reasons, anger rose up and lashed out and both found themselves filing restraining orders against the other as tensions exploded.

It was a long and painful season for them. The church staff and I reached out in every way possible. We met with them, recommended counselors, nursed each through their pain. Church folks watched after their kids when things were imploding at home. Some took food. All this to say, we gave them our best time and energy.

So it came as a shock when a fellow staff member and I received a scathing seven page single-spaced email from the wife. My staff member walked into my office and stated that this was the longest email she had ever received! After all the time and energy we had put into this woman, my first response was anger. But then we realized the pain this woman was in had made her hurt so deeply that the smallest thing seemed incredibly painful to her. Intense pain had made her hyper-sensitive.

When your world comes crashing down time and space shrink and you may become hyper-sensitive to your environment and those around you. I know I did. I couldn't believe that most of my friends made no effort to reach out. And most of those who did venture forth simply didn't understand the intense pain I was in. It really made me angry.

Looking back now I understand a little better. I now realize how my pain drove me to seek someone, *anyone*, who would understand. Few did. But the few who did saved my life.

If the people in your life seem insensitive or not to care, don't be surprised. Some really don't care. Some may care but are uncomfortable sitting with someone who is in such intense pain. Others shy away because they don't want to be reminded that this could happen to them.

But a few will get it. A few will understand. Thank God for these few. Seek them out. Ask them questions. Let them into your heart.

And release everyone else from the burden of sharing your burden. God knows who you need to help you through. Find those folks and be grateful to them and to God for what they give you (see Appendix C).

Think About It . . .

Who among your friends and/or family has failed to reach out to you? Release them from your anger. They don't understand and you can't make them understand. Instead . . .

. . . Ask God to send you a few, maybe even just one, to get you through. And . . .

. . . Determine that you will not be insensitive to the hurting. Further down the path, when God puts hurting people in front of you, love them as you have been loved.

Prayer . . .

Not everyone will understand. Not everyone will get it. God, thank you for the few who do. As I heal, help me to be one of those 'few' to the hurting and suffering in this world.

Day 34: When You Hurt You May Lash Out

The Word

Teach me knowledge and good judgment for I believe in your commands.
— Psalm 119.66

Thought for the Day

There are too many people today who instead of feeling hurt are acting out their hurt; instead of acknowledging pain, they're inflicting pain on others. Rather than risking feeling disappointed, they're choosing to live disappointed.
~ Brené Brown

No one likes to take their dog to the vet, least of all, the dog! We are shocked when our normally loving and tail-wagging dog suddenly bares his teeth and emits a low, menacing growl. What causes a friendly animal to transform into a frightening beast? The short and simple answer is, *pain.* When normally benign animals are cornered or hurt, they turn ugly. So do we. Hurt people hurt people.

When my life crashed around me my first reactions were benevolent. I tried to understand why others were coming against me. I tried to be gracious to those who had betrayed me. But then the reality of what I was losing began to sink in and I became angry.

I can illustrate this through a Facebook Messenger conversation with a longtime friend. It started with me explaining what had happened in my life the past two years. My friend acknowledged the difficulty of the situation, then wrote,

> *I will remind you that our God is big. Really big. He came to reconcile and leaves us with a ministry of reconciliation. He is most glorified when we are most like him.*

My response?

> *If I did not know God was big I would have put a .40 caliber bullet through my head a few months ago. Having to go through this with you just brings it all back so maybe I should just give the lite answer when someone I know hasn't heard.*

It should come as no surprise that I didn't get a response from him.

What happened in this conversation? My friend tried to understand, then he off-loaded the 'Sunday School answer' to my pain in a way that I heard as condescending and trite. This infuriated me more, and when he let the conversation drop, my anger only increased. I did *not* feel like a minister of reconciliation. I felt like I wanted to hurt him and all those who had wounded me so deeply.

When we are in severe pain we need to express it in ways that don't further alienate us from those around us trying to help. Ask God to give you one or two other guys who can absorb your pain without further hurting you.[68]

And then release anger through other means. For me, my bike is my outlet. I let the anger flow from my head down through my legs into the pavement. My record rides come when I am most angry. I can't over-emphasize the value of sweating. Men were made to fight. Channel that urge away from others and into the pavement or weights or MMA. *When you are angry and frustrated, get moving.*

[68]Brené Brown writes, *Most of us were never taught how to hold discomfort, sit with it, or communicate it, only how to discharge or dump it, or to pretend that it's not happening.* Brené Brown, *Rising Strong* (Random House, 2017), Kindle Location 859.

And if you are on the receiving end of someone who has been severely wounded, *leave the trite answers at home.* Instead, absorb their pain, even if it is directed at you. Hurt people lash out. Let them. Then, when the time is right, God will use you to mitigate some of their pain.

Think About It . . .

- What do you do when you are really hurt?
- What are some physical ways you can let pain out that are legal and only moderately dangerous?
- Who is the friend or counselor who is mature enough to sit with you in your pain?
- Who in your life needs you to sit with them in their pain?

Life Commitment . . .

I commit to releasing my hurt in as constructive a way as possible.[69]

---

[69]To read more, go to this website: http://www.charismanews.com/opinion/the-pulse/53573-15-ways-hurting-people-hurt-people.

Day 35: When You Hurt You May Be Willing to do Anything to Get Out of the Pain

The Word

Blessed is the man who does not walk in the counsel of the wicked or stand in the way of sinners or sit in the seat of mockers. But his delight is in the law of the Lord, and on his law he meditates day and night. He is like a tree planted by streams of water, which yields its fruit in season and whose leaf does not wither. Whatever he does prospers.

— Psalm 1.1–3

Thought for the Day

Our search for significance shows up in a lot of misdirected ways.

~ Tony Dungy

As we all know, the Chinese characters for the word *crisis* mean *danger* and *critical point.*[70] Crises push us to critical points where we can choose well or not.

Perhaps it was a crisis in your marriage that led you to choose to cheat on your spouse, and your divorce is the result. Perhaps you are the victim of a wayward or misguided spouse, and the divorce was a

[70]See https://en.wikipedia.org/wiki/Chinese_word_for_%22crisis%22 for a brief discussion about the common misinterpretation of this phrase.

complete surprise to you. Either way, you and I have choices to make from this point forward. The problem is that our intense pain can push us to make poor decisions with long-term consequences. The intensity of the pain can falsely make you believe you must make decisions *now.*

If there ever is a time when you need to slow down and seek God's wisdom and the wise direction of others, this is it. Don't make any huge decisions now. Stop, pray, talk with wise friends, seek out a counselor. Don't make any major decisions when you are hurting the most.

Paul Tripp says, *We all tend to surrender to and serve what we think will give us life.*[71] In your pain you may be led to believe that what gave you life before has radically failed, and it's time to try something new. If you turned to anything less than God to give you life, then, yes, it's time to try something new, or rather, *Someone* new. God is ready for you to surrender to him and find your life and significance in him. (See Appendix F)

One thing is guaranteed: If we seek life in things lesser than God, we will be disappointed, betrayed, damaged, and eventually, destroyed. Alcohol, drugs, sex, shopping, work, hobbies . . . these *horizontal* things will not deliver what only our vertical God can deliver.

And remember this: *Thinking and doing are two different things.* You have probably *thought* of doing one or more (or all) of the things listed above. But *thinking* and *doing* are two different things. You may *think* of doing a lot of things. Just *don't do* them.

Consider these things in your moment of crisis:

- How do you want to be remembered?

- How do you want your kids to think of you now?

- What is the cost of choosing poorly now?

---

[71]Paul David Tripp, *New Morning Mercies*, Kindle Location 4163.

Divorce strips away the things that gave us significance. Take the advice of Wayne Stiles who writes, *We need a different goal: faithfulness rather than significance.*[72]

In your time of crisis, choose to be faithful to God. In the end, faithfulness to him will pay off *now* and for *eternity.*

The most common ways men use to escape pain are pornography and alcohol. Below are resources to help you succeed against these quagmires of disaster:

Alcohol and Drug Addiction:

Alcoholics Anonymous: *www.aa.org*;
Celebrate Recovery (Christian-based recovery program for all addictions meeting in local churches): *www.celebraterecovery.com*

Pornography:

Be Broken Ministries: *2.bebroken.com* and,
Faithful & True Ministries: *www.faithfulandtrue.com*

Think About It . . .

Consider these good words from Paul David Tripp:

No person can be the source of your identity.
No one can be the basis of your happiness.
No individual can give you a reason to get up in the morning and continue.
No loved one can be the carrier of your hope.
No one is able to change you from the inside out.
No human being can alter your past.
No person is able to atone for your wrongs.
No one can give your heart peace and rest.
Asking another human being to do those things for you is like requiring him to be the fourth member of the Trinity and then

[72]Wayne Stiles, *Waiting on God: What to Do When God Does Nothing,* (Grand Rapids: Baker Books, 2015), 24.

judging him when he falls short. It simply cannot and will not work.[73]

Life Commitment . . .

I commit to finding my significance in God and not in another person, place or thing. From this point on my choices will be driven by being faithful to God, not easing my pain.

[73]Tripp, *New Morning Mercies*, Kindle Location 3960-3962.

Day 36: When You Hurt You May Question Everything

The Word

Trust in the Lord with all your heart and lean not on your own understanding; in all your ways acknowledge him, and he will make your paths straight. Do not be wise in your own eyes; fear the Lord and shun evil. This will bring health to your body and nourishment to your bones.

— Proverbs 3.5–8

Thought for the Day

We say that there ought to be no sorrow, but there is sorrow, and we have to accept and receive ourselves in its fires.

~ Oswald Chambers

THEY SAY THAT THE LITTLE TOE was given to us by God to show us where the furniture is in the middle of the night. If I slam my toe into furniture in the dark, the pain transmitted to my brain will cause me to question several things. *Have I lost my sense of direction in the dark? Has someone moved the furniture without me knowing? Am I getting old and losing my mind?*

The point is, every pain we experience causes us to question something. The deeper the pain, the more penetrating the questions.

When I was a chaplain at Children's Medical Center in Dallas I talked with a very confused father. His daughter was dealing with juvenile diabetes, and she was struggling. Her illness was serious but not life threatening. Just a few hundred feet away was the liver transplant unit. The kids in there were fighting for every moment of life.

But this dad was angry and upset, disproportionally so. As he looked out the window he shook his head and said to me, *I don't get it. I started going to church. I started giving money, lots of money. And my daughter is still sick.*

Without knowing it, this father had tried to bargain with God: *God, I will give my life to you, I will give my money to you. And if I do my part, you must do your part, and your part is to take this sickness away from my daughter.*

When his daughter remained sick, he questioned God. Instead of questioning God, he should have questioned his bargain with God. God cannot be manipulated into doing our bidding.

But this dad was hurting for his daughter, and his pain caused him to ask some tough questions.

Don't be surprised if you find yourself doubting beliefs you have deeply held. I know I did. I had given my life to the church. When I was booted out of the church I had faithfully served, I had serious doubts about the church at large. I had followed the right path regarding marriage. I had followed the rules. But my marriage didn't turn out the way I was promised it would. All I had believed in about marriage was up for review in my mind's eye.

When your ground is shaken, allow yourself to ask the hard questions, *but always come back to God.* Even if you doubt him, come back to him and ask him to give you just what you need to settle your heart and quiet your mind.

Take a look at Psalm 73. Here is a man who, in his pain, was questioning everything. Finally, he says, *When I tried to understand all this, it was oppressive to me till I entered the sanctuary of God; then I understood . . .* (Psalm 73:16–17)

God doesn't mind our questions. In the midst of our hard questions he always invites us into his sanctuary to experience his love and grace.

Think About It . . .

- What foundational beliefs have you questioned through this painful process?
- How can you know what beliefs should be ditched and which should be kept?

Life Commitment . . .

I commit to the truth. I commit to shedding old, false beliefs and finding the truth in God.

Day 37: When You Hurt You Don't Care

The Word

My people are fools; they do not know me. They are senseless children; they have no understanding. They are skilled in doing evil; they know not how to do good.

— Jeremiah 4.22

Thought for the Day

He has never called back one single sentence of comfort.

~ Spurgeon

As long as you are feeling your pain, you care. As long as you are questioning what you believe in, you care. As long as you are fighting to do the next right thing, you care. As long as you are struggling with decisions, you care.

But if you stop feeling, if you stop questioning, if you stop thinking, if you stop struggling, you don't care anymore. Even a man stuck in self-pity cares—if only for himself.

A man who doesn't care is a dangerous man indeed. But it's easy not to care. It's easy to throw up your hands and walk away. It's easy to fall into the pity pit and curl up in a ball and die. The easy way is not to care. The easy way is to give in to despair. The easy thing is to give up.

When you feel like that, *or if you stop feeling anything*, stop, pray, and find someone to talk with. And if you haven't gotten to this place, know that you very well might. Several times.

Don't give in to this strong pull to give in to the despair. Know that our enemy (Satan) wants to destroy you. His primary targets are families, churches, fathers, mothers, children. If you are human you are a target, and Satan's goal is destruction.

Push back. You are in a fight bigger than yourself. More is at stake than your immediate pain. What you do, how you respond, the choices you make will reverberate far wider *now* than you know and far *longer* than you can imagine.

Don't let your pain shrink your time and space to this tiny moment and this pinpoint of space. Allow God to expand your perspective of time—there is more to your life than this painful, present *now*.

Allow God to enlarge your space. If you give in to despair your space shrinks to nothing. If you push back and allow God to lead you through this, your place of positive, life-giving influence will expand far wider than you know.

Think About It . . .

- When have you despaired? What triggered that emotion? An email from your ex? A text from your bank warning of an overdraft? A bill from your lawyer? An ignored call to your child?

- What did you do? Dwell on it? Or give it to God?

- If you feel your time shrinking, pray. Breathe deeply. Relax into God and allow him to love you back into a larger time frame. If you feel your space shrinking, take a walk. Get outside and let God use the beauty of his creation to expand your space.

Prayer . . .

God, I am tempted to give in to the despair. The pain is too much, or so it feels that way right now. Give me strength to push back. Give me hope. Give me encouragement—put courage into my heart again. Help me see the bigger picture. Help me see beyond this moment. Help me see the future you have for me. Help me see the influence you can have through me to my children and to the world. Deliver me from the enemy.

Day 38: The Four P's of Identity

The Word

Those who are led by the Spirit of God are sons of God. For you did not receive a spirit that makes you a slave again to fear, but you received the Spirit of sonship. And by him we cry, "Abba, Father."

— Romans 8.14–15

Thought for the Day

We are never-ending. We are warriors and creators. We are divine and sacred and worthy. You are worthy without caveat or exception.

~ Teresa Pasquale

From the moment of our birth we are seeking our identity. The first task is to separate ourselves from our parents. But to define ourselves by what we are *not* leaves a huge hole. We fill that hole with things from the horizontal.

Richard Rohr writes:

> *Without a transcendent connection, each of us is stuck in his own little psyche, struggling to create meaning and produce an identity all by himself. When we inevitably fail at this—because we can't do it alone—we suffer shame and self-defeat. Or we try to pretend that our small universe of country, ethnicity, team, or denomination is actually the center of the world. This can bear dire results. We need a wider universe in which to realize our own significance and*

> *a bigger story in which to find meaning. Not only does a man need to hear that he is beloved, that he is a son, he needs to believe that he is a beloved son "of God."* [74]

Rohr identifies a man's horizontal pursuit of identity by the 'Four P's': *Possessions, Perks, Prestige, and Power.*[75]

Perhaps you are divorced because you sought your identity through one or more of these Four P's to the detriment of your marriage and family. Maybe you worked too many hours to attain these Four P's and the price was your family. Or maybe you have attained these Four P's, only to have divorce strip them away.

In the end, for every person on the planet, the great awakening is that *finding happiness, satisfaction and contentment in the horizontal is empty and fruitless.* The horizontal is composed of the *gifts.* True happiness, satisfaction and contentment are found (vertically) in the *Giver.*

And what does the Giver think about us? He radically, wildly, passionately loves us and pursues us!

The Bible says that Jesus began his ministry with his Baptism. Matthew says that *As soon as Jesus was baptized, he went up out of the water. At that moment heaven was opened, and he saw the Spirit of God descending like a dove and lighting on him. And a voice from heaven said, "This is my Son, whom I love; with him I am well pleased."* (Matthew 3.16–17)

The amazing thing about this is that God declared Jesus his Son and stated his love, pleasure and acceptance of him *before Jesus did anything.*

The same is true of us. *Because* you are a child of God, you are of immeasurable worth and happiness to God. And you are a child of God because he has declared you his son and paid the price through Jesus to make you his child.

Brennan Manning writes,

---

[74]Rohr, Durepos and McGrath, *On the Threshold of Transformation*, 254.
[75]Ibid., 95.

It takes a profound conversion to accept that God is relentlessly tender and compassionate toward us just as we are—not in spite of our sins and faults (that would not be total acceptance), but with them. Though God does not condone or sanction evil, He does not withhold His love because there is evil in us.[76]

Your identity is in God, the Giver, not in acquisition of the gifts. Your identity is as a child of God, not a product of this world. Your identity is rooted in the eternal, not the temporal. No one can take your identity in God away from you. He holds you safe and secure.

Think About It . . .

- Skip ahead to Days 58-63 to read what it means to be accepted by God.
- Think about what you have lost because of your divorce. What role did those things play in defining you? How can firmly rooting your identity vertically in God replace the pain of losing these horizontal things.
- In 100 years, what will the Four P's have given you (Possessions, Perks, Prestige, and Power)?
- In 100 years, what will having rooted your identity in God have given you?

Life Commitment . . .

Though building my identity around Possessions, Perks, Prestige, and Power is tempting, I choose to find my identity in God and in him alone.

[76]Brennan Manning, John Blase, and Jonathan Foreman, *Abbas Child: The Cry of the Heart for Intimate Belonging* (Colorado Springs: NavPress, 2015), 19.

Day 39: God is Your Anchor

The Word

We have this hope as an anchor for the soul, firm and secure.
— Hebrews 6.19

Thought for the Day

Ultimately, spiritual maturity is not about memorizing the Bible and mastering the spiritual disciplines. These are healthy things to do, but they are still only means to a greater end, which in itself is learning to love with God's love and learning to serve with God's power.
~ Gary Thomas

For a few years I had the privilege and joy of restoring a 28-foot sailboat and learning to sail it. There is nothing like the feeling of a massive boat moving silently through the water under wind power alone.

After the boat was habitable, my two older children and I would spend nights on Lake Travis. Lake Travis was formed upon the completion of Mansfield Dam in 1941. The dam backed up water between limestone hills. Most of the shore, therefore, consists of rocky cliffs. Those rocky cliffs gave new importance to correctly setting the anchor of my boat, especially if the wind was up!

I had never given much thought to how to anchor a boat—I just thought you tossed the anchor overboard and it would hold. But when you are on a sailboat surrounded by rocks, correctly setting the anchor takes on new meaning. The last thing you want is to wake up with the boat smashing against the rocks with your two kids inside.

On one trip a cold front was predicted to come in that Friday afternoon. Sure enough, the winds went from a southerly breeze of 10 mph to a northerly howler of at least 25 mph. We were determined to spend the night on the boat anyway, so we motored to our favorite spot. But I knew that with a strong northerly wind predicted through the night, setting the anchor was critical. I took my time choosing the spot and then worked to make sure the anchor would hold.

Through the night the wind buffeted our boat but the anchor held. The next morning we were where we planned to be—safe in the cove, ready for a breakfast of pancakes and sausage. All through the night the winds battered our sailboat. And through the night our boat swung back and forth, *but not too far back and forth because the anchor held.*

If you have set your anchor on one of the Four P's, Possessions, Perks, Prestige, and Power, you have wrongly set your anchor. The only anchor for your soul that will hold is God himself.

The Bible says, *We have this hope as an anchor for the soul, firm and secure.*

The Greek word translated *firm* is formed from the negative of *fail.* In other words, the writer says that Jesus is our anchor that will not fail.

The Greek word we translate as *secure* means *stable* and relates to walking on stepping stones that are sure and secure. From both the negative and the positive sides, the writer of Hebrews is confirming for us as clearly as possible that God is our only hope, an anchor that will hold us secure in the storm.

Like my sailboat, you and I may swing about when the winds blow, but if we remain anchored in God we will not be set adrift to crash into the rocks.

Think About It . . .

- Into what is your anchor set? Is your anchor holding?

- What steps can you take to set your anchor in God? (Reading this book is a good start!)

Life Commitment:

God is my anchor, my rock, my sure foundation. He will not be moved. Though I may waver between hope and fear, God will not waver. He holds me secure.

DAY 40: SUICIDE: STAY

THE WORD

The thief comes only to steal and kill and destroy; I have come that they may have life, and have it to the full.
— John 10.10

THOUGHT FOR THE DAY

It is crucial to see that deciding against the principle of suicide creates its own practical strengths: it commits one to the human project and to one's own life in a way that gives rise to solidarity and resilience. And when one speaks of such commitment to living, others may be encouraged to live and to find the resources to survive pain.
~ Jennifer Michael Hecht

NATIONAL SUICIDE PREVENTION LIFELINE: 800-273-8255. The information found in the next few days can also be found in Appendix A.

Divorced or separated men have a 39% higher suicide rate than their married counterparts. They are also more likely to take part in risky activities which increases their chance of early death.[77]

---

[77]Emma Innes, *Why Divorce is bad for a man's health: Separation increases the risk of early death, substance abuse, suicide and depression*, last updated October 2, 2013, accessed October 20, 2017, http://www.dailymail.co.uk/health/article-2440005/Divorce-mans-health-Separation-increases-risk-death-substance-abuse-suicide-depression.html. See also Augustine J Kposowa, *Marital*

If you have thoughts of taking your life you are not alone nor are you abnormal. I believe that the vast majority of people think of taking their own life at some point in their lives.

I know I did. For about four days a few months after my divorce was final, suicide became one of several options. I was shocked at how casually I thought of this option. As I considered what to do, suicide seemed a viable choice. Death by my hand was laid out there along with the other options on how to move forward out of the pain.

A newly divorced man named Philip writes:

> *As a divorced man, I can honestly say I contemplated suicide for the first time in my life during the first year or two of my separation. It's incredibly difficult to have your entire family life—children, home and even wife—pulled away from you. Prior to the divorce, I was very happy, making a good salary and living in a nice neighborhood. Soon after the divorce, I was saddled with very high child support payments, debt from legal fees and barely enough left over to pay the rent of my small one bedroom apartment.*[78]

Tremendous pain is caused through divorce because divorce creates so much loss. Add to this that our society largely ignores the intense pain caused by divorce. This further isolates divorced men in their suffering. We are, by nature, wired to get out of pain, and suicide is one way to escape.

H. Norman Wright says that there are four main reasons for suicide:

- **Depression [Rage]**—*The person is sitting on a high level of unacceptable rage that has developed because of a series of events in life over which he or she has no control. Eventually this repressed rage is turned against himself or herself in suicide.*

---

status and suicide in the National Longitudinal Mortality Study, Journal of Epidemiology Community Health 2000;54:254–261, accessed June 12, 2018, http://jech.bmj.com/content/jech/54/4/254.full.pdf.

[78]Jack Cafferty *Why does divorce make men more suicidal than women?,* last updated March 11, 2010, accessed July 13, 2017, http://caffertyfile.blogs.cnn.com/2010/03/11/why-does-divorce-make-men-more-suicidal-than-women/.

- **Relief of Pain**—*Those with high levels of pain usually have three choices: a psychotic distortion that reduces the pain, drugs or alcohol, or suicide. They often say, "I don't want to die, but I don't know any other way out—I just can't stand it."*

- **Revenge**—*Some [people] feel overwhelmed by hurt or rejection from another person. Their desire to hurt back is stronger than the desire to live.*

- **Hopelessness**—*Twenty-five percent of those who commit suicide do so after giving it quiet consideration and weighing the pros and cons of living and dying.*[79]

Teacher, author, and historian Jennifer Michael Hecht lost two friends to suicide. In her own grief she decided to research and write about it. She wrote her thoughts in a blog called "The Best American Poetry." In the blog she made an appeal to those contemplating suicide:

> *I want to say this,... Don't kill yourself. Life has always been almost too hard to bear, for a lot of the people, a lot of the time. It's awful. But it isn't too hard to bear, it's only almost too hard to bear...*
>
> *I'm issuing a rule. You are not allowed to kill yourself. When a person kills himself, he does wrenching damage to the community. One of the best predictors of suicide is knowing a suicide. That means that suicide is also delayed homicide. You have to stay.*
>
> *Don't kill yourself. Suffer here with us instead. We need you with us, we have not forgotten you, you are our hero. Stay.*[80]

When I was struggling those four days, here is (among other things) what I kept in my head that helped me choose to stay:

---

[79] H. Norman Wright, *The New Guide to Crisis and Trauma Counseling* (Ventura, CA: Regal Books, 2003), Kindle Locations 3120-3126.

[80] Jennifer Michael Hecht, *Stay: A History of Suicide and the Philosophies Against It* (New Haven: Yale University Press, 2015), 7-8 (emphasis mine).

- ***I did not want to add to the pain of others.*** If trauma has caused me tremendous pain, it is fair to assume that my suicide would traumatize the people I love the most. This is not right nor fair to them.

- ***I will get through this.*** Life has always been almost too hard to bear for a lot of the people a lot of the time. It's awful. But it isn't too hard to bear—it's only *almost* too hard to bear. What I feel today will not be what I feel tomorrow.

- ***If I take my life, this is what I will be remembered for.*** No matter all my accomplishments, the first thing people will think of when my name is mentioned will be that I took my life. I did not want that.

- ***By taking my own life, I may contribute to someone else's suicide.*** Survivors of those who take their lives are more likely to take their own life. I didn't want to potentially contribute to the death by suicide of anyone among my family or friends.

- ***I will deprive the world of what God has planned to do through me.*** I have much to offer this world. God showed me that I had many years to serve him and that many people would be helped if I chose to stay.

When I thought of these realities, suicide remained an option, but one among many options. If I had not considered these realities, suicide as an option could have become my *only* option, at least in my mind.

If you are thinking of suicide as one of several options, pay attention to your thinking. If you have come to the conclusion that suicide is your *only* option, your thinking has become distorted and you need immediate help. ***Call the suicide prevention hotline immediately*** – **800-273-8255**. Don't hesitate. Put this book down and call ***now***. Don't turn temporary moments of personal anguish into a permanent state of calamity for those around you.

Think About It . . .

- Is suicide one of several options you are considering? God has bigger plans for you than you can imagine. Don't cheat the world of what you have to offer.
- In your mind, is suicide becoming the *only* option? You need help. Call the suicide hotline: **800-273-8255**

Life Commitment . . .

"Life has always been almost too hard to bear, for a lot of the people, a lot of the time. It's awful. But it isn't too hard to bear, it's only almost too hard to bear." I commit to bearing through this terrible time of life, knowing that what is now will not always be. God is my hope. He will see me through to new life and new hope. I choose to stay.

Day 41: Suicide—Assessing Your Risk

The Word

The Lord is close to the brokenhearted and saves those who are crushed in spirit. A righteous man may have many troubles, but the Lord delivers him from them all.

— Psalm 34.18–19

Thought for the Day

It can be a tremendous comfort to learn that great minds have concluded that no individual need wonder whether his or her life is worth living. It is worth living.

~ Jennifer Michael Hecht

National Suicide Prevention Lifeline: 800-273-8255

On September 25, 2000, Kevin Hines jumped off the Golden Gate Bridge. He hit the water 220 feet below and lived to tell about it. He is only one of 33 among an estimated 2,000 people who have jumped to survive the fall. As I read his story his words leapt out at me:

> *In the midst of my free fall, I said to myself these words, words I thought no one would ever hear me repeat: "What have I done? I don't want to die. God, please save me!" As I fell, I somehow possessed the mind-set that all I wanted to do was live—by any means necessary.*[81]

[81] *He jumped off the Golden Gate Bridge . . . and lived!*, New York Post, last updated June 20, 2013, accessed July 13, 2017, http://nypost.com/2013/06/30/he-jumped-off-

I wonder how many of the more than 45,000 people who take their lives every year in the United States have had the same thought the moment after they jumped or pulled the trigger or hit the tree or swallowed the pills or cut their wrists.

Are you thinking of taking our life? Take your thoughts seriously. If you are thinking any of the following thoughts or taking any of the following actions, you are at a higher risk for attempting to take your life by your own hand.

Carefully consider these questions:

- How much of your 'brain space' is taken up by thinking of suicide? Are you thinking of ***how*** to do it? Are you considering what people would say? Are you thinking about suicide a large portion of your day?

- Are your thoughts turning into ***plans***? Have you thought of a ***time*** and a ***place***? Have you thought of ***how*** you would do it? Have you thought of how you would obtain the means to do it?

- ***Are you preparing others for your leaving?*** Have you told anyone you will miss them? Have you written out your will? Have you given away personal belongings? Have you obtained the means to do it such as purchasing a gun or obtaining pills? Have you rehearsed how you will do it?

- Have you decided if you want your attempted suicide to be your final act on earth, or do you plan for it to be only self-injurious, not lethal?

If you answered yes to any of these questions, I urge you, I plead with you, get help immediately. Call this number: **800-273-8255.**

---

the-golden-gate-bridge-and-lived/. See also his book, Kevin Hines, *Cracked, Not Broken: Surviving and Thriving After a Suicide Attempt,* (Lanham, MD: Rowman & Littlefield Publishers, 2013).

I want you to stay. I got up at 4:30 every morning for months so that I could write this book *so that you would choose to stay.* One reason I chose to stay is to help others in the same situation choose to stay. You are wanted and needed. Please stay.

What the Psalmist wrote 3,000 years ago is as true today as it was then: *The Lord is close to the brokenhearted and saves those who are crushed in spirit. A righteous man may have many troubles, but the Lord delivers him from them all.* (Psalm 34.18–19)

In 1997 my 50-year-old sister, Jackie, took her life. Don't do what my sister did. Please stay. I did, and I am glad I did.

Think About It . . .

- Go back over the questions listed above. If you are considering suicide as an option I urge you get help. Call the hotline. Call a pastor, a trusted and wise friend, a counselor.

Life Commitment . . .

I commit to staying. The world needs me.

Day 42: Suicide—Getting help

The Word

So do not fear, for I am with you; do not be dismayed, for I am your God. I will strengthen you and help you; I will uphold you with my righteous right hand.

— Isaiah 41.10

Thought for the Day

God's agenda is never elimination but transformation.

~ Richard Rohr

National Suicide Prevention Lifeline: 800-273-8255

Jesus said as recorded by the apostle John: *The thief comes only to steal and kill and destroy; I have come that they may have life, and have it to the full.* (John 10.10)

Brother, you are in a war and Satan is your enemy. Satan hates God, but since Satan can't destroy God, his driving passion is to deface God by defacing and/or destroying God's highest creation. That would be you. Suicide is the ultimate destruction of God's amazing creation.

King David wrote: *When I consider your heavens, the work of your fingers, the moon and the stars, which you have set in place, what is man that you are mindful of him, the son of man that you care for him? You made him a little lower and crowned him with glory and honor.* (Psalm 8:3–5)

Wow! You and I are God's amazing creation! No wonder Satan wants to take you out! **Don't let him!**

In my office I have a plastic anatomical human skull that can be taken apart. Inside is a model of the brain. Sometimes when people come into my office who are troubled and depressed, I take out my plastic skull and pull out the brain.

I say to them:

> *I know you are suffering and that you are in pain because of your loss. But did you know that you still have this amazing thing between your ears—your brain! Your brain is the second most incredible thing in all the universe. Did you get that? That three-pound mass of cells in your head is the second most astounding thing in the entire universe! The first is, of course, God himself. Whatever you have lost, you still have this amazing thing! And, you have God! What can be better than that?*

To take your life by suicide is to destroy this second most amazing thing in all the universe! Don't do it. Don't give Satan the victory. Don't let the thief come in and destroy. Instead, cry out to God. He WILL rescue you!

Yesterday I listed some questions to help you assess how much of a risk for suicide you are. Have you thought about those questions since then?

Whatever your answers, I urge you to get help. The journey you are on is a journey only you can make. Only you make the journey but you don't have to make the journey alone.

God knows the battle for your soul. God knows the war against your life. He wants you to win. He's on your side. Because he is for you, God will put resources in your path that will help you survive this journey and thrive on the other side. This book is one of those resources. It's no accident that you are reading this. God knew you would need this book to make it through this ordeal. He called me to write it and he called you to read it. This is evidence of God's loving care for you.

In addition to written resources, God has placed many other resources for you to tap into during this hard time. I urge you, please reach out and get the help you need.

The following are some suggestions. Perhaps these suggestions will be prompts God is putting in your path to help you right now.

- **Pray** to God. He is listening and much closer to you than you can imagine. He is eager to help you and see you through this. Praying is just talking to God and listening for his response. He longs to hear our cries (Psalm 62.8).

- **Friends**. We all need a few trusted, loyal, wise friends. Who can you call in the middle of the night who will listen to you, accept you for who you are, and help get you through it? Not everyone will help you but God will give you a few who will.

- **A Pastor**. Pastors are today's unsung heroes. Most pastors are amazing people who give themselves to helping people win victories over the enemy. If you don't have a church, ask around to find a church known for their love for God and their love for people. It takes courage to jump in, but do it. God works through his church. His church is there for you. If available, find a church with a strong and lively men's ministry.

- **A Counselor** or **Therapist**. God has put smart people on this planet who are committed to helping people get through hard times. You want this person to be honest and be able to gently confront you when necessary. To find a Christian Counselor in your area go to *Focus on the Family's Christian Counselor's Network.*[82]

For years I have told depressed people the same thing: Don't believe everything you are telling yourself right now. Your thinking is distorted. Instead, listen to what others are saying to you.

---

[82]https://ccn.thedirectorywidget.com/

How you are *thinking* now will change. You will have more positive thoughts as time goes by. Hold on!

How you are *feeling* now will change. You will feel better! Hold on!

Jennifer Hecht succinctly states: *Though we may refuse a version of life, we must also refuse voluntary death.*[83]

You are right to be upset about how your life is right now. Don't choose to change the state of your life, however, by ending it. That is a worse choice with far worse consequences. Instead, hang on, get the help you need, and watch God do his amazing work in your life.

Think About It . . .

- Get help. Really. Help will help more than you imagine right now.

Life Commitment . . .

I commit to getting the help I need to get through this.

[83]Hecht, *Stay*, 183.

Day 43: Homicide

The Word

Now Cain said to his brother Abel, "Let's go out to the field." And while they were in the field, Cain attacked his brother Abel and killed him. Then the Lord said to Cain, "Where is your brother Abel?" "I don't know," he replied. "Am I my brother's keeper?" The Lord said, "What have you done? Listen! Your brother's blood cries out to me from the ground."

— Genesis 4.8–10

Thought for the Day

The great malady of the twentieth century, implicated in all of our troubles and affecting us individually and socially, is "loss of soul." When soul is neglected, it doesn't just go away; it appears symptomatically in obsessions, addictions, violence, and loss of meaning.

~ Thomas Moore

On September 9, 1996, a beautiful young 23-year-old girl was shot and killed. The killer was her ex-boyfriend. He then turned the gun on himself.

Ami had just graduated with a degree in social work. She worked as a volunteer with the Austin Police Department and helped AIDS victims and disabled children and adults.[84] Ami's huge and generous heart was stopped by the irrational rage of an angry young man.

[84] *Ami Lunsford Memorial Scholarship in Victim Services*, accessed July 14, 2017. https://binged.it/2N2CTpO

As pastor to this family I saw firsthand the unbelievable damage caused by homicide. One thing I learned was that *painful circumstances can lead to murder.* No one would have guessed that Ami's murderer would have committed such a radical act.

Murders happen when people are enraged and take their rage to the next level. People don't just kill people. The pathway to murder starts with rage.

Are you angry at what has happened to you? In your anger do you have thoughts of taking someone's life?

Perhaps your wife cheated on you. Are you thinking of killing her lover? Do you have thoughts of killing her? If so, you would not be the first to think of and carry out murder in these circumstances. The reason I point this out is simply that murder happens, and murder usually begins with an angry male.

Consider these statistics:

- Males were convicted of the majority of homicides in the United States, representing 90.5% of the total number of offenders. (2014 stats)

- Females were most likely to be victims of domestic homicides (63.7%) and sex-related homicides (81.7%).

- Male perpetrators constituted 96% of federal prosecution on domestic violence.[85]

All this to say, it is possible that someone reading this could be thinking of homicide. If you are one of those men, don't do it. Murders happen when ordinary men are extraordinarily wounded. Hurts lead to rage which can lead to the actual act of murder. When murders are reverse engineered through their line of formation, it's clear that

[85] *Sex differences in crime,* Wikipedia, June 29, 2017, accessed July 14, 2017, https://en.wikipedia.org/wiki/Sex_differences_in_crime, from https://www.bjs.gov/content/pub/pdf/htus8008.pdf, Rep. No. NCJ 236018 (2011). *Homicide Trends in the United States, 1980-2008: Annual Rates for 2009 and 2010,* U.S. Department of Justice Office of Justice Programs, Bureau of Justice Statistics by Alexia Cooper and Erica L. Smith, BJS Statisticians.

most men who commit murder did not start out thinking they would do it. Their rage carried them along until the deed was done.

Believe it or not, there is actually help for those considering homicide. *http://www.savingcain.org/preventing-murder.html* is a great resource even if you are not thinking of murder as an option to handling your problems.

The author if this website, Yale lecturer James Kimmel, Jr, writes:

> *Research scientists have discovered that when we have been hurt or wronged, the desire to harm others activates the same pleasure centers of the brain activated by narcotics. This suggests that the desire to kill is a biological craving created inside the brain. If you are thinking about killing, you are not "evil." You are experiencing a brain-created desire to harm others and yourself. If your brain created it, then your brain can also make it go away. Help is available right now. The desire to kill can be overcome.*[86]

Think About It . . .

- Have you thought of killing someone because of the pain you are in?
- If you are thinking of homicide, go to the website *http://www.savingcain.org/preventing-murder.html* and follow the steps to getting the help you need.
- Remember that Satan's greatest desire is to destroy God's amazing creation. Don't let him win the victory. Self-destruction (suicide) and murder (homicide) are never part of God's plan. God is *for life*, yours and others.

Life Commitment . . .

God, help me see your incredible hand on my life. Preserve my life so I can give your life to others.

[86]http://www.savingcain.org/preventing-murder.html

Day 44: Larger Than Life

The Word

He who began a good work in you will carry it on to completion until the day of Christ Jesus.
— Philippians 1:6

Thought for the Day

The rat race speeds up... but it is still a race for rats.
~ Os Guinness

I slipped. I raged on Facebook against the unfairness I experienced. The conversation began when an old friend (literally, 81 years old, and a friend for 30+ years) asked how I was doing. The scab was pulled back and the blood began to flow. My friend is a saint—back in the 1980s when the AIDS epidemic was ravaging the homosexual population, she bucked the evangelical detestation of gays and embraced men who were dying young.

I knew she could take what I had to dish out, so I unloaded my anger and grief right there on Facebook. But a few days later I realized I had let my smaller self gain the upper hand. This was *not* how I wanted to be remembered. I wanted to be remembered as *larger than life...*

Richard Rohr describers this well:

> *We describe some people as larger than life. If we could see their history, we would learn that at some point they were led to the edge*

of their own resources and found the actual Source. They suffered a breakdown, which felt like dying. But instead of breaking down, they broke through!

Instead of avoiding, shortchanging, or raging against death, they went through death—a death to their old self, their small life, their imperfections, their illusory dreams, their wounds, their grudges, and their limited sense of their own destiny. When they did this, they came out on the other side knowing that death henceforth could do them no harm.

"What did I ever lose by dying?" they say. This process is supposed to be the baptismal initiation rite into Christianity, where we first "join him in the tomb" and then afterwards "join him in his resurrection" (Romans 5:4-5). We are all supposed to be larger-than-death men, appearing to the world as larger than life. This should be the definition of a Christian man.[87]

God began a good work when he brought you to the planet. That good work, however, is a work in progress and requires your cooperation. When we cooperate with him, we move past the big and little 'deaths' in our lives to his resurrection beyond. If we hang in there with him, he will bring this good work (you!) to completion.

What if we don't cooperate? Of all the mass shootings from 1982 to 2016, 79 were male shooters and three female.[88] That tells us something of the crisis among men in our world today. Obviously not all who fail to cooperate with God's transforming energy end up mass shooters. But those who fail to live within God's jet stream do end up causing death and destruction in many big and small ways along life's journey.

The pain of divorce squeezes our soul. What is leaking out of your soul today? What comes out will be how others define you . . . Larger than life or . . . crushed by death?

---

[87]Rohr, Durepos and McGrath, *On the Threshold of Transformation*, 283. Used with permission.

[88]Taryn Hillin, *Nearly All Mass Shooters Have One Thing in Common,* Fusion, accessed January 10, 2017, http://fusion.net/story/314137/what-mass-shooters-have-in-common/.

Think About It . . .

- Size matters. In your own eyes, are you small or large?
- When you are squeezed, what comes out? Patience, endurance, kindness? Or wrath, bitterness, rage?
- How do you want to be remembered?

Life Commitment:

I have a choice as to how cooperative I am with God's working in me. I commit to jumping into his jetstream and allowing him to do his work in me.

Day 45: What Does a Win Look Like?

The Word

For we are God's workmanship, created in Christ Jesus to do good works, which God prepared in advance for us to do.
— Ephesians 2.10

Thought for the Day

Information is not necessarily transformation.
~ Richard Rohr

At any point along our journey we need to ask ourselves, *"What does a win look like right now?"* If we have the wrong answer to this question, all our efforts are for nothing. All this pain is zilch, zero, nada!

Charlie Strong became the head coach of the University of Texas football team in 2014. At the time, UT President Bill Powers said that one of the reasons Strong was attractive was that he focused on the overall development of the student-athletes. Strong said *"I want to see [the players] develop on the field as well as off the field.... The program is always going to be about physical and mental toughness."*[89]

[89] Ted Madden, *UT introduces Charlie Strong as new Longhorns coach | kvue.com Austin,* (January 6, 2014) from Wikipedia, "Charlie Strong," accessed January 15, 2017, https://en.wikipedia.org/wiki/Charlie_Strong.

After three losing seasons, Strong was fired. In his press release after being fired Strong stated: "I do understand that it comes down to wins and losses, and we have not done our job in that area yet."[90]

What does a win look like at UT? The President of UT said that it looked like well-developed athletes. Strong agreed. But after three years it became apparent that for powerful alumni, the *real* win was a football program that won games. Player development took a distinct back seat.

What does a win look like in your life right now? Now is the best time to sit back and ask yourself how you want this time in your life remembered. As you think about what a win looks like for you, ask yourself, *How do I want my kids to remember me in this moment? What do I want people to say of me at the end of the day?*

In the next few days I want to suggest five 'wins' for you to consider. They are:

- Clarity
- Passion
- Solidarity with Others
- Solid Decisions
- Integrity

Think About It . . .

- What has winning looked like in your life up to now? How has that worked out for you?
- Do others consider you a winner? Why or why not?
- What does winning look like to God?

[90] *Texas football coach Charlie Strong fired after 3 years,* Last updated November 26, 2016, accessed January 06, 2017, http://kxan.com/2016/11/26/texas-football-coach-charlie-strong-fired-after-3-years/.

Life Commitment:

I commit to giving serious consideration to what really matters at the end of the season.

Day 46: The Win—Clarity

The Word

A bruised reed he will not break, and a smoldering wick he will not snuff out. In faithfulness he will bring forth justice.
— Isaiah 42.3

Thought for the Day

The pessimist complains about the wind; the optimist expects it to change; the realist adjusts the sails.
~ William Arthur Ward

A friend of mine was a mechanic at Carswell Air Force Base in Fort Worth, Texas. One day he came to church shaken. I asked what happened. He said that the day before, a French pilot was training in a fighter. The pilot came screaming over the runway upside down, then the pilot pulled 'up.' The problem was that 'up' to the pilot was, in reality, straight down onto the tarmac just outside the hanger where my friend was working on a plane. Imagine an F-16 slamming into the pavement at that kind of speed. This disaster happened because the pilot thought he was right-side-up when he was really up-side-down.[91]

Though the pilot was far more qualified and accomplished than probably almost anyone reading this, his *lack of clarity* led to death

[91] *List of accidents and incidents involving military aircraft (1980–89).* Wikipedia, accessed January 05, 2017, https://en.wikipedia.org/wiki/List_of_accidents_and_incidents_involving_military_aircraft_%281980%E2%80%9389%29

and destruction. He visualized the path ahead upside down, and that is where he ended up . . . or rather down.

Clarity begins with how you view God. He is for you, remember? He did not cause your pain but he can transform it. He will strengthen you so that in the end *you will get through this.* These are points of clarity you will want to drill into your mind and soul. You need to be clear about these truths about God and about yourself. Take a moment to visualize in your mind how these truths can work themselves out in your future.

Tony Dungy was head coach of the Indianapolis Colts from 2002 to 2008. He was the first African American football coach to win a Super Bowl (2006). He knows something about being clear about football and about life. He writes:

> *Visualization increases chances of success—not just in football but in any area of life. If we can't see ourselves succeeding . . . we won't have any confidence in those roles and be able to perform them well. But if we can see ourselves fulfilling our responsibilities effectively, achieving our goals, and relating to others healthily, we are much more likely to have the vision and the confidence to do those things. We tend to be able to accomplish what we can see.*[92]

In the wake of divorce you feel anything but successful. Don't let your present circumstances determine your future success. Picture yourself as successfully navigating through this storm and emerging stronger and more resilient than ever.

Think About It . . .

- Thinking back on your life, can you remember a time when you were really clear about what to do or what the future could hold for you?

- Are you confused or clear about things now?

[92]Tony Dungy and Nathan Whitaker, *The One Year Uncommon Life Daily Challenge*, Kindle Location 199.

- What specific areas are you confused about?

Life Commitment:

I commit to asking God to give me clarity about himself, his view of me, and how to think about and respond to my current situation.

Day 47: The Win—Passion

The Word

The heart of a man is like deep water.
— Proverbs 20.5

Thought for the Day

Do more than belong: participate.
Do more than care: help.
Do more than believe: practice.
Do more than be fair: be kind.
Do more than forgive: forget.
Do more than dream: work.
~ William Arthur Ward

I rode my bike over 5,000 miles last year. On one ride I was only two miles away from home when I noticed my front tire making an odd noise. Then it got really hard to peddle. My tire was flat to the ground. Most flats are slow leaks. Not this one. My tire was at zero psi and there was no moving forward without a fix. A big Texas thorn made short work of my tire and tube.

Divorce is a thorn that takes the air out of your life. Whatever passion you had before is gone. But why do we view the flat tire of divorce as a permanent state of deflation? When my bike stopped on the highway I didn't believe for a second that I would spend the rest of my life sitting on the side of the road with a flat tire. I didn't even believe that this flat could hold me up for more than 15 minutes!

But there is a difference between a tire and your soul. When a tire is flat, we know how to fix it. When the soul deflates we may not know how to patch the hole, blow it back up and get back on the road. But lack of knowledge is no excuse to sink into despair. It is possible to regain your passion. Or, more likely, to actually get a real passion for your life perhaps for the first time.

The truth is most men are stumbling through life with no sense of mission or purpose. If you are one of those guys, *now is your chance to discover who you are and what you are made to do.* In other words, this is your opportunity to slow down and look into the deep waters of your soul to find your passion.

John Maxwell asks penetrating questions: *Do you know your life's mission? What stirs your heart? What do you dream about?*[93]

If your highest goal in life is to have the best lawn in the neighborhood, you are off track. Now is the time to find out who you are and what you are made for. We will unpack this in the weeks ahead but for now, *know that your flat tire can be fixed!* Determine to seriously pursue finding and fulfilling your passion.

Here are some suggestions from Maxwell on discovering your passion:

1. *Get next to people who possess great desire [passion].*
2. *Develop discontent with the status quo.*
3. *Search for a goal that excites you.*
4. *Put your most vital possessions into that goal.*
5. *Visualize yourself enjoying the rewards of that goal.*[94]

A win looks like being CLEAR about where you are now and clear about your PASSION for your future.

Think About It . . .

- Do you know your life's mission?

---

[93]John C. Maxwell, *The Maxwell Daily Reader*, 385.

[94]John C. Maxwell, *Failing Forward: Turning Mistakes into Stepping-Stones for Success* (Nashville: Thomas Nelson Publishers, 2000), 171.

- What stirs your heart?
- What do you dream about?

Life Commitment:

I commit to asking God to give me clarity about who he wants me to be and what he wants me to do with the rest of my life.

Day 48: The Win—Solidarity with Others

The Word

Two are better than one, because they have a good return for their work:
If one falls down, his friend can help him up.
But pity the man who falls and has no one to help him up!
Though one may be overpowered, two can defend themselves.
— Ecclesiastes 4.9–12

Thought for the Day

A true friend knows your weaknesses but shows you your strengths; feels your fears but fortifies your faith; sees your anxieties but frees your spirit; recognizes your disabilities but emphasizes your possibilities.
~ William Arthur Ward

Every third Saturday at 7.30 in the morning a group of about 80 guys would meet in the basement of the church to have breakfast together, sing a few songs and hear words of encouragement and challenge. One morning I watched two men talk together. One was the owner of a large business he had built himself—marvelously successful by any measure of the world's standards.

The wealthy man was deep in a conversation with a man who had just lost his job. The amazing thing about this conversation was that this was just a conversation between two guys who loved God. The rich guy didn't see himself as better than the poor guy. The guy who just lost his job wasn't groveling before the rich guy. Instead, these were just two men, equal in the eyes of God, sharing life together.

This kind of camaraderie doesn't happen in our culture because men go it alone. We go it alone because we are designed to compete. In the hunter/gatherer days food sources were limited. You better be the guy to get the food for your family. Only one boy got the girl, so you better beat the other boys to the girl. It's all about competition. We are wired to find our place in the male order of things. I must find out who is above me and who is below me.

The problem with this way of doing life is that, by definition, *no one is beside me.* That's a lonely place.

When divorce slams you in the face, the loneliness only increases. Since men are not supposed to feel pain, we think we can't tell anyone, and if we do actually tell someone what's going on, we must pretend we are handling it with no problem. (See Appendix D)

But inside we're dying. We may find solace in a bottle or a pill or the internet. We may turtle up, hunkering down to ride out the storm. The problem with this strategy is that it never produces anything good. Left to our own thoughts, we go down destructive pathways. Left alone with no one to prop us up, we are unbalanced and eventually tump over.

Everything in you will tell you to pull back from life. Don't do it. Instead, believe what King Solomon said: *Two are better than one, because they have a good return for their work: If one falls down, his friend can help him up.*[95]

Think About It . . .

- On a scale of 0 to 10, (0 being not lonely at all to 10, absolutely completely lonely), how lonely are you?

0—1—2—3—4—5—6—7—8—9—10

[95]King Solomon, King David's son, ruled over Israel during its most prosperous and powerful days (970-931 BCE). He was famous for his wisdom, but in later life he gave up his godly principles to pursue pleasure at all costs. Like most men, Solomon did not finish well. Let's not be like most men!

- List two guys you know you can call anytime day or night for help.

_________________________ Phone # ___________

_________________________ Phone # ___________

- If the two lines above are BLANK, list two guys who you **THINK** might be willing to be your friend:

_________________________ Phone # ___________

_________________________ Phone # ___________

- Call the first one on your list. Take him to lunch or something. Be creative. It really can't be that hard to get together. Dogs do it. We can too.
- If none of the above work (or you just want to talk) give me a call (978.204.0480) or send me an email (dalebrown3@me.com)!

Life Commitment:

I commit to resisting the urge to turtle. I am asking God to bring into my life some other men who can walk beside me.

Day 49: The Win—Solid Decisions

The Word

If any of you lacks wisdom, he should ask God, who gives generously to all without finding fault, and it will be given to him. But when he asks, he must believe and not doubt, because he who doubts is like a wave of the sea, blown and tossed by the wind. That man should not think he will receive anything from the Lord; he is a double-minded man, unstable in all he does.

— James 1.5–8

Thought for the Day

The optimist lives on the peninsula of infinite possibilities; the pessimist is stranded on the island of perpetual indecision.

~ William Arthur Ward

As my life unraveled, decisions had to be made but I was not sure my heart, soul and mind were in a healthy place to move forward with any confidence. But another factor was at work. When life tumbles down you can become so disheartened that you really don't care what you decide.

God is not surprised at what has happened. He knows about your situation and he cares for you and is *for you*, even if the cause of the divorce lies mainly with you. He wants you to *do the next right thing* even if you have made many bad decisions up to now.

The best decision you can make right now is to make good decisions. Poor decisions now will only further tangle up the mess, and you really don't want that.

When divorce was headed my way, I yelled a lot. I cried. I cursed. But I didn't put a .380 bullet into my head. I didn't get in the car and start driving. Instead I called a good friend. Together we assessed the situation and made some solid short-term decisions to get me through the immediate crisis.

Now is the time when wins in the areas of CLARITY and SOLIDARITY will really pay off.

Seek clarity by *first* seeking God and asking him to guide you. James says, *If any of you lacks wisdom, he should ask God.* There's no *if* when it comes to whether I lack wisdom or not! I lack! But God is ready and eager to fill my lack.

Notice the promise that follows the invitation: *[Wisdom] will be given to him* because God is a generous giver and he gives to all, *without finding fault.* Whether perp or vic, God wants to guide you every step of this painful way. God speaks first and foremost through his Bible. Get a Bible and start reading. Start with reading the book of Psalms and the Gospel of John for right now. Seek God.

Second, trust that God will speak through smart people. This is where solidarity with a few good people will really get you through. Who do you need to contact? That depends on your situation, but you will most likely be helped by (1) a trusted friend, (2) a pastor, (3) a professional counselor, and (4) a lawyer.

The world may seem to be shifting under your feet. You may feel you are in a free fall. You may be raging at yourself, at your wife (or ex-wife), you may be sad beyond belief. You may be *like a wave of the sea, blown and tossed by the wind* as James says. But right now ask God for wisdom and let him lead you to smart people to get you through.

Your goal is to do the next right thing. Emotions may get in the way of making solid decisions. Ask God for direction and then get in touch with good people to stand with you and guide you through raging emotions and wild thinking.

Think About It . . .

- Do you believe God is the smartest being in all the Universe (and beyond) and that he wants to guide you for his glory and your good?
- If you are not sure, would you be willing to give him the chance to lead you?

Life Commitment:

I commit to praying for God's help and guidance and contacting smart people to help me through this.

I will call:

My good friend ______________________________

My pastor ______________________________

A counselor ______________________________

A lawyer ______________________________

Day 50: The Win—Integrity

The Word

But seek first his kingdom and his righteousness, and all these things will be given to you as well.
— Matthew 6:33

Thought for the Day

We do not think ourselves into new ways of living, we live ourselves into new ways of thinking.
~ Richard Rohr

A new couple at church asked to visit with me. We made the appointment and met a few days later. The issue at hand had to do with the husband's previous divorce. In the divorce process the man had not fully disclosed all his financial information. His ex-wife was suspicious (imagine that) and was pushing the issue through legal action. The man in my office wanted to know what to do.

Both the man and his new wife claimed to be good Christians, people of integrity. I sat there wondering why we were sitting there! Was there really a question here? I told the man he had to disclose all his financials. That was easy! Well, it was easy for me to say because it was easy for me to see. But when we are under fire, maintaining our integrity can be challenging.

The word *integrity* means *sound, whole, complete.* We get the word *integer* from it, which is a whole number. Integrity means being solid through and through. It means that what you see on the inside is reflected on the outside. It means that if you cut a watermelon in half you find watermelon inside. It means being undivided and true.

The only way to gain and maintain integrity is to *seek first [God's] kingdom and his righteousness.* In seeking his kingdom *first* we are trusting that *all these things will be given to [us] as well* because God is for us and is on our side, bending things toward his glory and for our good and the good of the world around us.

The man in my office that day was not seeking God's kingdom first. Though he said he was a follower of God, he really was not trusting God for his financial future. By not trusting God's provision for him he thought he had to lie to keep more of his money for himself and away from his ex-wife. Though he looked like a Christian on the outside, his decisions about his money indicated that he was not really seeking God's kingdom first.

Whether out of anger, fear, hurt, guilt, shame or desperation, when we are in the throes of divorce we may choose to take some shortcuts. Now is the perfect time to seek God, trusting that if you do the next right thing he will take care of all the rest. Don't compromise. Take the high road. You will not regret it and you will see God's incredible provision for you in every way.

Think About It . . .

- In what areas have you been tempted to compromise?
- What steps can you tak0e to keep you whole, sound, and complete?

Life Commitment:

I commit to seeking God first, trusting him for my future and proving my trust in him by making decisions that maintain my integrity.

Day 51: Fail Forward . . . But Not Flat on Your Face!

The Word

My flesh and my heart may fail, but God is the strength of my heart and my portion forever.

– Psalm 73.26

Thought for the Day

When we act, uncertainty chases us out into the open where opportunity awaits.

~ Marc and Angel Chernoff

My mom, who was 89 at the time, lived with us for seven months in New Hampshire. One winter day she determined to go on a walk. By this time we realized that resistance was futile so I told her to have a grand time. I watched all 85 pounds of her slowly make her way down the road. Then I forgot about her. I know. Not good.

About 20 minutes later I heard this 'ooohing' sound coming from the front yard. I jumped up to see her crumpled by the mailbox face down in the gravel between the yard and street. I dashed out the front door sure that one (or more) of our neighbors would call Adult Protective Services on me!

She had literally fallen flat on her face. Gravel was embedded in her forehead, her glasses were broken, and blood oozed from various wounds on her cheek and chin.

After an initial assessment I asked her if she thought she could get up with my help and walk to the house where we could clean her up. She responded with a hearty 'SURE!' She popped up and we went inside to dress the wounds!

Whether you are the one who initiated divorce or not, whether the divorce is mostly your fault or not, whether you believe your divorce is justified or not, *divorce feels like a failure.* Divorce is the ripping apart of a sacred bond you made with your partner. At some point, divorce feels like you fell flat on your face.

The question then becomes, what will I do about it? How you think about, feel toward, and behave in response to failure in general and your divorce in particular has huge consequences for the future. The next several days we will explore this topic of failure and how to respond to it.

One thing is certain: *Failure will **define** us, **refine** us or **redefine** us, but it will never leave us the same.*[96] A terrible thing happened. Don't let it define you. Let it ***refine*** you as you let God ***redefine*** you. You will not be the same. The question is, will you be better or worse? The answer depends on you.

In the introduction to this book I wrote words that ring true for you today:

> *You may be down, but brother, you are not out. You may be crushed, but my friend, you are not dead. You may be face down on the turf, but you will get up, take a deep breath, and get back in the game. Know this: No life has failed if God moves in, transforms, and transmits his grace, love and power to, in and through you.*

Think About It . . .

- When you failed as a child, how did people react to you?

[96] J. R. Briggs, *Fail: Finding Hope and Grace in The Midst of Ministry Failure* (Downers Grove, 2015), Kindle Location 1319.

- When you hear the word 'fail' what or who do you think about? What emotions come to the surface?

Life Commitment:

Failure is abominable. But failing to use my failure as a launchpad into a better future is worse. I commit to understanding failure and how God can use my failure to move me forward.

DAY 52: FAIL FORWARD (2)

THE WORD

We also rejoice in our sufferings, because we know that suffering produces perseverance; perseverance, character; and character, hope. And hope does not disappoint us, because God has poured out his love into our hearts by the Holy Spirit, whom he has given us.

— Romans 5.3–5

THOUGHT FOR THE DAY

When we fail we are merely joining the great parade of humanity that has walked ahead of us and will follow after us.

~ Richard Rohr

EVER HEARD OF TRAF-O-DATA? It was Bill Gates' first company.

Michael Jordan was cut from his high school basketball team.

Vincent Van Gogh sold only one painting in his lifetime.

Steven Spielberg was rejected from USC—twice.

Henry Ford was broke five times because his first businesses failed.

Twenty-Seven publishers rejected Theodor Geisel's first book. Theodor Geisel is better known as Dr. Seuss.

J. K. Rowling was divorced, broke and depressed while writing her first novel.

Colonel Sanders of Kentucky Fried Chicken had his chicken recipe rejected 1,009 times before a restaurant accepted it.

Walt Disney was fired by a newspaper editor. The reason? He "Lacked imagination and had no good ideas."

Lucille Ball was told by her drama instructors that she would never make it in theater and she should try another profession.

Elvis Presley was fired by the manager of the Grand Ole Opry after just one performance. The manager told him, "You ain't goin' nowhere, son. You ought to go back to drivin' a truck."

Jerry Seinfeld's career began when he walked out on stage, froze, and was eventually jeered and booed out of the club.

For decades Babe Ruth held the record for strikeouts.

Sidney Poitier was told by the casting director after his first audition, "Why don't you stop wasting people's time and go out and become a dishwasher or something?"

Thomas Edison was told by teachers that he was "too stupid to learn anything." He was fired from his first two jobs.

Stephen King's first novel (*Carrie*) was rejected 30 times. King threw it in the trash. His wife retrieved it.

Here is Tom Landry's coaching record of the Dallas Cowboys from 1960 to 1964:

Win	Loss	Tie
0	11	1
4	9	1
5	8	1
4	10	0
5	8	-

Every successful person has failed, some multiple times and some spectacularly (remember *New Coke*?) J. M. Barrie wrote, *We are all failures—at least, all the best of us are.*[97]

When we fail we feel like we are the only ones who have failed and that our failure is wildly public and depressingly permanent. Nothing is further from the truth. The harder the fall, the more amazing the summit when God pulls you up and out of that pit!

John Maxwell asks a good question: *If you've failed, are you a failure?* [98] God's answer for you is, *You are not a failure.* Failure is something that happens for a variety of reasons. Failure is a thing, not a person.

Think About It . . .

- When you read the list of names above and hear what others have said to them, what comes to mind?
- What do you think these people thought/have/did that pushed them past their failures?

Life Commitment:

If God uses only perfect people, he will have a short list! I'm not perfect but I know God can use me.

---

[97]J.M. Barrie, *J.M. Barrie Quotes*, BrainyQuote, accessed September 27, 2017 https://www.goodreads.com/quotes/288278-we-are-all-failures--at-least-the-best-of-us.

[98]John C. Maxwell, *Failing Forward: Turning Mistakes into Stepping Stones for Success* (Nashville, TN: Thomas Nelson, 2007), 23.

Day 53: Fail Forward (3)

The Word

Therefore, if anyone is in Christ, he is a new creation; the old has gone, the new has come!
— 2 Corinthians 5.17

Thought for the Day

Failure is an event. It is not a person.
~ Zig Ziglar

To many people, the Apostle Paul was an incredible failure. He didn't start out that way.

As a relatively young man—the man we know as the Apostle Paul (then named Saul)—was a rising star in the Jewish academy. Raised in a cosmopolitan city and attending the best schools, Paul's future was bright and secured. Paul's enthusiasm matched his great intellect. He fervently believed his zeal should be applied to stamping out the new sect of rebels led by the heretic named Jesus.

At this point Paul was a success according to the world—his zealotry was appreciated by his superiors and made him famous with the general population. The problem, however, was that Paul was using his energy *against* God instead of *for* him. While traveling from Jerusalem to Damascus Jesus confronted Paul in a vision. The experience literally knocked Paul off his feet.

When the Lord revealed himself to Paul (see Acts 9) Paul wisely chose to reject the dead tradition he had been taught for the living God he was encountering. God changed Paul's mind, heart and will that day. Paul went on to become the most effective missionary the world has ever seen. You and I live in a world shaped by God's work through Paul begun nearly 2,000 years ago.

Years later Paul put into words what he experienced that day: *If anyone is in Christ, he is a new creation; the old has gone, the new has come!* Paul, filled with zealous but misdirected hatred, became the bearer of the loving Good News of the very Christ he was determined to destroy.

If God can do that in Paul's life, he can do it for you. Your moment of failure is only a moment. Failure is an event. It is a thing that happens to you and sometimes because of you. *But it is not you.* Don't allow this failure to define you. Rather, let God *redefine* you!

Paul would later write to the church at Rome: *Do not conform any longer to the pattern of this world, but be transformed by the renewing of your mind.* (Romans 12.1)

What is the pattern of this world? The world sees failure as final. The world rejoices when you are down because, compared to you, they are up. The world loves victims because victims are helpless and easily manipulated. Paul tells us to reject this loser/victim mentality.

Instead, he says, *be transformed by the renewing of your mind.* The Greek word we translate as *transform* is *metamorfoo*, from which we get the word *metamorphosis.*

What happens when a caterpillar rejects its cocoon? It emerges transformed. It is metamorphosed into something so spectacular the ground can't hold it down!

The world defines success in a lot of bizarre, ridiculous ways. God defines success by allowing him to transform you into the man he purposed you to be.

Failure events are part of the process of this transformation. Whether you are the vic or the perp (or most likely a combination of the two), God can and will (and is!) using this event to transform you.

J. R. Briggs gives us God's perspective on your current crisis: *God is much more concerned about the transformation going on inside us than the circumstances going on around us.*[99]

Failure is not final. It is simply a launching point for a better you which means a better future *for* you.

Think About It . . .

- Do you believe that your failure will define you for the rest of your life?
- If you answered *yes* to the question above, open your mind to the possibility that God can use your failure to *refine* and *redefine* you.
- If you allowed God to use failure to refine and redefine you, what could your life look like?
- What is the cost of not allowing God to use failure to refine and redefine you?

Life Commitment:

God, I believe you can do for me what you did for the Apostle Paul. My failure can be the turning point in my life that I need. Here's my life . . . take me and refine and redefine me.

[99]Briggs, *Fail: Finding Hope And Grace In The Midst Of Ministry Failure,* Kindle Location 1428.

Day 54: Fail Forward (4)

The Word

For my thoughts are not your thoughts, neither are your ways my ways, declares the Lord. As the heavens are higher than the earth, so are my ways higher than your ways and my thoughts than your thoughts.

— Isaiah 55:8–9

Thought for the Day

The cross is evidence that in the hands of the Redeemer, moments of apparent defeat become wonderful moments of grace and victory.

~ Paul David Tripp

A long time ago (20 years) the hottest thing in computing was WYSIWYG—*What You See Is What You Get.*

In computerese, this meant that what you saw on the computer screen as you typed a document or presentation is what you would get when you printed it out. Today everything is WYSIWYG, but before WYSIWYG, your words appeared on a plain screen without formatting. The advent of WYSIWYG made writing and making presentations much easier.

Through over 30 years in ministry, one unequivocal truth I have learned is that **this is not a WYSIWYG world**. What appears to be a raging success often isn't. What appears to be utter failure is often a blessing.

The Bible is all over this. Joseph, sold into slavery, becomes second in command in all of Egypt. Later, the weak, depleted and powerless Hebrew slaves are freed from the grips of the world's greatest super-power eventually to become their own super-power. The Bible is full of these *Great Reversals.*

One of the greatest of Great Reversals is when a teenage Jewish girl is chosen to bear God's own Son into the world. When Mary heard the news she sang a song that is all about Great Reversals. Her song defies any notion that this is a WYSIWIG world:

> *My soul glorifies the Lord*
> *and my spirit rejoices in God my Savior,*
> *for he has been mindful*
> *of the humble state of his servant.*
> *From now on all generations will call me blessed,*
> *for the Mighty One has done great things for me—*
> *holy is his name.*
> *His mercy extends to those who fear him,*
> *from generation to generation.*
> *He has performed mighty deeds with his arm;*
> *he has scattered those who are proud in their inmost thoughts.*
> *He has brought down rulers from their thrones*
> *but has lifted up the humble.*
> *He has filled the hungry with good things*
> *but has sent the rich away empty.*
> *He has helped his servant Israel,*
> *remembering to be merciful*
> *to Abraham and his descendants forever,*
> *even as he said to our fathers.* (Luke 1.46–55)

Men, this song puts to rest the idea that the world or God's Kingdom is only about us! It also denies any thought that things are always as they appear to be. In God's Kingdom, rulers are brought down, the humble are lifted up. Those who *have* become those who *have not.* The hungry are filled. The lowly are esteemed and called blessed.

God is all about Great Reversals. This is not a WYSIWYG world. God is doing things behind the scenes of your life that are far more complex and incredible than you can imagine.

- What you see as a *dead-end* God sees as a *launchpad* into a life you never could have imagined.
- What you see as *downer* in life God sees as an opportunity *to lift you up.*
- What you see as *depletion* God sees as an opportunity to *fill you up.*
- What you see as an *end* God sees as a new *beginning.*

Don't believe me—believe a 15-year-old Jewish girl who lived 2,000 years ago!

Paul David Tripp's advice is timely:

> *Be careful how you make sense of your life. What looks like a disaster may in fact be grace. What looks like the end may be the beginning. What looks hopeless may be God's instrument to give you real and lasting hope. Your Father is committed to taking what seems so bad and turning it into something that is very, very good.*[100]

Think About It . . .

- Looking back on your life. when have you experienced a *Great Reversal*?
- What could a Great Reversal look like in your own life right now?

[100] Tripp, *New Morning Mercies*, Kindle Location 2285.

Life Commitment:

Though things look down now, I believe God can lift me up. Though things feel empty now, I believe God can fill me up. Though things look dark now, I believe God can light me up!

Day 55: Fail Forward (5)

The Word

This is what the Lord says:

Cursed is the one who trusts in man, who depends on flesh for his strength and whose heart turns away from the Lord. He will be like a bush in the wastelands; he will not see prosperity when it comes. He will dwell in the parched places of the desert, in a salt land where no one lives.

But blessed is the man who trusts in the Lord, whose confidence is in him. He will be like a tree planted by the water that sends out its roots by the stream. It does not fear when heat comes; its leaves are always green. It has no worries in a year of drought and never fails to bear fruit.

— Jeremiah 17.5–8

Thought for the Day

During crisis God seems to give us his presence at a depth we have not experienced in times of peace and calm.

~ J. R. Briggs

We have a huge problem and it is this: We have thought it best to live without God.

A great teacher and pastor of early last century says it best in his amazing book, *The Knowledge of the Holy*:

> *The teaching of Christianity is that man chose to be independent of God and confirmed his choice by deliberately disobeying a divine command. This act violated the relationship that normally existed between God and His creature; it rejected God as the ground of existence and threw man back upon himself. Thereafter he became not a planet revolving around the central Sun, but a sun in his own right, around which everything else must revolve.*[101]

I have watched many people take their last breath. Those who don't know God go silently. Those who know God go with an incredible hope filled with a firm and certain conviction of where they are headed. In the end, *these people know that they are completely dependent on God—nothing they have done, nothing they have acquired, nothing they have achieved will get them through.* The only thing going with them as their bodies fail is God's amazing and all-powerful presence.

The greatest gift this failure can give you is to make you realize you really need God. In fact, he is all you need and all you will have. He is all you really have now, you just didn't realize it.

It is true that

> *In the face of your failure, you can wallow in guilt and shame, beating yourself up because you did not do better and working hard to hide your failure from God and others. Or, in the brokenness and grief of conviction, you can run not away from God but to him. You can run into the light of his holy presence utterly unafraid, filled with the confidence that although he is righteous and you are not, he will not turn you away.*[102]

In the end, *God can fly faster than we can ever fall, and He swoops in under us to break the fall when He sees that we need His help.*[103]

---

[101]Tozer, *The Knowledge of The Holy: The Attributes of God, Their Meaning in The Christian Life* (New York: Harper & Row, 1961), 61.
[102]Tripp, *New Morning Mercies*, Kindle Location 1711.
[103]Keturah C. Martin, *Jesus Never Wastes Pain*, 333.

Think About It . . .

- Who or what have you relied on in the past to get you through tough times?
- What does relying on God look like to you right now? What does it look like to give your brain a break from trying to figure it out and just trust that he knows what is happening and can turn things around?

Life Commitment:

I think I am stubbornly independent but the reality is that I am radically dependent on God and others. Self-made men are poorly made men. I want to be re-made through complete dependence on God. I am unashamed to say that I need God—desperately.

Day 56: Fail Forward (6)

The Word

Christ Jesus came into the world to save sinners—of whom I am the worst. But for that very reason I was shown mercy so that in me, the worst of sinners, Christ Jesus might display his unlimited patience as an example for those who would believe on him and receive eternal life. Now to the King eternal, immortal, invisible, the only God, be honor and glory for ever and ever. Amen.

— The Apostle Paul, 1 Timothy 1.15–17

Thought for the Day

The pessimist sees difficulty in every opportunity. The optimist sees the opportunity in every difficulty.

~ Winston Churchill

Whether we survive a failure and then thrive afterward depends entirely on putting failure in perspective. This is a battle in your mind. It's a war for your soul and for your future. It is critical that you right-size your divorce and anything else in your life you or others perceive as failure.

First, know that failure is inevitable. I deluded myself that I could avoid failure if I just worked hard enough and kept everyone happy. While much of my hard work was driven by good motives, underlying it all was the fear of failure. Then I failed, spectacularly, at least in the world's eyes. I thought I could avoid failure. I couldn't. Nobody can. Life is incredibly fragile.

Second, know that failure is not the enemy. No one cruises through life making all the right decisions. No one takes the right path at every fork in the road. John Maxwell calls these wrong turns 'errors.' What we do with errors makes the difference between people.

Maxwell says, *Errors become mistakes when we perceive them and respond to them incorrectly. Mistakes become failures when we continually respond to them incorrectly.*[104] Mistakes, errors, bad decisions . . . these are unavoidable. But each of us can choose to respond to them by learning from them.

Third, determine to live life on the edge enough to fail some. *If you are not failing some, you are not living at all.*

At the beginning of every summer, some schools put a phrase on their sign that drives me crazy: *Be Safe!* What kind of message is that to send to our kids? Of course we don't want our kids to live unsafe lives, but we also don't want them to avoid risk! Every kid should have what I call 'summer legs.' Summer legs have scrapes on the knees from climbing over rocks, scratches on their shins from running through the forest, and sore muscles from living life!

Sumner Redstone said, *We all have to decide how we are going to fail, by not going far enough or by going too far.* That you are divorced now means that you risked loving and being loved in the most intimate and demanding of all relationships. Marriage is hard. Some are going to fail. But that you tried says that you were willing to take the risk.

Go back and read Day 52. Look again through that list of people. They either failed miserably or were told they were failures or both. How did they overcome? They viewed failure as a stepping stone instead of a brick wall. When they were told they *couldn't* or *shouldn't*, they dug down deep and determined they *would* just to show the world they *could*!

Read again what the Apostle Paul wrote: *Christ Jesus came into the world to save sinners—of whom I am the worst.* Ouch! Paul says that though he started off strong, eventually he was a huge failure.

---

[104]John C. Maxwell, *Failing Forward*, 18.

But Paul could see that what looked like a failure to him was really an opportunity for God to shine through him: *But for that very reason I was shown mercy so that in me, the worst of sinners, Christ Jesus might display his unlimited patience as an example for those who would believe on him and receive eternal life.*

In the long view, Paul could see how God worked in his life so that God could show off his mercy and glory.

God doesn't waste pain. He doesn't waste our mistakes. He doesn't cut us down when we fall short. In God's Kingdom, those who are down are lifted up, those who fall into the deepest pit are elevated to the highest summit. When people see what God does with our failures, they are amazed and know that only God could do such a cool thing!

No wonder Paul concluded his brief biographical foray with this exclamation: *Now to the King eternal, immortal, invisible, the only God, be honor and glory for ever and ever. Amen!*

Let God put that *Amen!* in your life by right-sizing your failures.

Think About It . . .

Who is winning that war in your mind right now? The *pessimist* who sees difficulty in every opportunity or the *optimist* who sees the opportunity in every difficulty?

Life Commitment:

Everyone fails. Some right-size their failures and move past them into God's future for them. I choose to move with God past my failure into the future he has for me.

Day 57: Fail Forward (7)

The Word

But he said to me, "My grace is sufficient for you, for my power is made perfect in weakness." Therefore I will boast all the more gladly about my weaknesses, so that Christ's power may rest on me. That is why, for Christ's sake, I delight in weaknesses, in insults, in hardships, in persecutions, in difficulties. For when I am weak, then I am strong.

— 2 Corinthians 12.9–10

Thought for the Day

You have brains in your head. You have feet in your shoes. You can steer yourself any direction you choose.

~ Dr. Seuss, Oh, The Places You'll Go!

Whether failure is a period or a comma is entirely up to you. Just know this: *Failure doesn't have to be a period.*

Too many people put a period in their life where a comma belonged. I think of men whose dreams are finished so they think they are too. They keep living but they are not alive. They keep going but without direction. They keep waking up but they are still just really sleeping.

Then I think of the tens of thousands of people in our country who put the ultimate period in their lives—they kill themselves.

My oldest sister chose this at the age of 50. She was a vibrant, brilliant, fun, glorious human being. She embraced life to the max. She was the first woman to graduate from Georgia Tech with a master's degree in Mechanical Engineering. She had three amazing children (who are still amazing). She was the ultimate big sister. She took me and others backpacking into the high country of Colorado— for over a week! We traipsed through the Arkansas Ozarks during Christmas vacation. It was 5°.

Suicide is a huge mistake. Suicide is a permanent (and terrible) solution to a temporary problem. Don't put a period where a comma belongs. Failure is a temporary problem; it's a comma, not a period (See Appendix A).

By the end of World War I, Winston Churchill was washed up as a politician. As Britain's Lord of Admiralty, he had planned and pushed for the attack on Turkey at Gallipoli. A million men fought on both sides. Over the course of eight months, over 135,000 died with nearly 400,000 wounded. Britain lost in total humiliation. Churchill was fired and thereafter excluded from any decisions regarding war.

But nearly 20 years later, it was Prime Minister Churchill who would lead the British when Britain alone faced the Nazi juggernaut. Imagine being Churchill leading Britain as Prime Minister. Here he was being tested at the very point where he previously had failed miserably.

Later Churchill would write, *Success is not final, failure is not fatal: it is the courage to continue that counts.* Churchill proved that with his life. So can you.

Bear Grylls says it like this: *Ever heard the phrase When you're in a hole, stop digging'? It's the same with mistakes. Don't give the mistake more power than it warrants by squandering precious time worrying about it. Yesterday is not ours to recover, but tomorrow is ours to win or lose.*[105]

Failures are commas, not periods. Don't put a period where a comma belongs.

---

[105] Bear Grylls, *A Survival Guide for Life: How to Achieve Your Goals, Thrive in Adversity, and Grow in Character* (New York: William Morrow, 2014), 235. Reprinted by permission of Peters Fraser & Dunlop (www.petersfraserdunlop.com) on behalf of Bear Grylls.

Think About It . . .

- Failure can lead one to seriously consider suicide. If you are contemplating suicide, call this hotline right now: 800-273-8255 or visit (https://suicidepreventionlifeline.org/). See also Appendix A to assess your risk for suicide. Take suicidal thoughts seriously.
- Six days ago we started this short series about failure. What has changed in how you view failure?

Life Commitment:

Success is not final, failure is not fatal: it is the courage to continue that counts. Though it is painful and though I don't know what the future holds, I commit to continuing this journey.

Day 58: Accepted by God (1)

The Word

Accept one another, then, just as Christ accepted you, in order to bring praise to God.

– Romans 15:7

Thought for the Day

People are suffering from an identity crisis. It seems everywhere we turn we see people striving to become someone or something that they perceive will bring them some sort of contentment when in reality the opposite is true.[106]

~ Perry Noble

From the beginning of my Christian experience I was told the amazing truth that I was accepted by God. Everyone seemed so excited to tell me this wonderful news. But try as I might, I could not wrap my head around what being accepted by God really meant. The reason is that my understanding of acceptance was based on my experiences of human 'acceptance.'

We are told that to accept others is a noble thing, part of our unique American experience of one another. Despite the mantra that we need to accept one another, my actual experience is that we don't accept each other for who we are. Instead, relationships are unpleasantly based on a cost-benefit analysis. If I can do something

[106]Perry Noble quoted in Mark Driscoll, *Who Do You Think You Are? Finding Your True Identity in Christ* (Nashville: Thomas Nelson, 2013), 7.

for you, you like me. If I am no use to you, you push me aside and move on to the next person to use.

For this reason, all this talk of acceptance was muddied in my brain until I ran across a new (and biblical) way of looking at things from the smart folks at an organization called Victorious Christian Living.[107]

Here's how this works: when someone says to me that God accepts me I automatically filter that statement through what I know of acceptance, which is to say, I define the word 'acceptance' by my experience of acceptance. The only experience I know of acceptance is from my life in the world.

How do I gain the world's acceptance? To get the world's ultimate approval/acceptance I follow a specific path. First, someone in the world (an **AUTHORITY** in my life) gives me their expectations. This authority can be parents, a teacher, an employer or anyone or anything in the world that has a measure of control over my life.

Next, I have to work to meet those expectations. I strive to *do* the things that I have been told I should do. I jump through all the right hoops to reach the goal, *which is acceptance by that authority in my life.*

I wrote on the first day of this guide:

> *The only question on my mind growing up was, "Am I good enough?" The answers from my dad and others were conflicted. On one hand, I was told I was special and nothing could stop me. I would be spectacular. On the other hand, if I was anything less than spectacular, it was my fault. Given the deluge of criticism I received, it seemed that though I was special, I pretty much never measured up to my specialness!*
>
> *Not to kick a dead horse till its teeth fall out, but most of us men grew up with this double message from our parents, our schools, our peers. To be accepted we had to jump through hoops that were*

[107]The teachings for the next several days come primary from *"Seven Areas of Life Training."* Victorious Christian Living International, accessed February 03, 2017, http://www.vcli.org/salt/.

> *just out of reach. The message we received was, you can do it but . . . you probably won't.*
>
> *Implicit in this message was that people were both for me and against me, both my friend and my enemy, my companion and my challenger. People were as likely to push me down as they were to help me up.*

Is this your experience of 'acceptance'? If this is the way God 'accepts' me, I think I will pass!

To be continued . . .

Think About It . . .

- When you hear the word 'acceptance' what first comes to your mind?
- What have you been told you must do to be accepted by the authorities (Parents, Teachers, Employers) in your life?
- When have you measured up? What were the consequences?
- When have you failed to measure up? What were the consequences?

Life Commitment:

It could be true that what I think about God's love and acceptance for me has been informed more by my experience of how the world defines love and acceptance than by what God says about me.

Day 59: Accepted by God (2)

The Word

We have the free gift of being accepted by God, even though we are guilty of many sins.

— Romans 5.16 (NLT)

Thought for the Day

I renounce the lie that I am too worthless to ever be accepted by God or people. I acknowledge that my value before God is so great He sent Jesus to die for me, and it is the value in His eyes which truly counts.

~ Keturah Martin

I was often told I was loved and accepted without condition, but it seemed to me that love and acceptance came with a lot of conditions. When I came home with A's on my report card, I got showered with praise and affection. When I came home with a single C in algebra, I never heard the end of it. All those A's didn't seem to cover over a C. The question I was always asking (and still ask in my weaker moments) is, *Am I good enough?* And usually the answer was, *Almost.*

When I worked hard to be good enough for the **AUTHORITIES** in my life, I got **AFFIRMATION**.

Affirmation is the second step in being accepted by the world. First, authorities lay out their **expectations**. If you meet these expectations, you get **affirmed**.

This is the way the world works whether you working on a Ph.D. or trying to get into a gang. The group says, "Do this, and we will accept you." You jump through the hoops, and if you succeed, they affirm you. If you keep it up, affirmation turns into **ACCEPTANCE**. You're in!

The downside of this is that if you fail to keep jumping through the hoops, you can be pushed back out. You can go from being *acceptable* to *unacceptable.*

This is the way of the world. Authorities give us expectations. We work hard to meet those expectations. If we do, we are affirmed, and if consistently affirmed, we are accepted.

Here's the thing: The motivation behind this dynamic at work in our world is *control.* Parents, teachers, employers—they all have to control us. The way they control us is to give or take away their acceptance of us. The emotion that accompanies and drives this process is *fear.* We *fear* not being accepted, and that fear motivates us to follow the rules.

Do you think God accepts or rejects you based on your obedience to his authority?

If you do, please explain these words from the Bible:

> *[We] know and rely on the love God has for us. God is love . . .. There is no fear in love. But perfect love drives out fear, because fear has to do with punishment.* (1 John 4.16–18)

Hopefully you are beginning to realize that being accepted by God means something significantly different than how the world accepts us.

Think About It . . .

- What is the most ridiculous thing you ever did in order to be accepted by a group?

- What are some ridiculous things people do to earn God's acceptance?
- Was there a time you felt like God accepted you?
- Was there a time when you believed God rejected you?

Life Commitment:

I think God's way of accepting me must be different than the world's way of acceptance.

Day 60: Accepted by God (3)

The Word

Do you want to get well?
– Jesus, asked of a lame man as recorded in John 5.6

Thought for the Day

If you obey for a thousand years, you're no more accepted than when you first believed; your acceptance is based on Christ's righteousness and not yours.
~ Paul David Tripp

For the past two days I have explained the way the authorities in our world accepts us. The **authorities** in our lives give us expectations. We try to meet them. If we do, we are **affirmed**. If we are affirmed enough, we are **accepted.** If we screw up, we can be unaccepted.

The purpose of this dynamic is ***control***, and the emotion used to control us is ***fear***.

Now, two simple questions: Is this the way God works? Is God's main goal to control you?

That leads to a next question: Do you think God has the power to control you?

The small town of Bertram is located northwest of Austin. This little town has the irritating habit of positioning one of their police cruisers somewhere along the highway that goes through their town. The cruiser is empty. But it is menacing. Every time I go through Bertram

I know the empty cruiser will be there. And every time I see that cruiser my heart skips a beat and I slow down out of fear of getting a speeding ticket!

Guys, if an empty police cruiser can control my behavior and strike fear in my heart, what can an all-powerful God do?

The prophet Jeremiah said,

> *God made the earth by his power; he founded the world by his wisdom and stretched out the heavens by his understanding. When he thunders, the waters in the heavens roar; he makes clouds rise from the ends of the earth. He sends lightning with the rain and brings out the wind from his storehouses.* (Jeremiah 10.12–13)

That's a powerful God! God could make you bend over double with excruciating pain right now. He could pop your head off or send you careening through space. *God can do to you whatever he wants!* So the question is, *What does God want?*

Here's what God wants: God wants you to experience his love so that you can respond to him in love. God does not want to control you out of fear but to woo you with his love. That's why God's acceptance of us begins with his love, not his expectations. First John 4.16 plainly states, *God is love. Whoever lives in love lives in God, and God in him.*

In the world's way of acceptance, you must earn the approval of the authorities. In God's Kingdom, ***God already approves you on the basis of what Jesus, his Son, did for you on the cross.***

God's way starts with acceptance. He accepts you right now before you do anything. He doesn't accept you based on your ability to obey His commands. You are accepted because Christ's death on the cross made you acceptable.[108]

When God looks at you he doesn't see your shortcomings, he sees his Son's righteousness. When God looks at you he doesn't see you falling short, he sees his Son lifting you up.

[108] *Seven Areas of Life Training*, Book 1, Lesson 4. VCLi, Version 2.0, 51.

That means that you have nothing to prove to God. Jesus has already bought God's approval of you. You cannot earn God's approval; his approval of you has already been purchased by his Son.

Neil and Joann Anderson say it like this:

> *We are not on a performance basis with God. He doesn't say, "Here are My standards, now you measure up." He knows you can't solve the problem of an old sinful self by simply improving your behavior. He must change your nature, give you an entirely new self—the life of Christ in you.*[109]

The world says, ***Perform***! God says, ***Receive***!

There is nothing you can do to add to or take away his love from you. When you do something good, God doesn't love you more. When you mess up, God doesn't love you less. His love is based on who he is not on what you do or don't do.

God's acceptance of us begins with his love for us, not his expectations of us.

Think About It . . .

- In what ways have you tried to earn God's approval?
- If you tried to earn God's approval, how did you know you got it (or not)?
- God's acceptance of us begins with his love for us, not his expectations of us. What could change in your life if you really believed this?

[109] Anderson and Anderson, *Daily in Christ: A Devotional* (Eugene: Harvest House Publishers, 1993), 105.

Life Commitment:

I give up! I give up trying to earn God's approval and love. Instead, I choose to simply receive his steadfast, never-changing love for me.

Day 61: Accepted by God (4)

The Word

For you did not receive a spirit that makes you a slave again to fear, but you received the Spirit of sonship. And by him we cry, "Abba, Father." The Spirit himself testifies with our spirit that we are God's children.

— Romans 8.16-17

Thought for the Day

Every day you preach to yourself some kind of gospel—a false "I can't do this" gospel or the true "I have all I need in Christ" gospel.

~ Paul David Tripp

When my wife met me upon my return from Africa and told me she was leaving me, the weight of her rejection drove me into the ground. I had worked hard all my life to earn the approval, affirmation and acceptance of the people in my life. No person's approval meant more to me than her's.

Just a few weeks before this happened, she had been on a business trip. On the way home she posted on Facebook that she couldn't wait to get home and go to church to hear her favorite preacher. She meant me! I beamed inside! A month later she told me she was leaving me. Coming to grips with these double messages is a challenge yet before me.

Every rejection stings because rejection goes against all that we have tried so hard to attain—the love, approval and acceptance of others. As now famously disgraced Lance Armstrong once said, *A boo is a lot louder than a cheer.*

The only thing that kept me going through that time was knowing that God did not reject me. Even though I am a divorced pastor, God has not divorced me. Though to many people in the world I am a failure because my wife rejected me, I know that in God's eyes, I am accepted and loved *no matter what.*

God begins by accepting us out of his love for us and based on Christ's death on our behalf. When we understand this amazing truth we understand and experience God's **AFFIRMATION**. God's affirmation of us is experienced as an emotion. We *feel* God's love for us. Just like we feel the fear of the rejection of the world, we can feel God's amazing love and acceptance of us!

The Apostle Paul wrote, *The Spirit himself testifies with our spirit that we are God's children.* (Romans 8.16). This is really good news! When we experience God's Spirit testifying with our spirit that we are his kids—accepted *because we are his kids*—we experience joy, peace, gladness . . . and the list of positive emotions goes on!

To the depth that I felt crushed by all that I was going through, God met me equally and even beyond with his Spirit gently holding my soul and reassuring me that I would be OK. I kept hearing him say, *I love you, you are OK. Just hold on and we will get through this. I will never leave you or forsake you.* I could receive no greater affirmation than that.

God first **ACCEPTS** us based on his love for us, not our performance for him. He then **AFFIRMS** us by reassuring us that we his kids and he will never leave us or forsake us.

Think About It . . .

- Have you experienced God's **peace** equal to or greater than your **anxiety**?

- Have you experienced God's **joy** equal to or greater than your **anguish**?

- Have you experienced God's **love** equal to or greater than your **anger**?
- If not, ask his Spirit to testify with your spirit that you are his son, and that you are accepted, affirmed and loved *no matter what* anyone else may say or do. Ask him to allow you to experience this truth deep in your soul as a good and strong emotion.

Life Commitment:

I choose to believe that God has accepted me first, and that he actually wants me to experience the reality of his acceptance of me resulting in the emotions of peace, joy and love.

Day 62: Accepted by God (5)

The Word

Before I formed you in the womb I knew you, before you were born I set you apart.

— Jeremiah 1.5

Thought for the Day

Because the Spirit of the Lord is in you, you are free to choose to live a responsible and moral life. You are no longer compelled to walk according to the flesh as you were before conversion. And now you are not even compelled to walk according to the Spirit. You are free to choose to walk according to the Spirit or to walk according to the flesh.

~ Neil Anderson

Everyone demands it for others but few want it for themselves. We decry others when they avoid it, but we crumple into a heap when others require it of us. We rail at others when it catches them in the act, but curl up into a ball of excuses when it exposes our shortcomings. What am I talking about? Accountability.

Everywhere we turn we hear the incessant call for more accountability. And yet when we are held accountable, we squeal and squirm. We scream at the referee who fails to call pass interference on the opposing team, but run like a hen when the finger is pointed at us.

From the world's perspective, accountability is all about fear. The boss lays down expectations. Then he/she holds us accountable. The thought of failing creates fear in us, and fear motivates us to meet expectations. If we meet expectations we get affirmed, and if affirmed enough, we feel accepted. Accountability is a big piece of the way the systems in the world work.

How does accountability work in God's Kingdom? If God starts with accepting us, and then he affirms us, where does accountability fit in?

Look at the first few lines of the 23rd Psalm:

> *The Lord is my shepherd, I shall not be in want.*
>
> *He makes me lie down in green pastures, he leads me beside quiet waters, he restores my soul.*
>
> *He guides me in paths of righteousness for his name's sake.* (Psalm 23.1–3)

This Psalm affirms what we have said about the way God accepts us. It starts off with the assurance that God is our good shepherd, and we know that shepherds accept their sheep the way they are.

The next few lines are all about affirmation: God leads me to green, abundant pastures and quenches my thirst at no cost. Green pastures and still waters are given to all sheep regardless of how 'good' or 'bad' they have been. He restores my soul *at no cost.* In other words, God accepts us and provides for us because he loves us, not because we have done anything to earn it.

But then comes accountability. Notice how David describes accountability in God's Kingdom: *He [God] guides me in paths of righteousness for his name's sake.*

God *does* hold us accountable. He doesn't let us live without limits. But the limits he sets are *for his glory* and *for our good.* God sets boundaries for us, but the purpose of those boundaries is that we may flourish into what we were meant to be. When we grow into his Kingdom people, the world takes notice and God gets the glory!

He *guides* us—he doesn't *drive* us—into the paths of righteousness so that we may flourish and in our flourishing, he may get the glory. God wants the best for us.

I confess that a few times I disciplined my children more to release my own anger than to guide them in life. Not God. His discipline is never to vent his own anger but *always* to nudge us back onto the path toward green pastures, smooth waters and soul restoration.

What if we stray *way* off the path? The Shepherd will pursue us (not hunt us down) to bring us back to the abundant pasture and thirst-quenching stream (see Luke 15.4-7).

God holds us accountable for our good and for his glory. He is motivated by his love for us, trusting that by loving us we will respond in love back to him. There is no fear in this equation. The world operates on the basis of fear. God operates on the basis of love. The difference between the two is utterly profound.

Think About It . . .

- If you go to church, why do you go?
- If you give money to your church or another charity, why do you give?
- If you pray, why do you pray?

Life Commitment:

I choose to believe that God is for me and has my best interests in mind, and that he holds me accountable not out of a motivation of control but out of pure love for me.

Day 63: Accepted by God (6)

The Word

Brothers and sisters, I do not consider myself yet to have taken hold of it. But one thing I do: Forgetting what is behind and straining toward what is ahead, I press on toward the goal to win the prize for which God has called me heavenward in Christ Jesus.

— Philippians 3:13-14

Thought for the Day

Jesus paid it all! There are no bills due for your sin! You are now free to simply trust and obey.

~ Paul David Tripp

One day I was driving along and I had a profoundly terrible thought. It was terrible because it was so incredibly untrue. The thought I had was this: *I bet I will get into heaven. I mean, I'm a pastor! Don't all pastors go to heaven because we are so good?*

The moment I thought it I realized how idiotic this was. The first bad thing about this thought was that whatever *good* I did could *never* add to God's love for me. I could *never* increase God's love for me by any good thing I did. He loves me now as much as he did when he decided in eternity past to create me. He loves me now as much as he did when his Son hung on a cross taking the hell I rightfully deserved for every sin I would commit in my lifetime. There is nothing good I could ever do to increase God's love for me. He loves me, period.

The second bad thing about this thought was that I am *not nearly as good as I had led myself to believe!* I am a self-centered sinful creature like everyone else. Which led me to this awesome reality: *There is nothing bad that I could ever do that would take away God's love for me.* He loves me, period. His love for me never changes.

God is not like the Greek gods who were just super-sized humans who pretty much screwed up the world with their super-sized but misdirected powers. God does not act like we do—he doesn't keep score of our good deeds and misdeeds—and love us depending on the score.

The world begins with rules to follow which may or may not lead to its acceptance of us. God is just the opposite—he begins by accepting us! No hoops to jump through, no demands to meet, no fear of falling short. God *begins* with accepting you because he profoundly, passionately, deeply and incessantly loves you.

If he wanted to control you out of fear, he could. Oh . . . he could! Instead of controlling you through fear he wants to woo you with his love. The basis of God's acceptance of you is love, not fear.

Think About It . . .

- Do you fear God or love him?
- What could you do to make God love you more?
- What does God think when you screw up?

Life Commitment:

I will live my life based on God's unchangeable love for me, not based on the fear of not meeting his or people's expectations of me.

Day 64: Walden Pond or the North Atlantic?

The Word

There is a time for everything, and a season for every activity under heaven.
— Ecclesiastes 3.1

Thought for the Day

I believe in process. I believe in four seasons. I believe that winter's tough, but spring's coming. I believe that there's a growing season. And I think that you realize that in life, you grow. You get better.
~ Steve Southerland

I can't remember where I read it, but someone said that while we yearn for a peaceful life on Walden Pond in summer, real life is more like the North Atlantic in winter! For the most part, we try to live on Walden Pond, and for most of our lives we may be able to manage life closer to Walden than the North Atlantic.

But inevitably something happens that flings you into the North Atlantic where the waves are huge and the water frigid.

Divorce did that for me. All the things I had worked for, the *stability and security* I sought, slipped right out of my hands. Maybe you had this same experience. You worked hard to provide for your family. You tried to be there for your kids, you sacrificed to secure a safe and stable home. Then the bottom dropped out.

The reality is this: Walden is an illusion. But so is the North Atlantic. Life is never as peaceful as Walden and it is never as completely terrifying as the North Atlantic.

I've had a 'Walden Pond' moment or two. It was great, but fleeting and still not deeply satisfying.

Then for three years I was flailing around in the North Atlantic with wind, water and waves crashing all around me. But just as Walden was not as great as promised, the North Atlantic was not as terrifying as imagined. The reason Walden disappoints and the North Atlantic not so terrifying is that our security and stability are not found in earthly circumstances.

Look at Psalm 46:

> *God is our refuge and strength, an ever-present help in trouble. Therefore we will not fear, though the earth give way and the mountains fall into the heart of the sea, though its waters roar and foam and the mountains quake with their surging.* (Psalm 46:1–3)

Did you get that second sentence? *Therefore we will not fear, though the earth give way and the mountains fall into the heart of the sea.*

Earth and mountains are supposed to be *stable*. They don't just collapse. Their collapse represents the Psalmist's worst calamity. But, he says, *because God is our refuge*, we will not fear *even if the most stable things we can imagine actually do collapse.*

If your life is more like flailing in the North Atlantic than sitting peacefully by Walden Pond, know that God is your refuge and strength and that, ultimately, nothing can shake you.

Think About It . . .

- Where are you right now: Walden Pond, the North Atlantic, or somewhere in between?

- Have you experienced moments of true peace due to positive circumstances? Did the peace last?

- When circumstances have felt like drowning in the North Atlantic, how did you feel? What did you do?
- What does it mean that God is our *refuge and strength*?

Life Commitment:

I am coming to realize that life is never as peaceful as Walden nor as completely terrifying as the North Atlantic. Security and safety are only found in turning to God to be my refuge and strength.

Day 65: Go With the Flow

The Word

See, I am doing a new thing! Now it springs up; do you not perceive it? I am making a way in the desert and streams in the wasteland.
— Isaiah 43.19

Thought for the Day

Often in the growth process we do not know what to do, or we do not want to do what we know we should do. This is where the "control" of the Spirit comes into play, and we must yield. We must submit to what the Spirit is telling us to do and allow him to have the reins of control moment by moment.
~ Henry Cloud

I mapped out my life carefully. I would get educated, get married, get a steady job, have some kids, retire comfortably and die peacefully. I would spend my last days in a house by a lake, reading good books beside the water in summer and by the fireplace in winter. My life would be predictable. My life would be peaceful. Most of all, my life would be stable.

In some ways that happened. I got educated. I pastored stable churches (or so I thought). We had the big house and the kids. I loved walking with my kids in the New England woods behind our home, working in the yard in the summer and working with wood in my basement workshop in the winter. I really craved this stability and worked hard to get it and protect it. I wanted what scientists and engineers call *homeostasis*.

The problem with stability is that life is intrinsically unstable. Life is not a quiet pool of water. It's a flowing river. Life is in motion and motion means change.

God knows this. The Bible is about a God who is in motion and it tells the stories of this God-in-motion sending his people in motion.

God calls Abram to get moving from the city of Ur to the yet-undisclosed Promised Land. He sends Jacob north to get a wife and Joseph south to Egypt by the most unlikely of means. God pulls his chosen people out of Egyptian slavery and then has them live a life of constant motion in the desert until they finally get a few hard-fought lessons under their belts.

God sends a very pregnant Mary from Nazareth to Bethlehem on the back of a donkey, then he sends the young family fleeing to Egypt as refugees. Jesus sends his disciples on all kinds of missions. He is always on the move, teaching and healing wherever he is.

God scatters the early church when they became too comfortable in their Jerusalem digs. He knocks Saul off a donkey and then Saul becomes Paul, the most in-motion man who ever lived, traveling well over 11,000 miles in his four recorded journeys.

A persecution in Rome sends Priscilla and Aquila fleeing to Corinth and then to Ephesus. Along the way they faithfully teach about the Jesus who had saved them . . . and who seemed to want them to keep moving!

If your life has been turned upside down by divorce and/or other circumstances, welcome to life. Life is about movement and change. Since nothing surprises God and God himself seems to relish movement, determine to quit fighting for stability in your circumstances and simply *go with the flow.*

God has you covered. He is *with* you and he is even *in front of you,* preparing your future for you. Stability is an illusion. Real life is in the river!

Think About It . . .

- How important is stability to you?
- When your life has been turned upside-down in the past, how did you handle it? Did you go with the flow or fight it every step of the way?
- What possibilities do you see for God to work in your future?

Life Commitment:

God is a God in motion. I will move with him.

Day 66: Flow With the Go

The Word

But as surely as God is faithful, our message to you is not "Yes" and "No." For the Son of God, Jesus Christ, who was preached among you by me and Silas and Timothy, was not "Yes" and "No," but in him it has always been "Yes." For no matter how many promises God has made, they are "Yes" in Christ.

— 2 Corinthians 1.18–21

Thought for the Day

Security is mostly a superstition. It does not exist in nature, nor do the children of men as a whole experience it. Avoiding danger is no safer in the long run than outright exposure. Life is a daring adventure or nothing at all.

~ Helen Keller

When hammered by life, recovery begins with a surrender to the flow . . . Go with the flow. The only way you can go with the flow with any sense of peace is to know that God controls the flow. God is with you, and he is in front of you. He has your future—he is in your future preparing a way for you.

But when life is caving all around us our natural reaction is to withdraw, hunker down and ride out the storm. We tend to pull back rather than risk reaching out.

For men, pulling back can be deadly. We can easily get lost in booze, pornography, video games, television . . . anything we think can fill the hole left by the rejection of our spouse or by the guilt of our own poor choices. We just want to be left alone and try to forget our pain.

Another factor is fatigue. When struggling through divorce our energy level drops. Getting through each day is like trudging through a snow-covered field with the wind howling against us rather than strolling through a green and sunny meadow.

This is definitely not the time to make major decisions. But it is also a mistake to turtle up and get lost in booze and porn.

God knows this and so he will send you opportunities to crawl out of the hole. Say yes to these opportunities.

Bear Grylls is a man who consistently said yes to the opportunities that came his way. Once he spent 18 months recovering from a skydiving accident. But when the opportunity came to say yes to jumping out of a plane again, he took it! His advice? *Say yes and try something, rather than saying no because you fear where a yes will take you.*[110]

He goes on to write, *More often than not, saying no means that nothing will change in your life. A yes, however, has the power to create change. And change is where we create room for success.*[111]

SAY YES! Say yes to God and the invitations he sends your way to get out of the hole. Say yes to people when they reach out to you. Say yes to opportunities to get out. Say yes to your own ideas . . . go take a hike, go on a trip, go to a movie. Go to church, a men's conference, a small group. Take a chance! What do you have to lose?

Think About It . . .

- What invitations have come your way that you have said no to? Was it helpful to stay hunkered down?
- What happened when you said yes?
- What can you say yes to today?

---

[110]Bear Grylls, *A Survival Guide for Life*, 36.
[111]Ibid.

Life Commitment:

I choose to believe that saying yes to the opportunities God puts in my path is better in the long run than playing it safe.

Day 67: It's a War

The Word

Finally, be strong in the Lord and in his mighty power. Put on the full armor of God so that you can take your stand against the devil's schemes. For our struggle is not against flesh and blood, but against the rulers, against the authorities, against the powers of this dark world and against the spiritual forces of evil in the heavenly realms.

— Ephesians 6.10–12

Thought for the Day

If you know the enemy and know yourself, you need not fear the result of a hundred battles. If you know yourself but not the enemy, for every victory gained you will also suffer a defeat. If you know neither the enemy nor yourself, you will succumb in every battle.

~ Sun Tzu, *The Art of War*

The worst thing you can do when going to war is to underestimate your enemy. The British underestimated the Americans and the Americans underestimated the Viet Cong.

Worse than underestimating your enemy is not realizing you have one. We experienced the terrible results of this fatal error on September 11, 2001. I experienced it in my church in New England. I never knew that guy was my enemy or that he was at war with me.

We are at war. This war is bigger than any battle fought between humans on earth. This war is cosmic. It's huge and it's ancient, going back to the beginning of time.

Before we were created, God had a worship leader who wanted to be God. There's only one God and he is (rightfully) jealous of his glory. The worship leader lost his bid to take God's place in the universe. The mutineer and his compatriots were kicked out of heaven. We know this mutinous worship leader as Satan and his fellow rebels as demons.

Ever since that terrible cosmic tragedy, Satan has done all he can to destroy and defame anything of God. The war was won but skirmishes continue. Since Satan can't get to God, he goes for what God loves—his children. The battleground of this war is our mind and heart.

On June 6, 1944, the largest assault in military history took place when the Allies invaded northern France. We know this as D-Day. The success of this initial battle to retake Europe spelled the end of Hitler and his murderous regime. Everyone knew it except Hitler.

Between Normandy and Berlin were 844 miles of German-infested hedgerows, forests, meadows and mountains. To complete the victory meant retaking all that ground stolen by Hitler.

Victory was *assured* on June 6, 1944, D-Day. But victory was not *fully realized* until May 8, 1945, V-E Day, when the Germans surrendered in Berlin. Between D-Day and V-E Day were 336 days and 844 miles of struggle. But each allied soldier fighting those 336 days and 844 miles knew Hitler was doomed.

We are living between a spiritual D-Day and V-E Day. Jesus stormed the beaches of Satan's stronghold on Good Friday. Jesus emerged victorious on Resurrection Sunday. The victory was won and secured 2,000 years ago. But the full benefits of that victory will not be realized until Jesus comes again and the Great Renovation of heaven and earth is complete.

Meanwhile, we fight on, knowing the victory is ours and the enemy is defeated.

How does this help with anger? It helps to know that the battle is bigger than you, your ex-wife, your boss, your flat tire, your ______________ (fill in the blank). The real enemy is not a human or situation or circumstance on earth. Your real enemy is Satan, and his target is your head and heart.

It helps to know that a good choice in the midst of your anger scores a victory that rings throughout heaven.

It helps to know the battles are temporary. Eventually you will have rest from this struggle. It helps to have hope. It helps to be angry at the real enemy and to know he is ultimately defeated forever.

Think About It . . .

- Have I been fighting the right enemy?
- If all this is true, what does a real victory look like?

Life Commitment:

I will know the enemy and I will know myself and my God, so I need not fear the result of a hundred battles.

Day 68: God Wins

The Word

Since everything will be destroyed in this way, what kind of people ought you to be? You ought to live holy and godly lives as you look forward to the day of God and speed its coming. That day will bring about the destruction of the heavens by fire, and the elements will melt in the heat.
But in keeping with his promise we are looking forward to a new heaven and a new earth, the home of righteousness. So then, dear friends, since you are looking forward to this, make every effort to be found spotless, blameless and at peace with him.

— 2 Peter 3.11–14

Thought for the Day

This is the good news of the gospel. Peace came. Peace lived. Peace died. Peace rose again. Peace reigns on your behalf. Peace indwells you by the Spirit. Peace graces you with everything you need. Peace convicts, forgives, and delivers you. Peace will finish his work in you. Peace will welcome you into glory, where Peace will live with you in peace and righteousness forever. Peace isn't a faded dream. No, Peace is real. Peace is a person, and his name is Jesus.

~ Paul David Tripp

John O'Donohue writes, *It is strange to be here. The mystery never leaves you alone. Behind your image, below your words, above your thoughts, the silence of another world waits.*[112]

[112] O'Donohue, *Anam Ċara*, Kindle Location 283.

This mystery is not only *in* you but far *beyond* you. There is far more *in* you than you can possibly imagine, and there is far more *beyond* you than you can possibly fathom.

We live out our earthly lives on an extremely thin line (about 10 feet?) where rock and air meet. We exist on a tiny speck of rock in a universe of perhaps a trillion galaxies. Go outside tonight and look up. You will be humbled. It is, indeed, strange to be here.

But we *are* here and we are here because God made us to be here. We are his glorious creation, the ones he has made to love and from whom love is desired. As weird as it is for us as men to hear it, we are in the middle of a love story.

It makes sense, doesn't it? In the end, don't all good things come down to love, and all the heartache and suffering of life to misplaced love?

All love stories are about love in the midst of conflict and war. The epic stories we tell and the movies Disney makes are not creations of our imagination. They are echoes of the deeper reality we seek while stumbling around in our foggy world.

We are in a love story, but a love story gone awry. The battle rages and casualties mount. But here's the thing: as in our epic tales and delightful movies, *in the end, love wins.*

This is crucial for you to understand. In the end, love wins. In the end, God wins. You are on the winning team.

How does this help you manage your suffering? If you know you are on the winning team, you can endure anything until the victory is complete. If you know you are on the winning team, everything *now* becomes training for the ultimate victory *later.* You and I can endure hardship because we know the victory is coming.

The Apostle Paul says it like this:

> *For our light and momentary troubles are achieving for us an eternal glory that far outweighs them all. So we fix our eyes not on what is seen, but on what is unseen. For what is seen is temporary, but what is unseen is eternal.* (2 Corinthians 4.17–18)

Knowing you are on the winning team lets you look beyond your current troubles to the victory that is on the way.

Think About It . . .

- What am I here for?
- If this is a war, whose side am I on?
- What would change in my attitude if I really grasped that in the end, all that matters is that God wins?

Life Commitment:

It's Friday, but Sunday's coming! I can make it until Sunday.

DAY 69: THINKING ABOUT FORGIVENESS

THE WORD

He does not deal with us according to our sins, nor repay us according to our iniquities. For as high as the heavens are above the earth, so great is his steadfast love toward those who fear him; as far as the east is from the west, so far does he remove our transgressions from us. As a father shows compassion to his children, so the Lord shows compassion to those who fear him. For he knows our frame; he remembers that we are dust.

— Psalm 103.10-14

THOUGHT FOR THE DAY

Resentment is like drinking poison and then hoping it will kill your enemies.

~ Nelson Mandela

FORGIVENESS IS TOUGH. It's a journey. It's a process. Today I simply ask you to consider what forgiveness might look like in your life . . . forgiveness of your ex, forgiveness of yourself, forgiveness of anyone else involved in the pain you find yourself in right now.[113]

---

[113] The difficult and complicated topic of forgiveness is covered more thoroughly in the second book in this series, *Daily Survival Guide for Divorced Men, Book 2: Days 92-180.* The best book on forgiveness is Everett Worthington, *Forgiving and Reconciling: Bridges to Wholeness and Hope.* Downers Grove: InterVarsity Press, 2003.

Think About It . . .

- How have I experienced forgiveness from others in my life?
- What barriers to forgiving others are in my life right now?
- What will I gain by forgiving the people in my life who have hurt me?
- What would I gain by not forgiving them?

Life Commitment:

I commit to giving consideration to forgiveness.

Day 70: Between Surviving & Thriving

The Word

It is good and proper for a man to eat and drink, and to find satisfaction in his toilsome labor under the sun during the few days of life God has given him.

— Ecclesiastes 5.18

Thought for the Day

To be broken is no reason to see all things as broken.

~ Mark Nepo

I described earlier what I experienced when I walked in from a 38-hour journey from Tanzania that October day only to have my wife inform that she was leaving me. I was crushed beyond words. My thoughts spiraled out of control as my soul struggled to figure out what *had happened*, what *was happening* and *what could possibly happen* to my future.

I distinctly remember saying to myself that my goal was to ride this wave, to grab on to the Rock and hold on through the storm. I knew that whatever my long-term future looked like I would never make it there if I didn't survive this short-term hurricane.

When people are devastated by crushing news the first order of business is survival. But God made us for more than mere survival. He designed us to thrive as we live out the purpose for which he created us.

I fervently believe you will survive and I believe you will thrive. That's why the mission statement for Men's Divorce Recovery says:

Men's Divorce Recovery exists to Empower Divorced Men through Support, Knowledge and Encouragement to ***Survive and Thrive beyond their divorce*** *to become Resilient, Strong and Wise men in their world.*

You may be in survival mode. You are riding out the storm. You are clinging to the Rock. Survival for you may look doubtful. If surviving seems iffy, thriving will definitely seem a distant, diminishing hope.

But here is some hope for you right now: There is a place between merely surviving and totally thriving. It is in this place that God will give you some moments of enjoyment.

As you move through the survival stage you can expect God to give you moments of pleasure and happiness. They will probably be brief but these moments are real.

These glimpses of joy and hope may come from the things that gave you joy before like hiking or woodworking or reading or fishing. As you regain strength, try to do some of the things that brought joy to you in the past.

On the other hand, God may bring some new things into your life. Who knew bird watching could be so energizing! The symphony? Seriously? Country music? Rap? OK, maybe we're pushing the limits! Or maybe not.

You just never know what God will do in your future! Just know this: He loves you and has a plan for you that will include your deepest desires coupled with the world's greatest needs. It is in that happy place that you will know you are thriving. Until then, look for some spots along the trail where the views are stunning, the breeze refreshing, the water crystal clear.

Think About It . . .

- Where are you on this journey? Are you in survival mode? Are you fully thriving? Or are you somewhere along the path between these two places?

- As you think of your life right now, where are some places of enjoyment and happiness?

- Has God brought into your life some new desires? Has he put you into unexpected places of hope and healing?

Life Commitment:

Even if life looks totally black right now, I can expect God to bring into my life some new places of happiness and enjoyment, even if briefly.

Day 71: What You Hear is Important

The Word

Whether you turn to the right or to the left, your ears will hear a voice behind you, saying, "This is the way; walk in it."
— Isaiah 30.21

Thought for the Day

Those who trust His voice must learn to hear it above all other voices out there. And the only way to do that is to hear the other voices and still choose His.
~ ChrisTiegreen

Remember Elijah, the prophet? (see Day 30). He was a mighty man when facing off with the prophets of Baal. But when Queen Jezebel threatened his life he ran! The Bible says that *"Elijah was afraid and ran for his life"*! (https://www.biblegateway.com/passage/?search=1+Kings+19&version=NIV1 Kings 19.3) Man, that's low!

Elijah hit the mother of all lows: *He came to a broom tree, sat down under it and prayed that he might die. "I have had enough, Lord," he said. "Take my life; I am no better than my ancestors." Then he lay down under the tree and fell asleep.* (vs. 4–5)

Life can turn on a dime. We can go from the mountaintop of success to the pit of despair with just a few shifts in circumstances. We can go from amazing strength and confidence to debilitating weakness. In those moments it may seem God has left us. *Exactly the opposite is true.* God is ready to fill us up when we are emptied out.

In Elijah's 'broom tree' moment God gave him food and sleep. Then God called him to the mountain:

> *And the word of the Lord came to [Elijah]: "What are you doing here, Elijah?"*
>
> *He replied, "I have been very zealous for the Lord God Almighty. The Israelites have rejected your covenant, broken down your altars, and put your prophets to death with the sword. I am the only one left, and now they are trying to kill me too."*
>
> *The Lord said, "Go out and stand on the mountain in the presence of the Lord, for the Lord is about to pass by."*
>
> *Then a great and powerful wind tore the mountains apart and shattered the rocks before the Lord, but the Lord was not in the wind.*
>
> *After the wind there was an earthquake, but the Lord was not in the earthquake.*
>
> *After the earthquake came a fire, but the Lord was not in the fire.*
>
> *And after the fire came a gentle whisper. When Elijah heard it, he pulled his cloak over his face and went out and stood at the mouth of the cave.* (1 Kings 19.9–13, emphasis mine)

Earth, wind and fire . . . we live in a cacophony of sound. Just look at a cable news channel. On the television screen are multiple inputs of information—a talking head, pictures, tickers, sidebars, etc. Unbelievable!

God is not in this noise. His voice is *above* and *beneath* and *beyond* the noise.

God wants to guide you. He longs to show you the way. The key is to be still and listen for his gentle whisper. The key is to be still and listen for his *above and beneath and beyond voice.* If you are under the broom tree wishing you had never been born, *you can expect God to speak to you.*

When he does, you can be amazed but don't be surprised. His conversation with us is to be the norm, not the exception.[114]

God knows your troubles. He hears your cry. He is ready to provide for you (food and sleep) and to talk with you (*after the fire came a gentle whisper*). At the right time he will give you a new mission, a new purpose for the rest of your life. And he will let you know that you are not alone.

As you read the end of Elijah's story (below), notice how God speaks to Elijah, affirming him, calling him, guiding him:

> *When Elijah heard [God's voice], he pulled his cloak over his face and went out and stood at the mouth of the cave.*
>
> *Then a voice said to him, "What are you doing here, Elijah?"*
>
> *He replied, "I have been very zealous for the Lord God Almighty. The Israelites have rejected your covenant, broken down your altars, and put your prophets to death with the sword. I am the only one left, and now they are trying to kill me too."*
>
> *The Lord said to him, "Go back the way you came, and go to the Desert of Damascus. When you get there, anoint Hazael king over Aram. Also, anoint Jehu son of Nimshi king over Israel, and anoint Elisha son of Shaphat from Abel Meholah to succeed you as prophet.*
>
> *Jehu will put to death any who escape the sword of Hazael, and Elisha will put to death any who escape the sword of Jehu. Yet I reserve seven thousand in Israel—all whose knees have not bowed down to Baal and all whose mouths have not kissed him."* (1 Kings 19.13–18)

---

[114]Dallas Willard reminds us that *God wants to be wanted, to be wanted enough that we are ready, predisposed, to find him present with us. And if, by contrast, we are ready and set to find ways of explaining away his gentle overtures, he will rarely respond with fire from heaven. More likely, he will simply leave us alone; and we shall have the satisfaction of thinking ourselves not to be gullible.* Willard, *Hearing God*, 273.

Think About It . . .

- How has God spoken to you in the past?
- What did Jesus mean when he said in John 10.27 "My sheep listen to my voice; I know them, and they follow me"?
- If you have not heard God speak to you, ask him to. Then take some time to read the Bible (his main voice to us), be still in his presence, and open your heart and mind to the possibility that he really does want to speak to you, guiding you through this storm and giving you a new purpose for your life.

Life Commitment:

I believe God wants to speak with me, guiding me through this storm into a future with a mission and a purpose.

Day 72: What You Say is Important

The Word

From the fruit of his lips a man enjoys good things, but the unfaithful have a craving for violence.
— Proverbs 13.2

Thought for the Day

What starts out as a sound, ends in a deed.
~ Abraham Joshua Herschel

It is entirely possible that you are divorced because of things you said or didn't say. In fact, it is *inevitable* that this is the case. As I look back on my marriage I know I should not have said some things. And I know that some things were never said that I most certainly should have said.

Our words are the currency of relationships. It is said that only 7% of communication is in our actual words, the rest is through body language. I really doubt that. The content of our words is critical, far beyond a mere 7%.

Gary Thomas is right when he says:

> *The mouth reveals what the heart conceals. If we allow our tongues to become God's servants, there is no end to the good God can do through us. There is no limit to the encouragement he can*

> *unleash, the number of people he can turn from their sins, and the communities he can build.*[115]

First we make our choices, then our choices make us. We can and must make good choices with our words. The power to hurt or to heal with our words is incredible.

Remember James, the Christian leader who shepherded the early church through incredible persecution? He has some things to say about the tongue:

> *The tongue is a small part of the body, but it makes great boasts. Consider what a great forest is set on fire by a small spark. The tongue also is a fire, a world of evil among the parts of the body. It corrupts the whole person, sets the whole course of his life on fire, and is itself set on fire by hell.*
>
> *All kinds of animals, birds, reptiles and creatures of the sea are being tamed and have been tamed by man, but no man can tame the tongue. It is a restless evil, full of deadly poison.*
>
> *With the tongue we praise our Lord and Father, and with it we curse men, who have been made in God's likeness. Out of the same mouth come praise and cursing. My brothers, this should not be.* (James 3.5–10)

The trouble with our words is that we always feel justified in saying them *when we say them.* Always. The fact that we often regret what we have said is proof that we are sometimes not truly justified in what we say.

Given this reality, choose to use words well in this crisis of divorce. How you and I respond is important and will shape the lives of those around us, especially our children.

A couple of thoughts to leave you with:

---

[115] Gary Thomas, *Holy Available: What If Holiness Is About More Than What We Don't Do?* (Grand Rapids: Zondervan, 2009), 75-76.

Raise your words, not your voice. It is rain that grows flowers, not thunder. (Rumi)

The secret of being boring is to say everything. (Voltaire)

Think About It . . .

- I have most regretted what I have said. My second greatest regret is what I did not say. What do you need to say?
- The Apostle James wrote, *The tongue is a small part of the body, but it makes great boasts. Consider what a great forest is set on fire by a small spark. The tongue also is a fire.* Fires cause damage but they can be put out. What fires have you started with your tongue that need to be quenched? What life-giving words do you need to say to put out those fires?

Life Commitment:

Though I feel justified when I say what I say, I know that, in retrospect, I am often not. I will think before I speak.

Day 73: You Aren't as Brilliant as You Think

The Word

He has showed you, O man, what is good. And what does the Lord require of you? To act justly and to love mercy and to walk humbly with your God.

– Micah 6.8

Thought for the Day

What it all boils down to is this: one day a man must wake up and realize, "I'm a complete dumb ass, and I'm sick and tired of being sick and tired." Mature spirituality might well begin only at that point.

~ Richard Rohr

When my son was 13-years-old he traveled with us to Tanzania. It so happened that the local Masai clan was gathering from miles around for their annual initiation ceremony. A good friend (who was Masai) invited us to the celebrations.

We arrived at the local boma (village) where we joined the men around campfires feasting on the roasted meat of freshly slaughtered cattle. Our friend explained to us that the next morning at dawn all the boys who turned 13 the year before would line up and be circumcised. The manlier the boy, the less noise he made when the knife was applied!

The next morning, back at our hotel, I greeted my 13-year-old son with a well-received salutation: *It's a good day to be an American!*

Every boy wakes up with a simple question: *Am I good enough?* The answer to that question depends entirely on where the boy lives. If he is Masai and lives in Tanzania, the question is answered by silently enduring excruciating pain. If he lives in Vanuatu, a small island nation in the middle of the South Pacific, the answer is found in diving off a 100-foot tower with vines tied around his ankles. The closer he gets to the ground without smashing into it, the more of a man he is considered to be.

The *real* answer to this question is that *apart from walking humbly with God, we are not good enough.* But we sure think we are! The proof of this is our completely culturally conditioned standards of 'manliness.'

John Calvin wrote,

> *Until God reveals himself to us, we do not think we are [persons]... we think we are gods; but when we have seen God, then we begin to feel and know what we are. Hence springs true humility, which consists in this, that a [person] make no claim for himself [herself], and depend wholly on God.*[116]

Mac Davis was right when he sang, *Oh Lord it's hard to be humble / When you're perfect in every way.*

We really are not as strong, good or as smart as we think. The sooner we realize this, the faster we can start to grow.

Thomas Keating notes that

> *The spiritual journey is not a career or a success story. It is a series of humiliations of the false self that become more and more profound. These make room inside us for the Holy Spirit to come in and heal. What prevents us from being available to God is gradually evacuated. We keep getting closer and closer to our center. Every now and then God lifts a corner of the veil and enters*

[116]John Calvin, quoted in Robert J. Wicks, *Spiritual Resilience: 30 Days to Refresh Your Soul* (Cincinnati: Franciscan Media, 2015), Kindle Location 910.

into our awareness through various channels, as if to say, "Here I am. Where are you? Come and join me.[117]

We really are not as brilliant as we think, and that's a good thing. When we come to the end of ourselves we find God waiting to get us moving into the real journey to manly success: *To act justly and to love mercy and to walk humbly with your God.*

Think About It . . .

- What is the most humiliating experience you have ever had? What did it feel like? What did you learn?
- In what ways did your culture define 'manhood'?
- In what ways does God define manhood?

Life Commitment:

I am not as smart as I think. And in the end, that's a good thing. God is smarter and stronger than me. I bow before him and submit to his greatness.

[117]Thomas Keating, *The Human Condition: Contemplation and Transformation* (New York: Paulist Press, 1999), 38.

Day 74: Between Fear and Hope

The Word

So do not fear, for I am with you; do not be dismayed, for I am your God. I will strengthen you and help you; I will uphold you with my righteous right hand.

— Isaiah 41.10

Thought for the Day

Everything can be taken from a man but one thing: the last of the human freedoms—to choose one's attitude in any given set of circumstances, to choose one's own way.

~ Viktor E. Frankl

Think about this (I realize this is a big bite, but it's worth it!):

> *Hope is a disposition of the soul to persuade itself that what it desires will come to pass, which is caused by a particular movement of the spirits, namely, by that of mingled joy and desire. And fear is another disposition of the soul, which persuades it that the thing will not come to pass.*
>
> *And it is to be noted that, although these two passions are contrary, one may nonetheless have them both together, that is, when one considers different reasons at the same time, some of which cause one to judge that the fulfilment of one's desires is a straightforward matter, while others make it seem difficult.*[118]

[118]René Descartes et al., *The Passions of The Soul: And Other Late Philosophical Writings* (Oxford: Oxford University Press, 2015), 264.

Every person lives between hope and fear. When things are going well, hope dominates your 'brain space.' When things get tough, fears can (and do) set in. Your brain is saturated by worrying thoughts provoked by fear.

Your soul is always in a tug-of-war between hope and fear. Usually these two emotions are in balance. But when something really bad or really good happens, hope and fear get out of balance. This creates a sense of disequilibrium that is unsettling to our soul.

There are two things to say about this:

First: Know deep in your soul that *God is the God of hope*, and *he will not be moved*:

> *Many are saying of me, "God will not deliver him." But you are a shield around me, O Lord; you bestow glory on me and lift up my head. To the Lord I cry aloud, and he answers me from his holy hill. I lie down and sleep; I wake again, because the Lord sustains me. I will not fear the tens of thousands drawn up against me on every side.* (Psalm 3.2–6)

God is your anchor, your rock, your foundation. He will not be moved. Though you waver between hope and fear, God will not waver. He is solid when we are not.

Second, *know that your goal is to keep moving.*

Hope and fear can paralyze your life. On one hand, if hope runs rampant, complacency and laziness can slow or halt our growth. As Descartes says, *When hope is so strong that it altogether drives out fear, its nature changes and it becomes complacency or confidence.*[119]

On the other hand, if fear completely takes over, paralysis can lead to self-destruction. Descartes writes: *When fear is so extreme that it leaves no room at all for hope, it is transformed into despair; and*

[119]Ibid.

this despair, representing the thing as impossible, extinguishes desire altogether, ***for desire bears only on possible things.***[120]

God is the critical ingredient Descartes leaves out: God is the bearer and bringer of impossible things, therefore ***all things are possible for you that fit within God's will.*** Since God is unequivocally for you and on your side, you can be sure that his will is good and right and true.[121]

When fear come crashing in, take a deep breath, pray to God for comfort, peace and wisdom, and allow him to reassure you that you will make it and you will be OK. God will do this. He *longs* to do this for you. And God will keep you moving. He will keep a dream before you that drives you to move out of complacency (from too much hope) and out of despair (when you feel like giving up).

Think About It . . .

- Are you more hopeful or more fearful right now?
- What fears are roiling around your head right now?
- What hope is God giving you?

Life Commitment:

I will always live between hope and fear. I choose to give my fears to God and allow him to replace them with hope in his good will toward me and his desire to fulfill his purpose for me.

---

[120]Ibid. Emphasis mine.

[121] *Therefore, I urge you, brothers and sisters, in view of God's mercy, to offer your bodies as a living sacrifice, holy and pleasing to God—this is your true and proper worship. Do not conform to the pattern of this world, but be transformed by the renewing of your mind. Then you will be able to test and approve what God's will is—his good, pleasing and perfect will.* (Romans 12.1-2)

Day 75: Ultimate Hope

The Word

Since, then, you have been raised with Christ, set your hearts on things above, where Christ is seated at the right hand of God. Set your minds on things above, not on earthly things. For you died, and your life is now hidden with Christ in God. When Christ, who is your life, appears, then you also will appear with him in glory.

— Colossians 3.1–4

Thought for the Day

If you don't keep the eyes of your heart focused on the paradise that is to come, you will try to turn this poor fallen world into the paradise it will never be.

~ Paul David Tripp

A good friend of mine who had been through a hard time once told me, *If you don't have Jesus, this world is as good as it gets. If you do have Jesus, this world is as bad as it gets.*

If this world is all there is, *all your happiness depends on how things are going for you now* because now is all you have. Whatever future you have is limited by death, so you are driven to wring out of life all that you can while you can. The clock is ticking.

Charles Darwin wrote, *A man who dares to waste one hour of time has not discovered the value of life.*"[122] He is right. But if death ends

[122] Charles Darwin, *Life and Letters of Charles Darwin* (Rare Books Club, 2016), Kindle Location 3485.

it all, time becomes a ruthless taskmaster demanding that you get everything you can out of every minute of this life.

But if you *do* have Jesus, *this life is as bad as it gets* because through Jesus, *this life is not all there is.* In fact, because of Jesus, we have an eternity of problem-free living waiting for us!

Divorce puts an end to many dreams. At the very least, divorce slows life to a crawl. As you emerge from this dark place, you may resent the time you lost as you experience the pain of shattered dreams. If you believe this life is all there is, your resentment and anger will grow into bitterness because of lost time.

But if you believe in heaven, if you believe the best is yet to be, you will be able to bear the losses with patience and grace. I am not saying this is easy, but it is true that heaven gives you an amazing hope. Heaven frees us from the tyranny of having to get it all now. Heaven gives us room and freedom to live on earth.

Heaven is our ultimate hope. Heaven is forever and it is good. Heaven is home.

Think About It . . .

- What do you believe about heaven?
- What would change in your thinking, emotions and actions today if you really believed that this life is not all there is, that there is an amazing heaven waiting for you?

Prayer:

God, deliver me from the tyranny of time. Let heaven settle deep in my soul. Let heaven give me room to breathe, space to live as fully as I can now on earth, knowing that true life awaits me in eternity.

Day 76: Thin Skin, Hard Heart Or...

The Word

When [Jesus] saw the crowds, he had compassion on them, because they were harassed and helpless, like sheep without a shepherd.

— Matthew 9.36

Thought for the Day

[God] will use the brokenness of the world that is your present address to complete the loving work of personal transformation that he has begun.

~ Paul David Tripp

It's crazy how our culture glorifies people who have a *thin skin* and *hard heart.* Movies and TV celebrate 'tough guys' who take quick and violent action against anyone who slightly provokes them. Their 'toughness' is measured in how violently they respond to the slightest offense rather than their ability to absorb offenses without being rattled.

Thin-skinned people are easily provoked. A simple phrase or look can offend them. Everything is about them so anything or anyone who makes them uncomfortable in any way *gets under their skin.* They wear their feelings on their sleeve, which means that everyone knows what they are feeling, which is usually anger at some offense.

Thin-skinned people have a hard heart. Since they believe they are the center of the universe they lack the ability to put themselves in the other's shoes. They can't envision what it is like to be the other person because their imagination is limited to their own narrow lives.

Thin-skinned, hard-hearted people are usually angry, resentful, and bitter. And they let the world know it because they don't care how their words fall on others. Though they are easily offended, they believe others should not be. Thin-skinned, hard-hearted people believe they should be allowed to criticize everyone else. But when criticized, thin-skinned, hard-hearted people react with disbelief, anger and hostility. They can dish it out but they can't take it.

Thin-skinned, hard-hearted people believe they are powerful and that their angry outbursts show them to be so. In reality, however, thin-skinned, hard-hearted people have given their power away to others.

Thin-skinned, hard-hearted people are the opposite of self-differentiated. Their thoughts, emotions and actions are completely controlled by what other people think, feel, say and do. They believe that they are controlling others when, in fact, they are controlled *by* others.

Jesus was not like this. Jesus had a thick skin, that is, he was able to hear what others said and then respond (or not respond) according to what God the Father wanted, not according to his own wants or desires.

For example, during this trial before Pilate, Jesus fearlessly spoke truth to power. At the same time, he allowed Pilate to send him to the cross for crimes he didn't commit because Jesus knew that his death would bring life to us.

Jesus' thick skin allowed him to take what others were dishing out against him. At the same time, his soft heart drove him to act with complete compassion toward those who were hurting.

We are to be like Jesus, not Charlie Sheen. We are to be like Jesus, not the Godfather.

Divorce is a radical assault on our soul. It slams through our skin and slashes our heart. If left unchecked, the wounds of divorce can make our skin thinner and our hearts harder.

This is your moment to allow God to transform your thin skin and hard heart. God can thicken up your skin and soften your heart. Everything in you right now is reinforcing the old thin-skinned, hard-hearted person you were. Push back on that. Surrender to God's work of transformation. Let him toughen up your skin and soften your heart.

Think About It . . .

- How thin is your skin? How hard is your heart? You can measure both by simply thinking about what you *think*, how you *feel* and what you *do* when you are criticized.
- What would change in your life if you were more like Jesus—thick-skinned and soft-hearted?

Prayer:

God, show me where my skin is thin and my heart is hard. I want you to thicken my skin and soften my heart.

Day 77: Weak Enough, Strong Enough

The Word

This is how we know what love is: Jesus Christ laid down his life for us. And we ought to lay down our lives for our brothers.

— 1 John 3.16

Thought for the Day

Love must be learned, and learned again and again; there is no end to it. Hate needs no instruction, but waits only to be provoked.

~ Katherine Anne Porter

A few days ago I mentioned the various ways cultures define manhood. In Boston it's about brains. In Kyle, Texas, it's about having the biggest, baddest truck in the parking lot. Modern western cultures define manhood in terms of power—the more the better.

Football fans know about power. That hit in 2006 when Sheldon Brown (Philadelphia Eagles) laid it on rooky Reggie Bush (New Orleans Saints)? Or the Jason Varitek-Alex Rodriguez Brawl of 2004? Or Scott Stevens, NHL's one-man wrecking crew? We think these guys are powerful.

Male images of power almost always involve a man *powering over* somebody or something.

That's not the Jesus way. Don't get me wrong. Jesus was powerful. He was the most powerful human walking the earth when his sandaled feet cruised through Israel. He could stop wind and waves and blabbing idiots with his words. He could walk for untold miles and lay his head down for a good sleep anywhere. He could take the flesh-ripping lashing of the Romans and still keep going.

But the deeper power of Jesus was not in his powering over others but in his willingness to be weak enough to be strong enough to truly love.

Jesus was a warrior. But he was the perfect warrior. He fought the right *enemy* at the right *time against* the right *people for* the right *people* with the right *weapon* with the right *strength* and the *perfect motive.*

Sometimes the power of Jesus was to physically power over the enemy. The cleansing of the Temple comes to mind. He handily overturned the tables of the money changers and cleared the courtyard. But usually Jesus demonstrated his power through what the world would perceive as weakness.

Are you weak enough and yet strong enough to love? Perhaps a better way to look at this is to substitute the world 'weak' with 'tender.' Are you tender enough and yet strong enough to love? Are you tender enough to have an open heart, to have the confidence to express sympathy and compassion toward another? Are you strong enough to have an identity that can push against the tough guy persona our world loves so much?

Think About It . . .

- If you could have any super power, what would it be?

- How do you respond when someone powers over you?

- When have you used raw power to get your way? How did that feel?

- When have you expressed your strength through tenderness? What was the result?

- Who in your life needs your strength expressed through tenderness?

Prayer:

God, show me where I have used power to my advantage. Help me be strong enough to be weak (tender) enough to really love those in my life.

Day 78: God Restores

The Word

And the God of all grace, who called you to his eternal glory in Christ, after you have suffered a little while, will himself restore you and make you strong, firm and steadfast. To him be the power for ever and ever. Amen.

— 1 Peter 5.10–11

Thought for the Day

Fell sorrow's tooth doth never rankle more
Than when he bites, but lanceth not the sore.[123]

~ Shakespeare
The Life and Death of Richard the Second
ACT I, SCENE III.

Divorce is about loss. Whether you are the primary cause or not, divorce results in devastating costs. Is it possible to regain what has been lost?

Our English word *restore* comes from the French—from *re* which means *back again* and *stauro* which means *to stand, to be firm.*[124]

Divorce knocks us off our feet. In the old days, to be knocked to the ground in battle was the quickest way to death. For a warrior to

---

[123] *Sorrow hurts most when you treat the pain it creates without curing the cause.* http://nfs.sparknotes.com/richardii/page_46.html

[124] *"Restore," Online Etymology Dictionary*, accessed July 19, 2017, http://www.etymonline.com/index.php?allowed_in_frame=0&search=restore. Our English word *restaurant* comes from the same root as our word, *restore*, and means *food that restores.*

live, he had to get back up on his feet. God will do this for you—he will pick you up and restore you to a position of strength stronger than you were before.

Don't take my word from it. Consider these promises from God's Word:

> *And the God of all grace, who called you to his eternal glory in Christ, after you have suffered a little while, will himself restore [mend] you and make you strong [stable], firm [to make strong of soul and body so you can stand up] and steadfast [to establish].* (1 Peter 5.10–11, AMP)

> *Though you have made me see troubles, many and bitter, you will restore my life again; from the depths of the earth you will again bring me up. You will increase my honor and comfort me once again.* (Psalm 71:20–21)

> *I will repay you for the years the locusts have eaten—the great locust and the young locust, the other locusts and the locust swarm—my great army that I sent among you. You will have plenty to eat, until you are full, and you will praise the name of the Lord your God, who has worked wonders for you; never again will my people be shamed. Then you will know that I am in Israel, that I am the Lord your God, never again will my people be shamed.* (Joel 2.25–27)

> *"But I will restore you to health and heal your wounds," declares the Lord, "because you are called an outcast, Zion for whom no one cares."* (Jeremiah 30.17)

> *Instead of their shame my people will receive a double portion, and instead of disgrace they will rejoice in their inheritance; and everlasting joy will be theirs.* (Isaiah 61.7)

> *Return to your fortress, O prisoners of hope; even now I announce that I will restore twice as much to you.* (Zechariah 9.12)

> *The Lord is my shepherd, I shall not be in want. He makes me lie down in green pastures, he leads me beside quiet waters, he restores my soul.* (Psalm 23.1–3)

Does God automatically restore what we have lost? The answer is no. What are the conditions, then, for restoration?

The following verses show us:

Repent*, then, and turn to God, so that your sins may be wiped out, that times of refreshing may come from the Lord, and that he may send the Christ, who has been appointed for you—even Jesus. He must remain in heaven until the time comes for God to restore everything, as he promised long ago through his holy prophets.* (Acts 3.19–21)

> God wants us to come to him in humility and submit to his Lordship. Just as a train must submit to the rails to run free and do what trains do best, so we willingly 'place' ourselves on God's 'rails' in order to move forward. For a more thorough explanation of how to come to God, go to Appendix F.

After Job had prayed for his friends*, the Lord made him prosperous again and gave him twice as much as he had before.* (Job 42.10)

> Part of our restoration will be moving forward in the process of forgiveness. Job had some friends who were unhelpful to him in his time of need. When Job forgave them, God was free to move forward toward Job's restoration.

But ***seek first his kingdom and his righteousness****, and all these things will be given to you as well.* (Matthew 6:33)

> As you give yourself to God your priorities will change. The things of God will become primary in your life. God's Kingdom will become your first focus. As that happens, the things of earth will grow less important, and you will know and experience God's gracious provision for your every earthly need.

The next few days we will talk about how you can regain what you lost through your divorce. It all begins with your willingness to allow God to lead you: *Our response to God determines His response to us.*[125]

[125]Henry Blackaby and Richard Blackaby, *Experiencing God Day-By-Day* (Nashville:

Kristin Armstrong has these hopeful words for us: *God will restore your life. In all the ways you think you need it, and in intimate areas where you aren't even aware of your need.*[126]

Think About It . . .

- What have you lost?
- What do you expect God to restore to you?
- What steps do you need to take to make room in your life for God to work? How do you place yourself on God's 'rails' so your train can move freely and fast, fulfilling your purpose?

Prayer . . .

Restore to me the joy of your salvation and grant me a willing spirit, to sustain me. (Psalm 51.12)

B&H Publishing, 2006), Kindle Location 3450.

[126] Armstrong, *Happily Ever After*, Kindle Location 3377.

Day 79: Regaining Your Footing

The Word

Therefore, my dear brothers, stand firm. Let nothing move you. Always give yourselves fully to the work of the Lord, because you know that your labor in the Lord is not in vain.

— 1 Corinthians 15.58

Thought for the Day

If you have an unsatisfied heart now, outward accomplishments won't change a thing. Know who you are on the inside and what God has done to make you who you are. That's where your identity comes from. Who you are is not a vocational question. Your identity is defined by the God who made you, and it doesn't change with circumstances.

~ Tony Dungy

It was 1992, the Barcelona Olympics. British runner Derek Redmond started off strong in the 400 meter semi-finals, but at the 150-meter mark his hamstring ripped. Pain drove him to the ground. As the medical crew approached to carry him from the track, Redmond waved them off, deciding that even if he limped across the finish line dead last, he *would* finish. In that moment he says that he thought to himself, *I remembered where I was—the Olympics—and I knew I had to finish.*

Redmond stood up and started hobbling down the track. It was then that his dad, Jim Redmond, ran onto the track, pushing past a security guard to get to his son. Father and son finished the race,

Derek leaning on his father's shoulder for support. The crowd, 65,000 strong, jumped to their feet, cheering on father and son.

You may feel you are down on the track with your dreams shattered, your soul ripped to shreds, and no hope of finishing. In this moment *remember* ***where*** *you are and* ***who*** *you are and* ***who God your Father is.***

You are God's son, a trophy of his grace, a man of God who has a mission to accomplish, a purpose to fulfill.

God is there, next to you, hand outstretched, to lift you back to your feet and get you to the finish line.

Derek Redmond says that as his dad helped him toward the finish line, his father said to him, *Don't worry, you've got nothing to prove, you are a champion to us, we'll be back to do this together.* I can't think of any words I would want to hear more from my dad if I were limping along the track dead last in front of 65,000 people.

God says the same to you: *Don't worry, you've got nothing to prove, you are a champion to us, we'll be back to do this together.*[127]

Ask God to give you strength to get back on your feet. Ask God to give you a steady hand to right yourself as you stand. Ask God to point you in the right direction. And ask God to give you a shoulder to lean on as you head toward the finish line.

There was no prouder man in Barcelona than Jim Redmond on the day he helped his son across the finish line. God feels the same about you.

Think About It . . .

- In your mind picture the entire race Derek Redmond ran that day. Where are you on that race? At the starting line? Hurtling down the first 150 meters? Or down on the track in agony trying to decide what to do? Limping along alone toward the finish line? Leaning on dad's shoulder as you move down the track?

- Where does God fit into your race?

[127]Watch this video to hear Redmond explain that day: https://www.youtube.com/watch?v=kjkBPthoYVg

- What do you believe God is saying to you right now?

Life Commitment . . .

I commit to crossing the finish line. I may be slow and a bit gimpy, but I will cross the finish line with God at my side.

Day 80: Regaining Your Hope

The Word

May the God of hope fill you with all joy and peace as you trust in him, so that you may overflow with hope by the power of the Holy Spirit.

— Romans 15.13

Thought for the Day

Hope in the Christian's life is not wishful thinking. It is confident expectation.

~ Henry Blackaby

Hope is a hard and strange and marvelous thing. On one hand, we must live in what we call the 'real' world, that is, the world where pain really hurts, decisions have consequences, and the future seems up for grabs.

On the other hand, the Christian lives in the *really* real world. He/she knows that this is not a WYSIWYG world (see Day 54)—what seems permanently devastating can be used by God in amazing ways to turn around our lives and circumstances.

God is not surprised by our circumstances, he loves us, he is for us, he died and rose again to be with us is. But this radical hope in a materially invisible God is sometimes challenging to maintain through hard times.

The writer of Psalm 43 demonstrates the emotional roller-coaster of living through tough times while still grounding his hope in God:

Vindicate me, O God, and plead my cause against an ungodly nation; rescue me from deceitful and wicked men.

You are God my stronghold.

Why have you rejected me? Why must I go about mourning, oppressed by the enemy?

Send forth your light and your truth, let them guide me; let them bring me to your holy mountain, to the place where you dwell.

Then will I go to the altar of God, to God, my joy and my delight. I will praise you with the harp, O God, my God.

Why are you downcast, O my soul? Why so disturbed within me?

Put your hope in God, for I will yet praise him, my Savior and my God. (Psalm 43:1–5)

Let's walk through this Psalm. The Psalmist is hurting. He has been falsely accused and the cost has been high. Real life is incredibly painful for him in the moment. For you and me, divorce has caused real pain and huge losses. But then, is not God still God? The writer thinks so. He emphatically states: *You are God my stronghold.*

But the question remains: Why all this pain? The writer does what we do—he swings between anger and hope, frustration with God and radical reliance upon him:

Why have you rejected me? Why must I go about mourning, oppressed by the enemy? Send forth your light and your truth, let them guide me; let them bring me to your holy mountain, to the place where you dwell.

The writer then imagines himself further down the road. The pain is less and God is victorious:

Then will I go to the altar of God, to God, my joy and my delight. I will praise you with the harp, O God, my God.

The writer then reflects back on his previous thoughts and admonishes himself with these words:

> *Why are you downcast, O my soul? Why so disturbed within me? Put your hope in God, for I will yet praise him, my Savior and my God.*

If your emotions are swinging wildly between amazing hope and despair, you are not alone. Everyone swings between hope and despair (See Day 74). The difference between those with God and those without is that ***those whose hope is in God come back from the brink of despair to rest in God***. We settle our souls in God and find him a place of amazing refuge, comfort, strength and enduring hope.

Eugene Peterson writes,

> *Without hope a person has basically two ways to respond to the future, with wishing or with anxiety. Wishing looks to the future as a fulfillment, usually miraculous, of desire. It expends its energy in daydreaming and fantasy. Anxiety looks to the future as a demonstration of inadequacy—present weakness is projected to the point of disaster.*
>
> *Hope is a response to the future that has its foundation in the promises of God. It looks at the future as time for the completion of God's promise. It refuses to extrapolate either desire or anxiety into the future, but instead believes that God's promise gives the proper content to it.*[128]

Your future belongs to God. Wishful thinking will not deliver you out of your troubles and, instead, set you up for unrealistic expectations. Anxiety will take energy away from what you need to do now. Instead of dreaming about a blissful future or losing yourself in anxiety, *lean back into God. Settle your hope upon him* and *expect him to do amazing things.*

---

[128]Peterson, *God's Message for Each Day: Wisdom from the Word of God* (Nashville: Thomas Nelson, 2006), 233.

Why are you downcast, O my soul? Why so disturbed within me? Put your hope in God, for I will yet praise him, my Savior and my God.

Think About It . . .

- Are you living in a fantasy world or, at the other extreme, overcome by anxiety?
- What does resting in God look like to you? How has God helped you so far? What do you expect God to do in your future?

Prayer . . .

Lord God, only you can deliver me out of my troubles. My hope is in you, and my promise is that you get all the praise when you deliver me out of this mess.

Day 81: Regaining Your Strength

The Word

Do you not know? Have you not heard? The Lord is the everlasting God, the Creator of the ends of the earth. He will not grow tired or weary, and his understanding no one can fathom. He gives strength to the weary and increases the power of the weak.
Even youths grow tired and weary, and young men stumble and fall; but those who hope in the Lord will renew their strength. They will soar on wings like eagles; they will run and not grow weary, they will walk and not be faint.

— Isaiah 40:28–31

Thought for the Day

It is not the critic who counts; not the man who points out how the strong man stumbles, or where the doer of deeds could have done them better. The credit belongs to the man who is actually in the arena, whose face is marred by dust and sweat and blood; who strives valiantly... who at the best knows in the end the triumph of high achievement, and who at the worst, if he fails, at least fails while daring greatly.

~ Teddy Roosevelt

Life is hard enough as it is. Just the day-to-day regimen of work, family life and attention to personal needs takes an enormous investment of energy. At the time of my divorce I was using 110% of my energy. Then came the news that fateful Friday afternoon. The next weeks and months would see my available energy drop to half or less of what it had been. Divorce sucks the energy out of your life.[129]

Logistically, energy must be diverted to figuring out the legal and financial aspects of this new reality.

Emotionally, whether you wanted it or not, anxiety, worry and despair take the wind out of your sails. Just when you need *more* energy to meet enormous challenges, your energy level drops dramatically. Charles Spurgeon said, *Anxiety does not empty tomorrow of its sorrows, but only empties today of its strength.*[130] No truer words could be said.

When divorce comes into your life, here are some tips on wisely investing the energy you have and working to get your strength back:

- *Invest in time with God.* Spending time with God will give you energy, not take it away. Getting up an hour earlier to be with God will *not* make you more tired. Your true strength comes from God. Time with him will put energy *into* you, not take it away.

- *Lower your expectations of what you can accomplish.* No one expects a patient who just had open-heart surgery to run a marathon the next day. Or week. Or year. Dial back what you expect to get accomplished. This will most likely *not* be the most productive time in your life. That's OK. As you heal, strength will return. There will be times of amazing productivity in the future. It is winter, now, however, not spring.

---

[129] Grissom and Leonard note that, *Ideally, the amount of energy you expend each day is equally balanced across the physical, emotional, mental, and spiritual aspects of your life. But during and after a separation or divorce, your energy distribution is much different. As much as 85 percent of your energy can be diverted to dealing with the emotional upheaval, leaving only 15 percent to deal with all your physical, mental, and spiritual demands.* Steve Grissom & Kathy Leonard, *Divorce Care: Hope, Help, and Healing During and After Your Divorce* (Nashville: Thomas Nelson, 2005), 43.

[130] Quoted in Wayne Cordeiro, *Leading on Empty: Refilling Your Tank and Renewing Your Passion* (Minneapolis, MN: Bethany House, 2009), Kindle Location 835.

- *Invest in your children.* Divorce takes energy away from kids and puts it squarely on adults. Your kids are hurting and now, more than ever, need your attention. Don't rail about your spouse to them. Love them, listen to them, hug them. (See Day 24)

- *You must keep working*, so think about what you must do at work to get you by. When you are working, *work*. Concentrate, focus, get the job done. Don't waste time at work worrying about your personal life.

- As painful and distasteful as it is, *invest concentrated energy on the legal and financial aspects* of divorce. Bear down and focus. Push through.

- *Exercise.* I can't emphasize enough how sweating will give you energy. Don't go for the marathon, just move your body some every day. A little goes a long way. (See Day 31)

- *Sleep.* A common experience for the newly divorced is to want to curl up in bed and escape through sleep. This is normal since your mind is working hard to process all that is happening. Sleep, but don't sleep too much. If you *just* want to sleep that could be a sign of depression. You will need more sleep but not too much. (See Day 30)

- *Don't waste your energy* or *money* on anxiety, drugs, alcohol, pornography, buying stuff or escaping to the Caribbean. That's stupid and only makes things worse. *Don't make things worse.*

Pastor Wayne Cordeiro writes:

> *Each of us has a finite amount of energy to invest each day, and how we invest that will make all the difference . . .. I measure my energy in bursts or pockets of energy. I have found that I have about seven bursts of energy each day that I can invest. I must choose wisely where and when to invest these pockets of life vitality,*

because (as the used-car dealer says on the TV ads) when they're gone, they're gone.[131]

You *will* get your strength back. It will take some time but you will be strong again. Invest the energy you have now wisely.

Think About It . . .

- How is your energy level?
- What things deserve your pockets of energy right now?
- What can you quit doing or leave off your schedule?

Prayer . . .

God, I am beat. Restore to me my strength. Let me draw upon you and invest what you give me in what matters most.

[131] Ibid., Kindle Location 1653.

Day 82: Regaining Your Financial Health

The Word

I know what it is to be in need, and I know what it is to have plenty. I have learned the secret of being content in any and every situation, whether well fed or hungry, whether living in plenty or in want. I can do everything through him who gives me strength.... And my God will meet all your needs according to his glorious riches in Christ Jesus.

— Philippians 4.12–13, 19

Thought for the Day

Wherever God sends us, He will guard our lives. Our personal property and possessions are to be a matter of indifference to us, and our hold on these things should be very loose. If this is not the case, we will have panic, heartache, and distress. Having the proper outlook is evidence of the deeply rooted belief in the overshadowing of God's personal deliverance.

~ Oswald Chambers

Divorce takes money away in amazing ways. Standards of living drop for both parties when divorce hits. This is a hard reality.

I have a good friend who was making well into the six figures when his wife divorced him. The financial impact on him was extreme as it is for all of us. Anxiety over finances can be overwhelming and depressing.

Push back on financial anxiety with these realities:

- *Know that God will provide.* The overarching theme of the Bible is that God loves us. The two most poignant and tangible ways God shows his love for us are his presence with us and his provision for us. All through the Bible we see God providing for his people, often when it looked like all resources were dried up. Pray to God for his provision. And start giving. Choose an amount to give away, and despite the seeming lack of logic in doing it, give it away. God blesses an open hand.

- *Remember that loss is part of everyone's life.* You may have believed that your financial trajectory would always be up and to the right on the chart. You worked hard, you saved, you invested. Divorce takes much of that away and this can really hurt. Know this: financial reversals for many reasons are part of nearly everyone's life. They survived and so will you.

- *This is an opportunity to evaluate what is important.* Money is king in our culture. I'm convinced that our culture esteems a rich scoundrel over a poor saint. That's the world's view. God's view is that he owns every single resource and he can give and take away at will. He will not leave us without, but he also wants us to give careful consideration to our money and other resources.[132]

- *Follow God's path for you.* If you submit to the Lordship of Christ in your life, your financial picture may look very different in the future, but if Christ is Lord of your life, *whatever your finances are, you will be happy and satisfied.* Trust in God to provide.

---

[132]Patrick Morley reminds us that *All the benefits of prosperity are temporal. All the risks of prosperity are eternal. No matter how affluent and influential we become in the prosperous, material world, we will not find eternal profit from temporal kingdoms. Despite all our prosperity, we must still come daily to the foot of the Cross of the Lord Jesus Christ to inherit an eternal kingdom.... Tread lightly in temporal kingdoms, for all our plans will come to an end, and then we die. The only profit that matters is an eternal one.* Patrick Morley, *Devotions for The Man in The Mirror* (Grand Rapids: Zondervan, 2015), Kindle Location 174.

Carefully and prayerfully consider what Jesus said,

> *Therefore I tell you, do not worry about your life, what you will eat or drink; or about your body, what you will wear. Is not life more important than food, and the body more important than clothes? Look at the birds of the air; they do not sow or reap or store away in barns, and yet your heavenly Father feeds them. Are you not much more valuable than they? Who of you by worrying can add a single hour to his life?*
>
> *And why do you worry about clothes? See how the lilies of the field grow. They do not labor or spin. Yet I tell you that not even Solomon in all his splendor was dressed like one of these. If that is how God clothes the grass of the field, which is here today and tomorrow is thrown into the fire, will he not much more clothe you, O you of little faith?*
>
> *So do not worry, saying, 'What shall we eat?' or 'What shall we drink?' or 'What shall we wear?' For the pagans run after all these things, and your heavenly Father knows that you need them. But seek first his kingdom and his righteousness, and all these things will be given to you as well. Therefore do not worry about tomorrow, for tomorrow will worry about itself. Each day has enough trouble of its own.* (Matthew 6.25–34)

The key is to lay it all before God, seeking his will first.

Think About It . . .

- How has God provided for you in the past?
- What are your chief financial concerns right now?
- Pray to God, giving your financial worries to him. Ask him to re-order your priorities. Ask him to give you strength to follow his plan for your money.

Life Commitment . . .

I commit my financial concerns to God, expecting him to meet all my needs but not all my wants. I ask him to help me know the difference.

Day 83: Regaining Your Standing with Your Kids

The Word

He will turn the hearts of the fathers to their children, and the hearts of the children to their fathers; or else I will come and strike the land with a curse.

— Malachi 4:6

Thought for the Day

In my career, there's many things I've won and many things I've achieved, but for me, my greatest achievement is my children and my family. It's about being a good father, a good husband, just being connected to family as much as possible.

~ David Beckham

I GAVE MYSELF AS MUCH AS POSSIBLE to my children. Divorce suddenly ripped one of them away from me just at the time in life I believed he needed me most. Divorce left my two older children wondering what happened to their family and who I was as a dad and husband. Being a good husband and father were high values to me. Divorce seemed to tell my children and the world that I had failed on both counts. That was a huge blow.

As the pain of divorce ripped through me I was angry. It was difficult not to express that anger to my children. Because I was ambushed by my ex-wife I wasn't given the opportunity for any discussion with her or with my children. I was suddenly left without wife and the one child remaining at home was now gone with her. I had to do something, say something. Your situation is different, but the confusion is the same. Now, imagine being one of your kids. They are struggling with the same turbulence and confusion as you are.

I don't know your situation with your children. What I *do* know is that your kids need you to do these things for them:

- *Love your kids.* One of the most painful results of divorce is the separation of children from their parents. Our kids are hurting *but they probably won't show it.* Most kids can't express their emotions with words (most of us adults can't either!). Children go silent. Adults misinterpret this silence. When asked how their kids are doing, most couples will say that their children are 'handling it really well.' Their evidence for this assessment is that their children aren't saying much. The kids aren't saying much because they are hurting inside! They are as lost, confused, disoriented and wounded as anyone else. Your children NEED YOUR LOVE, understanding, attention, and lots of hugs. Put yourself in their shoes and love accordingly.

- *Assure your kids that this is not their fault.* It is common for children to blame themselves. Go overboard in assuring them the divorce is not their fault. And it is NOT their fault. Adults caused this disaster. The adults need to own it.

- *Be willing to answer any questions your children have.* The right knowledge can help children disentangle themselves from the mess. Be willing to own up to your piece, give a fair assessment of your spouse's role, and then promise to move forward together.

- *Develop a new and independent relationship with each child.* As I struggled with trying to figure out how to be with my kids, especially my then 15-year-old son, a wise woman gave the following advice: *You can and need to develop an independent relationship with each of your children.* Up to this moment in my life my kids had been *our* kids. My relationship with them had always been in the deeply embedded context of their mother.

Divorce changed all that. I needed to develop a separate relationship with my children completely independent of their mother.

- *Tell them the truth.* Have enough respect for your children to tell them the truth. Our children are far more capable of receiving the truth and correctly processing it than we give them credit for. Be honest with your kids as far as is appropriate (telling your five-year-old that you had an affair and that's why mommy kicked you out is not appropriate).

- *Assure them that they will be cared for.* Children of any age are concerned that they will have a home to live in and food to eat. Assure your children that they will always have what they need.

- *Keep your promises.* Show up when you say you will and pay for what you promised to pay for. Taking your anger out on your kids through breaking promises to them is low and only hurts your kids who have been hurt enough.

As I write this I am about to embark on a four-day trip to the Texas coast with my two sons, age 16 and 26. As I prayed about this trip I asked that God would give me the best words to say throughout the trip—words of encouragement, affirmation, and blessing. I prayed God would put moments in our trip when I would be able to speak honestly about the divorce, assuring them that this was not their fault. I prayed that God would empower our time together and enable me to lead them as their father in spite of what has happened.[133]

[133]The following books are good resources for helping your kids through divorce: John W. James, Russell Friedman and Leslie Matthews, *When Children Grieve: For Adults to Help Children Deal with Death, Divorce, Pet Loss, Moving, and Other Losses* (San Francisco: HarperCollins, 2001); Jean McBride, *Talking to Children About Divorce: A Parent's Guide to Healthy Communication at Each Stage of Divorce: Expert Advice for Kids' Emotional Recovery* (San Antonio: Althea Press, 2016).

Think About It . . .

- Think back to your childhood. What scared you? What made you anxious?
- How did the adults in your world help or hurt you when various crises came into the family?
- Take some time to really put yourself in your children's place. If you were them, what would you be thinking and feeling? What would you want your dad to *say* to you? What would you want your dad to *do* for you?
- Make a plan. Plan when you will see them, what goals you have for their relationship with you, what you will say to them, what you will do as you listen to them.
- For more help, review Day 24.

Life Commitment . . .

I commit to my children. I commit to praying for them by name every day. I commit to being fully invested in their lives by giving them undivided attention, listening to them and expressing my love for them. I realize that how they see me as their earthly father will influence their view of their Heavenly Father. I commit to representing God to them as best as I can.

Day 84: Regaining Your Manhood

The Word

Be on your guard; stand firm in the faith; be men of courage; be strong. Do everything in love.

— 1 Corinthians 16.13–14

Thought for the Day

The masculine identity in America and other Western nations is confusing, nebulous, and arbitrary, and often seems politically incorrect in modern society.

~ Bret Stephenson

Divorce is an epic fail on many levels but certainly in the area of what it means to be a man. Nothing pulls at our manhood so much as divorce. But, for whatever reason, our divorce happened. What has happened has happened. But what *will* happen is up to us.

I was once friends with a golfer on the Senior Pro Tour. I picked his brain about a lot of things, because, as we all know, golf can teach us valuable stuff about life. I asked him what he did when he hit a really bad shot. He said, *Well, Dale, I've seen men wrap golf clubs around trees in anger or walk away in disgust. But I never did that. I just figured that it was best to not worry about how the ball got there. Instead, I needed to play the ball from where it lay.*

When divorce pushes us face-down, we have choices to make. Like Derek Redmond in the 1992 Olympics, we can choose to be taken out of the race on a stretcher or we can choose to get up and move forward with God's help. Your goal from this point forward should be to be a better man, that is, to get up and move forward. Your goal should be to finish well (See Day 88).

To illustrate what this might look like for you, I pulled this quote by Brett Stephenson about the nature of manhood in our culture. As you read it, consider what makes a good man, and think about what kind of man you want to be from this point forward. If you ask God for help, he will give it. He will show you the next steps to take to either become the man he intended you to be or to regain the manhood you lost when divorce took you down.

> *The concept of masculinity in our culture has shifted dramatically over time. As we become less and less clear with each generation on what healthy masculinity is, it becomes hard to agree on what is expected of boys as they mature. Differences in just a couple of generations serve as testament to this.*
>
> *For example, in the world of movies there have always been heroes for us to identify with. Typical movie heroes of the 1940s were Bogart, John Wayne, Cary Grant, and Clark Gable. They were strong and tough, but not necessarily the biggest and baddest guys around. They often portrayed fairly ordinary men; their personification of ideal masculinity arose from their confidence, their values, and their resolve.*
>
> *Contrast that with the profile of modern heroes like Arnold Schwarzenegger in the eighties and nineties and Vin Diesel and The Rock today. The current model of a hero is truly larger than life, often assisted by technological invention such as bionics, genetic manipulation, and/or some serious weaponry. This new breed of hero, unlike those of yesteryear, is an image unattainable by the common boy who doesn't have personal trainers and mega-million-dollar computer effects to enhance him.*[134]

A random Google search for 'values of a man' yielded this result. These are worthy goals for each of us. Where we fall short, may God give us wisdom and strength to move forward.

---

[134]Bret Stephenson, *From Boys to Men: Spiritual Rites of Passage in an Indulgent Age* (Rochester, VT: Park Street Press, 2006), 25. Used with permission.

- Loyalty
- Respect
- Action
- Ambition
- Compassion
- Resilience
- Risk
- Centeredness
- Self-esteem
- Wisdom[135]

Think About It . . .

- What kind of man would your friends say you are? Your kids? Your ex-wife?
- What kind of man do you want to be a year from now? Five years?
- How do you want to be remembered?

Prayer . . .

God, give me wisdom, insight, revelation, motivation, and strength to become a better man. I answer to you first. I want to be a godly man.

---

[135]Vasco Patrício, *10 Values Every 20-Something Man Should Strive To Embody,* last updated August 6, 2015, accessed July 21, 2017, http://elitedaily.com/life/10-values-gen-y-men/635340/.

Day 85: Regaining Pride—The Right Kind!

The Word

When pride comes, then comes disgrace, but with humility comes wisdom.
— Proverbs 11.2

Thought for the Day

Failing in love is better than succeeding in pride.
~ Eugene Peterson

My first real head-on confrontation with my pride happened at 22,000 feet in a twin-engine Beechcraft King Air somewhere over Zimbabwe. Our 7-year-daughter lay on a stretcher in front of me, delirious, stomach distended with an unknown diagnosis and terrifyingly uncertain prognosis.

After graduation from seminary we had followed God's call to teach for a year in Tanzania. On Valentine's Day, 1996, Lindsey became sick to her stomach. The next 48 hours would see her condition rapidly deteriorate. We decided to drive to Nairobi for help. In Nairobi the doctors encouraged us to evacuate her by air to South Africa.

The story has a happy ending. We landed in Johannesburg where Lindsey received amazing medical care. She recovered and is now a beautiful, brilliant biologist working at a biotech startup in Boston. That's a story for another book.

Up to that moment on the plane from Nairobi to Johannesburg I was certain of my identity and proud of it. I was a newly graduated

Ph.D. who was on the cusp of what was sure to be a brilliant career as a pastor after a teaching stint in the wilds of Africa. I was full of energy, confidence, intelligence and pride. Things had gone my way and I was sure the positive trend would continue.

But as I looked with despair at my daughter on the stretcher, God hammered into me the stark reality that none of the things I was proud of in my life—none of my accomplishments, none of my schooling or experience—could help her as she lay at the brink of death. As I watched Lindsey writhe in pain on the stretcher, I was brought to my knees in humility.

Oswald Chambers reminds us that,

> *The underlying foundation of Jesus Christ's kingdom is poverty, not possessions; not making decisions for Jesus, but having such a sense of absolute futility that we finally admit, "Lord, I cannot even begin to do it." Then Jesus says, "Blessed are you . . ." (Matthew 5:11). This is the doorway to the kingdom.*[136]

Men hate this. We were born to win. We live for competition. We dream of being strong and victorious. But Jesus shows us another way. The way up is down. The way to wisdom is across the river of pain. We learn when we fall. We find God and our true strength when we fail.

Pride is the opposite of all that. But can we have any kind of pride at all?

Nehemiah was commissioned by God to lead in rebuilding the destroyed city of Jerusalem. When he first saw the city he was dismayed. Instead of being discouraged, however, he was energized.[137] He gathered the leaders and said to them, *You see the trouble we are in: Jerusalem lies in ruins, and its gates have been burned with fire. Come, let us rebuild the wall of Jerusalem, and we will no longer be in disgrace.... The God of heaven will give us success.* (Nehemiah 2:17, 20).

---

[136]Oswald Chambers, *My utmost for His Highest: Selections for The Year* (Uhrichsville, OH: Barbour and Co, 1992), 203.

[137]The story of Nehemiah is found in the Old Testament of the Bible titled *Nehemiah.* It's a quick and exciting read.

With God's command, strength and protection, the people rebuilt the walls. It was an extraordinary feat that took enormous energy and courage. Their success was due to God's help and the hard work of the people. Together, something amazing was accomplished that still inspires almost 2,500 years later.

Nehemiah had much to be proud of, but his was the right kind of pride. Thanks went to God *first* because it was God's strength supplied to his people that made the task possible. But it was also the effort of the people that built the wall.

Like Jerusalem, your life may be in shambles. But with God's help and your cooperation and energy, something new can rise from the ashes. You have been brought low, but God will not leave you there. In due season he will lift you up and together, you and God will look back on something amazing you built together. This is the right kind of pride, pride in our amazing God and what he can do through willing, available *and humble* servants.

> *Humble yourselves, therefore, under God's mighty hand, that he may lift you up in due time. Cast all your anxiety on him because he cares for you. Be self-controlled and alert. Your enemy the devil prowls around like a roaring lion looking for someone to devour. Resist him, standing firm in the faith, because you know that your brothers throughout the world are undergoing the same kind of sufferings.*
>
> *And the God of all grace, who called you to his eternal glory in Christ, after you have suffered a little while, will himself restore you and make you strong, firm and steadfast. To him be the power forever and ever. Amen.* (1 Peter 5.6–11)

Think About It . . .

- How has human pride caused you to be where you are today?
- Have you embraced the 'humbling'?
- What could God be calling you to join him to do today?

Prayer . . .

Lord God, I have been brought low. It hurts. But what would hurt more is if I waste this pain by wallowing in it. Instead, I submit to this humbling and ask you to take the pieces of my life and accomplish what you will to build your Kingdom. Whatever good comes of the rest of my life, I give you the credit and glory.

Day 86: Regaining Your Courage

The Word

Have I not commanded you? Be strong and courageous. Do not be terrified; do not be discouraged, for the Lord your God will be with you wherever you go.

— Joshua 1.9

Thought for the Day

Courage is not the absence of fear, but rather the judgment that something else is more important than fear.

~ Ambrose Redmoon

The American Heritage Dictionary says that *courage is the state or quality of mind or spirit that enables one to face danger, fear, or vicissitudes with self-possession, confidence, and resolution.*

The root of our word courage comes from the Latin *cor* which means *heart.* Your heart is your inner being, your thoughts, your desires and your will. We can have a strong heart, which means a heart that is sure, confident and leaning in the right direction. Or your heart can be weak—fearful, timid, flighty, and leaning in the wrong direction.

Painful and frightening life experiences weaken our heart. Just like a blow to the leg weakens it and makes walking difficult, so hard experiences take courage out of our hearts and make living difficult.

Discouragement takes courage out of our heart. *Encouragement* puts courage back in the heart. God wants your weakened heart to have courage. Courage comes into your heart when you believe the right things about God and about yourself.

Are you strong enough to get through this? Your answer will reveal what you believe about your sources of strength and perseverance.

Does God have your best interests in mind, making all things work for his glory, your good and the good of the world? A resounding *Yes!* to that question will put courage into your heart. A wavering or faltering *Maybe* will take courage away.

Let God put courage back into your heart. To have courage, receive and believe in a mission bigger than yourself.

Courage is not the absence of fear, but rather the judgment that something else is more important than fear. What is more important than your fear? I suggest first thinking of your kids. They are far more important than anything you can fear. I suggest thinking of the amazing good God can do in your life if you give yourself to him and the task he has for you in his Kingdom. If one life is significantly changed because of your story, isn't that one life worth pushing past this fear?

Audrey Lorde writes, *When I dare to be powerful, to use my strength in the service of my vision, then it becomes less and less important whether I am afraid.*[138]

What are you really living for? The suffering of divorce can clarify the answer to this question for you. When you have a mission and purpose bigger than yourself, courage comes flowing in!

Believe in a God big enough to accomplish his mission through you. God is far beyond anything you and I can imagine. I believe one of our first responses to arriving in heaven and seeing God's glory will be, *Why did I worry so much? Why was I so discouraged?*

Consider these passages from the Bible:

> *But God made the earth by his power; he founded the world by his wisdom and stretched out the heavens by his understanding.*

[138] "Audre Lorde Quotes." BrainyQuote, accessed July 25, 2017. https://www.brainyquote.com/quotes/quotes/a/audrelorde357287.html.

(Jeremiah 10.12)

Finally, be strong in the Lord and in his mighty power. (Ephesians 6.10)

For God did not give us a spirit of timidity, but a spirit of power, of love and of self-discipline. (2 Timothy 1.7)

Bear Grylls writes,

> *Real courage is about how we react in the face of overwhelming odds. And it is impossible to be courageous if you aren't also afraid. Courage involves facing our fears, and walking through them. It is not about having no fear, but it is about doing what is necessary despite the fear.*[139]

Let God put courage into your heart today.

Think About It . . .

- What is most frightening to you?
- How can one or more of the truths above speak against your fear?
- What action(s) do you need to take to demonstrate power over your fear?

Life Commitment . . .

I am not a coward and I will not be ruled by fear. My God will move me boldly into the future he has for me, and I want to be there with him, side-by-side.

---

[139]Bear Grylls, *A Survival Guide for Life*, 183. Reprinted by permission of Peters Fraser & Dunlop (www.petersfraserdunlop.com) on behalf of Bear Grylls.

Day 87: Occupation or Vocation?

The Word

__Fight__ the good fight of the faith. __Take hold__ of the eternal life to which you were called when you made your good confession in the presence of many witnesses. In the sight of God, who gives life to everything, and of Christ Jesus, who while testifying before Pontius Pilate made the good confession, __I charge you to keep__ this command without spot or blame until the appearing of our Lord Jesus Christ, which God will bring about in his own time—God, the blessed and only Ruler, the King of kings and Lord of lords, who alone is immortal and who lives in unapproachable light, whom no one has seen or can see. To him be honor and might forever. Amen.

— 1 Timothy 6.12-16, emphasis mine

Thought for the Day

Grace not only forgives you, but enables you to live for something hugely bigger than yourself. Why go back to your little kingdom of one?

~ Paul David Tripp

LET'S GO BACK TO OUR MISSION STATEMENT:

Men's Divorce Recovery exists to empower divorced men through support, encouragement and knowledge to __survive and thrive beyond their divorce__ to become resilient, strong and wise assets to their world.

God has something much bigger for you than just punching a clock until you can hit a little white ball around a nicely manicured lawn. He calls us to a life of risk and adventure, not for our own sakes but for the sake of the world.

Divorce may be tearing you down so God can rebuild you into the man he called you to be—a strong, confident man, given over to God and to the world he created, using your male energy for others instead of yourself.

Do you merely have an *occupation*? Or has God called you into his *vocation*? The root meaning of the word *vocation* means *voice.* You hear it in other words like *vocal.* To fulfill God's mission in your life means *hearing his voice in your life and following him into the task into which he calls you.*

How do you live in the power and energy of your *vocation* rather than merely live in the drudgery of an *occupation*?

First, *Till the Soil.*

If the farmer wants a crop in the fall he tears up the soil in the spring. God can't plant a vision, a dream, a mission into a hard, bitter, crusty heart. Take the plow to your heart. We do that by practicing the Spiritual Disciplines, the *habits of the heart* that make room for God to speak to us (see Day 5). If you plow the soil of your heart God will honor your movement toward him by speaking to you. Be patient. The farmer doesn't plow and plant on Monday and get the harvest on Friday!

Second, *Listen for God's Call.*

The call of God upon our lives is *God's call.* He initiates and invites. We don't come up with a good idea and then ask him to bless it. We don't ask God to join us in *our* mission. No, this is about God, not us. Let God speak. Expect him to speak! He has a huge mission in this world! Why would he not call you to your place in that mission?

Henry Blackaby writes:

> *The most dramatic changes in your life will come from God's initiative, not yours. The people God used mightily in Scripture were all ordinary people to whom He gave divine assignments that they never could have initiated. The Lord often took them by surprise, for they were not seeking significant mandates from God. Even so, He saw their hearts, and He knew they were trustworthy.*
>
> *The Lord may be initiating some new things in your life. When He tells you what His plans are, trust Him and walk closely with Him. Don't let the busyness of your present activity keep you from experiencing all that God has in store for you. You will see Him accomplish things through your life that you never dreamed were possible* (Eph. 3:20).[140]

Third, *Trust.*

Trust that the call is from God. God wants you to do his will. He is for you! He wants you to succeed for his glory, for your good, and for the good of the world!

Trust that he will accomplish his will through you. I heard the testimony of a man named Jimmy Heald. By all accounts, Jimmy should be dead. Growing up with drug abusing parents, his dad was murdered when Jimmy was a boy, his mom hooking. But God reached Jimmy, rescued him, and set him on a path to becoming a staff member of a large, growing new church, all in the course of a few years! Jimmy could testify from his own amazing experience: *If God is calling me to it he will see me through it.*[141]

Fourth, *Obey.*

C.S. Lewis throws down the challenge before us: *[God] is calling us. It remains with us to follow or not, to die in this winter, or to go on into*

[140]Blackaby and Blackaby, *Experiencing God Day-By-Day*, Kindle Location 3510.
[141]Sermon by Jimmy Heald, Real Life Church, Austin, Texas, 2017

that spring and that summer.[142]

Divorce brings winter, but if we wait patiently, winter turns to spring. This is *always* true in the earth, but *only* true in our lives if we plow the soil, let God plant the seed, and then obey him through the summer to the harvest. If God calls, obey. Don't hesitate.

Think About It . . .

- Have you heard God speak to you?
- Have you heard God call you to a ministry inside the church or beyond its walls?
- Consider this statement by Rick Warren: *God never wastes anything. He would not give you abilities, interests, talents, gifts, personality, and life experiences unless he intended to use them for his glory.*[143] What abilities, interests, talents, gifts, and life experiences do you have that God is calling you to use for others?

Life Commitment . . .

Life is too short to spend it on myself. I give myself to God, asking him to plant the seed of his vision for my life in my heart. I will hear and respond to him in obedience.

[142] C. S. Lewis and Walter Hooper, *The Business of Heaven: Daily Readings from the Writings of C.S. Lewis* (London: Fount, 1999), Kindle Location 1828.

[143] Rick Warren in Erik Rees, *S.H.A.P.E.: Finding and Fulfilling Your Unique Purpose for Life* (Grand Rapids: Zondervan, 2006), 6.

Day 88: Finishing Well

The Word

> *For I am already being poured out like a drink offering, and the time has come for my departure. I have fought the good fight, I have finished the race, I have kept the faith. Now there is in store for me the crown of righteousness, which the Lord, the righteous Judge, will award to me on that day—and not only to me, but also to all who have longed for his appearing.*
>
> — 2 Timothy 4.6–8

Thought for the Day

> *According to legend, the Great Plains warriors would say to their sons first thing in the morning, "It is a good day to do great things."*
>
> ~ Richard Rohr

Here's what I have observed from watching men die:

- Few men have thought about life, how they will end theirs, and if they have much to celebrate or regret. Most men, it would seem, really have lived lives of quiet desperation.[144]

[144] Henry David Thoreau wrote: *The mass of men lead lives of quiet desperation. What is called resignation is confirmed desperation. From the desperate city you go into the desperate country.... A stereotyped but unconscious despair is concealed even under what are called the games and amusements of mankind.* Henry David Thoreau, *Works of Henry David Thoreau* (Boston: MobileReference.com, 2008), Kindle Location 5599.

- Not a single man has ever said to me, *I had the best lawn in the neighborhood* or *I wish I had spent more time at the office* or *How 'bout them Cowboys?*
- Most highly successful men (high achievers such as physicians, lawyers, successful businessmen) go out kicking and screaming. They are angry that they have to die. But death is beyond their control and they hate that.
- Godly men are few and far between. These few men are gentle, humble, and full of joy when they die. They are grateful for the lives they were given and they are full of hope for the new life they know is coming.

These observations bring up important questions:

- Why do so few men think deeply about their lives?
- Why do so many men spend their lives in such trivial pursuits such as football fanaticism or having the perfect lawn?
- Why do highly successful men end life so angry?
- Why are so few men finishing well?

We've always heard that life is a journey. When we were young we believed the journey would last forever. There comes a time, however, when we know it won't. For many men that time comes in the middle of life and it comes like a train barreling down the tracks.

Perhaps you are in this moment as you face your divorce. *This is a moment all men face* whether brought on by divorce, a job loss, financial ruin, a health crisis or any number of catastrophic events.

It's at this point that you and I decide how we will finish the journey. Imagine your life 30 years from now. When you are an old man, how do you want people to think of you? What do you want to be remembered for? What kind of man do you want to be?

Most men don't think this through and consequently, most men don't finish well. Your personal disaster has given you the opportunity not to be one of those men.

At this point in the journey men have a choice to make: (1) keep trying to be 'the man,' (2) surrender to anger and cynicism, ending up a bitter old man, or (3) humble yourself before the King of kings and join him in the adventure he has for you.

If you choose to surrender to God, you will end well. Determine that at the end of the day, you will be able to say with the Apostle Paul: *I have fought the good fight, I have finished the race, I have kept the faith.*

Think About It . . .

- Are you still defining yourself by what you have, what you did (or do), and who or what you control?
- Have you given in to bitterness, determined to make it to the end with gritted teeth?
- Have you surrendered to God and heard his call upon the rest of your life?

Life Commitment:

I don't want to end up a bitter old man. I want God to use me as he sees fit, and, at the end of the day, finish well.

Day 89: Steady Strum

The Word

By the grace God has given me, I laid a foundation as an expert builder, and someone else is building on it. But each one should be careful how he builds. For no one can lay any foundation other than the one already laid, which is Jesus Christ.

— 1 Corinthians 3.10–11

Thought for the Day

The Mission of Men's Divorce Recovery is to Empower Divorced Men through Support, Encouragement and Knowledge to Survive and Thrive beyond their divorce to become Resilient, Strong and Wise Assets to their World

I've been playing the guitar for only a few years and it's been good for my soul.

As a new student to the guitar, I have realized that it takes both the left and right hands doing the right things at the right time to make good sound. But my hands do different things.

The notes established by the fingers of the left hand pushing down on the strings on the fretboard are the foundation of good sound. To make solid and clear sound, the fingers must be on the fretboard pushing down hard in the right place at the right time. No matter how great my strumming, if my fingers on the left hand are weak and/or misplaced, the sound will be muddled and out of tune.

At the same time, the right-hand strums or picks. Unlike the fingers of the left hand—which must be firm, secure, stable and tight—the right hand is free to strum or pick as the song dictates.

What is true of my guitar is true of my life. On the one hand, my life must be pushing in on the right foundation. Like the fingers of my left hand on the fretboard, I must have a firm grasp of my values, my convictions—the things in my life I am willing to die for and will not give up at any cost. I must be clear and firm about the principles, values and core truths that define the 'sound' of my life.

Some men have found it helpful to ask God to give them a personal Mission Statement. God clearly gave me mine: *My life mission is to fervently love God and people, expressing this love frequently and persevering in it forever.*

I have not always strummed well to this mission statement, but at least I have something to ground me.[145]

With my foundation firmly in place, I am free to strum or pick as life demands. Sometimes I can strum my life with a slow, steady peaceful rhythm. At other times I have to strum hard and fast to make the music that fits the moment. At other times, finessed picking sounds best. As a beginning guitarist, I'm still working on strumming. Finessed picking is sometime in my future!

As we come to the close of this devotional, think about your core truths. What are your values? Are you pushing down hard on these values? Are these truths deeply ingrained in our soul and second nature to you?

How about your strumming? Do you know when to strum slow and when to strum fast?

Think About It . . .

- Do you have a Mission Statement? If not, check out *The Purpose-Driven Life* by Rick Warren to figure out yours.

[145]For help with developing your own Mission Statement, see Rick Warren, *The Purpose-Driven Life* (Cleveland: Findaway World, 2005), 312-319.

Life Commitment:

I may not be Jimi Hendrix on a real guitar, but with God's help and the right values, I can strum well to life.

Day 90: Moving into the New Normal

The Word

When you were dead in your sins and in the uncircumcision of your flesh, God made you alive with Christ. He forgave us all our sins, having canceled the charge of our legal indebtedness, which stood against us and condemned us; he has taken it away, nailing it to the cross. And having disarmed the powers and authorities, he made a public spectacle of them, triumphing over them by the cross.

— Colossians 2.13-15

Thought for the Day

Attitude is everything—or at least a great, big piece of everything! Check your attitude as you do small tasks and then take on greater things.

~ Tony Dungy

Twice in two years I experienced moments that I knew everything changed for me, and not for the better.

The first was December 16, 2013. By the time I left what should have been a routine meeting of my church's elders, I understood that I could not trust them or my staff anymore. At that point everything I had believed in and worked so hard for radically changed. The foundation of my vocational life was shattered. The future of what I had worked so hard for was completely up for grabs.

The second came nearly two years later. On October 23, 2015, I arrived home after a two-week teaching trip to Africa only to have my wife meet me in the carport of the church parsonage and tell me she had left me. As I walked into the house I knew that my life was further radically changed. I knew that I was losing things I had worked hard to achieve. I knew the losses would pile up and would be felt for years to come. I knew that the things by which I identified myself were being stripped away before my eyes.

The journey since those moments has been like something I have never experienced. I cannot find words to wrap around the heartache and pain.

But this I know: *God has walked with me every step of this treacherous path.* Whatever was normal before is gone and can't be recovered. But with God at my side, he is moving me into a new 'normal,' whatever 'normal' is.

You can't let what has happened to you or what you have done to others stop you in your tracks now. Too much is at stake and God has so much planned for you.

Life is more like pedaling a bike uphill than it is a cruise downhill. If you are going uphill and you stop pedaling, you tump over! So... keep pedaling!

In the end, I want to be able to say with the Apostle Paul: *I have fought the good fight, I have finished the race, I have kept the faith.* (2 Timothy 4:7)

Think About It . . .

- What is 'normal' to you?
- How has your life been turned upside-down?
- What could a new 'normal' look like to you?
- What steps do you need to take today to move into the future God has for you?

Life Commitment:

God is for me. He has a future for me that includes a deeper, richer, more profound life. I want to live for him and eternity rather than for myself and this brief life on earth. I want to fight the good fight, finish the race, keep the faith.

Day 91: The Next Right Thing

The Word

In all my prayers for all of you, I always pray with joy because of your partnership in the gospel from the first day until now, being confident of this, that he who began a good work in you will carry it on to completion until the day of Christ Jesus.

– Philippians 1:4-6

Thought for the Day

Perhaps it's not such a bad thing to come to the end of your rope if at the end of your rope you find a strong and willing Savior.

~ Paul David Tripp

You will find yourself at your wits' end but at the beginning of God's wisdom. When you come to your wits' end and feel inclined to panic—don't! Stand true to God and He will bring out His truth in a way that will make your life an expression of worship.

~ Oswald Chambers

With time, great good can come from great sorrow.

~ Desmond Tutu

Every spiritual problem has an individual genesis and therefore requires an individual exodus.
~ Gary Thomas

AHHH, WHAT A TIME IN WHICH TO LIVE! Everything seems to be getting stronger and lighter with so many choices it leaves the head spinning! One such product caught my attention recently: Duct Tape.

Duct tape was the brainchild of Vesta Stoudt, mother of two Navy sailors in World War II. Working in a factory making ordnance, she had the idea for duct tape as a way to seal ammo boxes so that the boxes would stay closed but could also be easily opened during battle.

She wrote the President who forwarded her idea to the War Production Board. They sent it to Johnson & Johnson who developed duct tape.[146] Today duct tape comes in so many colors and patterns it boggles the mind. Not only is it strong, it's pretty. Go figure.

Competition to produce ever-better duct tape is fierce. I recently saw one such product: T-Rex Duct Tape. I haven't bought any yet but I probably will before the zombie apocalypse. It pays to be prepared.

What caught my eye about the T-Rex Duct Tape ad was its tag line: *T-Rex Ferociously Strong Tape . . . All Weather, Works Longer, Holds Stronger.*

Guys, I want to be like T-Rex Duct Tape: *Ferociously Strong, All Weather, Works Longer, Holds Stronger.*

In the end, this is who God calls us to be: *Ferociously Strong, All Weather, Working Longer, Holding Stronger.*

The circumstances of my life caused me to change residences five times in 38 months, and this for a guy who really likes to hang out in the same place forever! In my last move I ran across a box that had been sealed long ago with duct tape. The gray plastic top layer was either faded to white or completely gone. The fabric showed underneath. But it was still holding.

The grind of life can weather us. Traumatic events like divorce can rip us apart. But in the end, we want to be *Ferociously Strong, All Weather, Working Longer, Holding Stronger.*

---

[146] *Duct tape*, Wikipedia. July 28, 2017, accessed August 11, 2017. https://en.wikipedia.org/wiki/Duct_tape.

By now this truth has sunk into you: Whatever happens *circumstantially* in your life is secondary to what is going on *spiritually*. And above all, by now you understand that what God wants—more than anything—is for ***you to come to him so he can invade your soul and grow you into the man he calls you to be.***

Circumstances are what they are. I certainly didn't want to lose two churches and a wife in 18 months. In fact, I worked like heck to keep that from happening, but it happened anyway. I didn't choose to have my life turned upside-down and to lose hundreds of thousands of dollars in the process. But it happened.

What I did choose to do was to go to God. In him I found something, or rather Someone, who could never be taken away from me. I found my Heavenly Father, my *true* Father, glad to receive me, eager to comfort me, and firmly calling me into a future with him.

I know God did not cause my life to fall apart—people did. But I also know God is the pro at taking the horrible things in our lives and, with our cooperation, turning them into amazing displays of his grace, love and strength.

Tony Dungy captures this reality:

> *Have you thought about all the events that led up to this moment in your life—why you're here, how you've been shaped, what caused you to read this book or seek God's plans for your life? Have you wondered how much of it is accidental or random and how much is designed? I believe God knew exactly where you would be right now and exactly what you would be like. He knew about your passions and gifts and the platform you have. In fact, I believe He was very purposeful in designing your life. He made you to be uniquely significant and to have an eternal impact on the world around you.*[147]

When life comes crashing in we can either choose hope or despair, action or depression, life or suicide.

---

[147] Dungy and Whitaker, *The One Year Uncommon Life Daily*, Kindle Location 202.

In the introduction of this book I wrote:

> *Right now you are in pain and you are looking for relief. Know this: Our God who created a world of immense variety has many tools to get back on your feet and back in the game. And he will do it! You will get through this! But right now you are face down on the turf wondering if your playing days are over. They're not. You are God's son, and he doesn't leave his kids on the field alone and bleeding. His specialty, in fact, is taking wounded warriors and rehabilitating them into magnificent men who give back to the very world that beat them to the ground.*

My hope and prayer is that you know this reality more *now* than when you began reading this book.

Life will continue to be a challenge. As long as we have breath on this planet we will struggle. But how much better to know this world is not all there is? How much better is God's invitation into a future with him? How much better to know that God can turn your pain into promises for others? How much better to know that your life counts and can be spent doing things of eternal significance?

It all begins when we say *Yes* to God. As Henry Blackaby points out, *Our response to God determines His response to us.*[148] Have you said *yes* to God? He has already said *yes* to you! With God at your side your future is far brighter and more significant and meaningful than you can imagine!

In the old days they said . . . *Nulla tenaci invia est via . . .* (*For the tenacious, no road is impassable*).

In today's language we might say: *Ferociously Strong, All Weather, Working Longer, Holding Stronger.*

Think About It . . .

- Where are you with God?

[148]Blackaby and Blackaby, *Experiencing God Day-By-Day*, Kindle Location 3450.

- What are your next steps? See the resources and suggestions at the end of this book and on Men's Divorce Recovery website (http://www.mensdivorcerecovery.org/).

Life Commitment:

I am a wounded warrior being rehabilitated into a magnificent man who will give back to the very world that beat me to the ground. In God's strength and love, I am ferociously strong, working longer, holding stronger.

Next Steps

Men's Divorce Recovery exists to Empower Divorced Men through Support, Knowledge & Encouragement to Survive & Thrive Beyond their Divorce to Become Resilient, Strong & Wise Men.

It's one thing to get this info in your head. How do you let it soak down into your heart and out through your hands into your daily life? Try these next steps to continue your journey of hope and healing.

STAY CONNECTED to a community of men committed to finishing well despite the traumas we have been through:

MDR **WEBSITE**: MensDivorceRecovery.org

MDR **Facebook page**:
https://www.facebook.com/mensdivorcerecovery/

ATTEND AN MDR EVENT (See the website for dates & locations):

An MDR Weekend Conference.

A 6-Week Recovery Group. (Recovery groups include S-GROUPS (Survive Groups) for men in the immediate crisis of divorce and T-GROUPS (Thrive Groups) for men ready to take the next step with God)

An MDR Retreat.

An MDR week-long extended Outdoor Expedition.

KEEP PUTTING THE GOOD STUFF IN YOUR HEAD!

Read *Quick Start Guide for Divorced Men: Help & Hope* now if you haven't already.

Read the second volume of *Daily Survival Guide for Divorced Men: Surviving & Thriving Beyond Your Divorce: Book 2: Days 92-180.*

Read the newsletter and blog here:
http://mensdivorcerecovery.org/mdr-blog

Watch our Videos and listen to the podcasts on specific topics related to divorce and recovery, accessible through the website, Facebook and LinkedIn.

Go to counseling. I know this is hard but you will be rewarded for the time and money you invest in yourself, and you have potential to avoid the mistakes of your past and give a much better life to your children now and a partner in the future. Contact me for references in your area.

Men's Divorce Recovery website
http://www.mensdivorcerecovery.org/

Was this book helpful? If so, please write a review!

Here's how to write a review of this book:

1. 1. Go to the Amazon page were my book is sold under this title: *Daily Survival Guide for Divorced Men: Surviving & Thriving Beyond Your Divorce Days 1-91*
2. Under the title, click "Customer Reviews."
3. On the next page click the 'Write a Customer Review".
4. Click the number of stars you give my book... then
5. Write your review... then post it!

Thank you!

Appendix A: Suicide Risk Assessment

Words of Life

In all my prayers for all of you, I always pray with joy because of your partnership in the gospel from the first day until now, being confident of this, that he who began a good work in you will carry it on to completion until the day of Christ Jesus.

— Isaiah 41.10

The Lord is close to the brokenhearted and saves those who are crushed in spirit. A righteous man may have many troubles, but the Lord delivers him from them all.

— Psalm 34.18–19

A Good and True Thought

God's agenda is never elimination but transformation.

~ Richard Rohr

National Suicide Prevention Lifeline: 800-273-8255

Divorced or separated men have a 39% higher suicide rate than their married counterparts. They are also more likely to take part in risky activities which increases their chance of early death.[149]

[149] *Why Divorce is bad for a man's health: Separation increases the risk of early death, substance abuse, suicide and depression,* Emma Innes, last updated October 2, 2013, accessed October 20, 2017, http://www.dailymail.co.uk/health/article-2440005/Divorce-mans-health-Separation-increases-risk-death-substance-abuse-suicide-depression.html

If you have thoughts of taking your life you are not alone nor are you abnormal. I believe that the vast majority of people think of taking their own life at some point in their lives.

I know I did. For about four days a few months after my divorce was final, suicide became one of several options. What was strange about this was how casually I laid this option on the table. As I considered what to do, suicide seemed a viable choice. Death by my hand was laid out there with other options on how to escape the pain.

A newly divorced man named Philip writes:

> *As a divorced man, I can honestly say I contemplated suicide for the first time in my life during the first year or two of my separation. It's incredibly difficult to have your entire family life—children, home and wife—pulled away from you. Prior to the divorce, I was very happy, making a good salary and living in a nice neighborhood. Soon after the divorce, I was saddled with very high child support payments, debt from legal fees and barely enough left over to pay the rent of my small one bedroom apartment.*[150]

Tremendous pain is caused through divorce because divorce creates so much loss. Added to this is the fact that our society largely ignores the immense pain divorce causes. This creates more isolation for the divorced man which only increases the pain (see Appendix C). Suicide can seem like one way to escape our pain.

Edwin Shneidman writes:

> *Suicide haunts our literature and our culture. It is the taboo subtext to our successes and our happiness. The reporting of a suicide of any public figure disturbs each of us. Amid our dreams of happiness and achievement lurk our nightmares of self-destruction. Who is not mindful of the potential self-defeating elements within our own personality? Each new day contains the threat of failure and*

[150] *Why does divorce make men more suicidal than women?* Jack Cafferty, last updated March 11, 2010, accessed July 13, 2017, http://caffertyfile.blogs.cnn.com/2010/03/11/why-does-divorce-make-men-more-suicidal-than-women/.

assaults by others, but it is the threat of self-destruction that we are most afraid to touch, except in our secret moments or the hidden recesses of our minds.[151]

H. Norman Wright believes there are four main reasons for suicide:

- **Depression [Rage]**—*The person is sitting on a high level of unacceptable rage that has developed because of a series of events in life over which he or she has no control. Eventually this repressed rage is turned against himself or herself in suicide.*
- **Relief of Pain**—*Those with high levels of pain usually have three choices: a psychotic distortion that reduces the pain, drugs or alcohol, or suicide. They often say, "I don't want to die, but I don't know any other way out—I just can't stand it."*
- **Revenge**—*Some [people] feel overwhelmed by hurt or rejection from another person. Their desire to hurt back is stronger than the desire to live.*
- **Hopelessness**—*Twenty-five percent of those who commit suicide do so after giving it quiet consideration and weighing the pros and cons of living and dying.*[152]

Though there are many reasons we may want to take our lives, it is a always bad choice. The story of Kevin Hines is instructive. On September 25, 2000, Kevin jumped off the Golden Gate Bridge. He hit the water 220 feet below and lived to tell about it. He is only one of 33 people to have survived the fall among an estimated 2,000 people who have jumped.

As I read his story his words leapt out at me:

---

[151]Edwin Shneidman, *The Suicidal Mind* (Oxford: Oxford University Press, 1995), Kindle Location 60.

[152]H. Norman Wright, *The New Guide to Crisis and Trauma Counseling* (Ventura, CA: Regal Books, 2003), Kindle Locations 3120-3126.

In the midst of my free fall, I said to myself these words, words I thought no one would ever hear me repeat: "What have I done? I don't want to die. God, please save me!" As I fell, I somehow possessed the mind-set that all I wanted to do was live—by any means necessary.[153]

I wonder how many of the more than 45,000 people who take their lives every year in the United States have had the same thought the instant after they jumped or pulled the trigger or hit the tree or swallowed the pills or cut their wrists?

Teacher, author, and historian Jennifer Michael Hecht lost two friends to suicide. In her own grief she decided to research and write about it. She wrote her thoughts in a blog called "The Best American Poetry." In the blog she made an appeal to those contemplating suicide:

I want to say this, . . . Don't kill yourself. Life has always been almost too hard to bear, for a lot of the people, a lot of the time. It's awful. But it isn't too hard to bear, it's only almost too hard to bear . . .

I'm issuing a rule. You are not allowed to kill yourself. When a person kills himself, he does wrenching damage to the community. One of the best predictors of suicide is knowing a suicide. That means that suicide is also delayed homicide. You have to stay.

I'm throwing you a rope, you don't have to explain it to the monster in you, just tell the monster it can do whatever it wants, but not that. Later we'll get rid of the monster, for now just hang on to the rope. I know that this means a struggle from one second to the next, let alone one day at a time.

Don't kill yourself. Suffer here with us instead. We need you with

[153] *He jumped off the Golden Gate Bridge . . . and lived!* New York Post, last updated June 20, 2013, accessed July 13, 2017, http://nypost.com/2013/06/30/he-jumped-off-the-golden-gate-bridge-and-lived/. See also his book, Kevin Hines, *Cracked, Not Broken: Surviving and Thriving After a Suicide Attempt,* (Lanham, MD: Rowman & Littlefield Publishers, 2013).

us, we have not forgotten you, you are our hero. Stay.[154]

When I was struggling those four days, here is what I kept in my head in order to choose to stay:

- ***I will get through this.*** Life has always been almost too hard to bear for a lot of the people, a lot of the time. It's awful. But it isn't too hard to bear, it's *only almost* too hard to bear. What I feel today will not be what I feel tomorrow.
- ***I would severely hurt the people I love the most***—my (now wife) Kelly, my kids and many others. I knew the pain I was in. Why would I want to increase the pain of those I love? Even if you have convinced yourself that the people in your life don't love you or care (a distortion of your thinking for sure) they do care and you will hurt them immeasurably. I didn't want to add pain to the world.
- ***If I take my life, this is what I will be remembered for.*** No matter all my accomplishments, the first thing people will think of when my name is mentioned will be that I took my life. I didn't want that.
- ***By taking my own life, I may contribute to someone else's suicide.*** Survivors of those who take their lives are more likely to take their own life. I didn't want to potentially contribute to the death by suicide of anyone among my family or friends.
- ***I will deprive the world of what God has planned to do through me.*** God showed me that I had many years to serve him and that many people would be helped if I chose to stay. I have much to offer this world. I really do and so do you.
- ***Why would I destroy this most amazing of all creations, my body?*** I would never take a hammer to a Ferrari! Why would I destroy my body which is exponentially more wonderful than a Ferrari?

[154]Jennifer Michael Hecht, *Stay: A History of Suicide and the Philosophies Against It* (New Haven: Yale University Press, 2015), 7-8 (emphasis mine).

- I would be making a decision which belongs to God alone.
- I would defame God's reputation in the world.
- It would show a lack of trust in God's plan for my life.
- It would show a lack of trust in God's ability to provide for me.
- It would show a lack of trust in God's ability to restore to me what has been stolen.
- It is only almost too much to bear. This will pass. ***God has me and it will be OK.***

When I thought of these realities, suicide remained an option, but one among many options. If I had not considered these realities, suicide as an option could have become my *only* option, at least in my mind. If suicide becomes the *only option*, alarm bells should be going off in your head.

Assessment

Are you thinking of taking our life? Take your thoughts seriously.

If you are thinking of suicide as one of several options, pay attention to your thinking. Seek out professional help now to assess how serious your situation is. If you are not sure, **go to the website at the bottom of this page** to take this simple risk assessment.[155]

If you have come to the conclusion that suicide is your *only* option, **YOUR THINKING HAS BECOME DISTORTED AND YOU NEED IMMEDIATE HELP.**

*Call the suicide prevention hotline (***800-273-8255***) immediately.* Don't hesitate. Put this book down and call **NOW**.

[155]https://www.choosehelp.com/topics/depression/suicide-risk-assessment-the-sbq-r-a-4-question-test

If you are thinking any of the following **thoughts** or taking any of the following **actions**, you are at a higher risk for attempting to take your life by your own hand. Ask yourself these questions:

- ***How much of my 'brain space' is taken up by thinking of suicide?*** If your thoughts are dominated by reasons why you should take your life, you are at higher risk for following through. ***Now is the time to seek help.***
- ***Are my thoughts turning into plans?*** Have you thought of a ***time*** and a ***place***? Have you thought of ***how*** you would do it? Have you rehearsed how you would do it? Have you obtained the ***means*** to do it such as purchasing a gun or obtaining pills? If you are thinking any or all of these thoughts, **STOP** and **SEEK HELP** immediately.
- ***Am I considering what people would say?*** If you are thinking of how people will react to your suicide, **STOP** and get help immediately.
- ***Am I preparing others for my leaving?*** Have you told anyone you will miss them? Have you written out your will? Have you given away personal belongings? If you are doing these things, **STOP and seek help immediately**.
- Have you decided if you want your attempted suicide to be your final act on earth, or do you plan for it to be only self-injurious—that is, not lethal? In other words, are you using a means that will lead to sure success or a means that may leave you here but injured? **Either way, your thinking is distorted and you need to STOP and get help now.**

If you answered yes to any of these questions, I urge you, I plead with you, get help immediately. Call this number: **800-273-8255**.

What the Psalmist wrote 3,000 years ago is as true today as it was then: *The Lord is close to the brokenhearted and saves those who are crushed in spirit. A righteous man may have many troubles, but the Lord delivers him from them all.* (Psalm 34.18–19)

In 1997 my 50-year-old sister, Jackie, took her life. Don't do what my sister did. Please stay. I did, and I'm glad I did.

I and many others want you to stay. I would imagine that if the people in your life got inside your head right now and knew your thoughts, they would be traumatized and horrified. They would want you to get help now.

I got up at 4:30 every morning for months so that I could write this book *so that you would choose to stay.* One reason I chose to stay is to help others in the same situation choose to stay. You are wanted and needed. Please stay.

From a spiritual perspective (which is the eternal and thus most important perspective), you and I are in a war and Satan is your enemy. Satan hates God, but since Satan can't destroy God, his driving passion is to deface God by defacing and/or destroying you. Suicide is the ultimate destruction of God's amazing creation.

King David wrote: *When I consider your heavens, the work of your fingers, the moon and the stars, which you have set in place, what is man that you are mindful of him, the son of man that you care for him? You made him a little lower and crowned him with glory and honor.* (Psalm 8:3–5)

Wow! You and I are God's amazing creation! No wonder Satan wants to take you out! **Don't let him!**

In my office I have a plastic anatomical human skull that can be taken apart. Inside is a model of the brain. Sometimes when people come into my office who are troubled and depressed, I take out my plastic skull and pull out the brain.

I say to them:

> *I know you are suffering and that you are in pain because of your loss. But did you know that you still have this amazing thing between your ears—your brain! Your brain is the second most incredible thing in all the universe. Did you get that? That three-pound mass of cells in your head is the second most astounding*

thing in the entire universe! The first is, of course, God himself. Whatever you have lost, you still have this amazing thing! And, you have God! What can be better than that?

To take your life by suicide is to destroy this second most amazing thing in all the universe! Don't do it. Don't give Satan the victory. Don't let the thief come in and destroy. Instead, cry out to God. He WILL rescue you!

I urge you to get help. The journey you are on is a journey only you can make. Only you make the journey but ***you don't have to make the journey alone.***

God knows the battle for your soul. God knows the war against your life. He wants you to win. He's on your side. Because he is for you, God will put resources in your path to help you survive this journey and thrive on the other side. This book is one of those resources. It's no accident that you are reading this. God knew you would need this book to make it through this ordeal. He called me to write it and he called you to read it. This is clear evidence of God's loving care for you.

God has given many resources for you during this hard time. I urge you, please reach out and get the help you need. The following are some suggestions. Perhaps these suggestions will be prompts God is putting in your path to help you right now.

- **Pray** to God. He is listening and much closer to you than you can imagine. He is eager to help you and see you through this.

- **See a Counselor** or **Therapist**. God has put smart people on this planet who have committed themselves to helping people get through hard times. Ask around for a counselor or therapist who is known for his/her skills in helping people through hard times. You want someone who is tender and compassionate. You also want this person to be honest and be able to gently confront you when necessary.

- **Call a Friend**. We all need a few trusted, loyal, wise friends. Who can you call in the middle of the night who will listen to you, accept you for who you are, and help get you through? Not everyone will help you but God will give you a few who will. If you have no one at this time, pray for God to send someone. He will. You will be amazed when he does!

- **Call a Pastor**. Pastors are today's unsung heroes. Most pastors are amazing people who have given themselves to helping people win victories over the enemy. If you don't have a church, ask around to find a church known for their love for God and their love for people. It takes courage to jump in, but do it. God works through his church. His church is there for you. If available, find a church with a strong and lively men's ministry. Pastors get calls all the time from desperate people. They are used to these calls and welcome them.

- This website has hotlines for all kinds of problems.[156]

For years I have told depressed people the same thing: *Don't believe everything you are telling yourself right now. Your thinking is distorted. Instead, listen to what others are saying to you.*

If you need more encouragement to push against thoughts of suicide...

Don't put a period where a comma belongs. Tens of thousands of people in our country put the ultimate period in their lives—they kill themselves. But crushing life problems are only commas. Don't make a comma into a period.

Suicide is a huge mistake. Suicide is a permanent (and terrible) solution to a temporary problem. Failure is a temporary problem. You will move past this time into a better future.

Be assured that how you are thinking now will change. You will have more positive thoughts as time goes by. Hold on!

How you are **feeling** now will change. You will feel better! Hold on!

[156]https://brokenbelievers.com/2011/01/23/247-crisis-lines/

There are many kinds of treatment for struggling folks like you and me—medications, talk therapy, etc. There is help and that should give you hope.

Jennifer Hecht succinctly states: *Though we may refuse a version of life, we must also refuse voluntary death.*[157]

You are right to be upset about how your life is right now. Don't choose to change the state of your life, however, by ending it. That is a worse choice with far worse consequences. Instead, hang on, get the help you need, and watch God do his amazing work in your life.

[157] Hecht, *Stay*, 183.

Appendix B: Homicide Risk Assessment

On September 9, 1996, a beautiful young 23-year-old girl was shot and killed. The killer was her ex-boyfriend. He then turned the gun on himself.

Ami had just graduated with a degree in social work and worked as a volunteer with the Austin Police Department. She helped AIDS victims and disabled children and adults.[158] Ami's huge and generous heart was stopped by the irrational rage of an angry young man.

As pastor to this family I saw firsthand the unbelievable damage caused by homicide. One thing I learned was that *painful circumstances can lead to murder.* No one would have guessed that Ami's murderer would have committed such a radical act.

Murders happen when people are enraged and take their rage to the next level. People don't just kill people. The pathway to murder starts with rage.

Are you angry at what has happened to you? In your anger do you have thoughts of taking someone's life?

Perhaps your wife cheated on you. Are you thinking of killing her lover? Do you have thoughts of killing her? If so, you would not be the first, and if you carried it out you would not be the first to commit murder in these circumstances. The reason I point this out is simply that murder happens, and murder usually begins with an angry male.

It is entirely possible that someone reading this could be thinking of homicide. If you are one of those people, don't do it.

Murders happen when ordinary men are extraordinarily wounded. Hurts lead to rage which can lead to the actual act of murder. When murders are traced back through their sequence of formation, it's

[158] *Ami Lunsford Memorial Scholarship in Victim Services,* accessed July 14, 2017, http://endowments.giving.utexas.edu/ami-lunsford-memorial-scholarship-in-victim-services/

clear that most men who commit murder did not start out thinking they would. Their rage carried them along until the deed was done.

Believe it or not, there is help for those considering homicide. The *Saving Cain* website is a great resource even if you are not thinking of murder as an option to handling your problems.[159]

The author if this website, lawyer and author James Kimmel, Jr, writes:

> *Research scientists have discovered that when we have been hurt or wronged, the desire to harm others activates the same pleasure centers of the brain activated by narcotics. This suggests that the desire to kill is a biological craving created inside the brain. If you are thinking about killing, you are not "evil." You are experiencing a brain-created desire to harm others and yourself. If your brain created it, then your brain can also make it go away. Help is available right now. The desire to kill can be overcome.*[160]

If you are thinking of taking someone's life, call the National Suicide Prevention Lifeline: **800-273-8255**. Though this hotline is for people considering suicide, they know how to help someone thinking of taking another's life.

Brother, I know the rage. Don't let that rage overtake you. Don't rage against yourself. Don't rage against others. Hold on. Get the help you need. And know that things will get better.

I wish I had my sister back. She was an amazing woman who had much to offer to the world. I wish I had Ami back. She was so young with so much potential. Rage took both of these beautiful people. If I may say it, you are beautiful too and so are the people in your life, even those who have caused so much pain in your life. Give God the pain, get the help you need, and live for another, better day. It will happen. You will see if you just hold on.

Remember that Satan's greatest desire is to destroy God's amazing creation. Don't let him win the victory. Self-destruction (suicide) and

---

[159]http://www.savingcain.org/preventing-murder.html
[160]http://www.savingcain.org/preventing-murder.html

murder (homicide) are never part of God's plan. *God is for life*, yours and others.

Appendix C: Understanding Differences in People's Reaction to Death and Divorce

One of the most difficult things for me to process through this divorce experience has been the near complete lack of empathy, sympathy and support from long-time friends and family. As a pastor for over 30 years, I know hundreds of people and those people know me. As a friend and pastor I have walked with them through all sorts of troubles. Yet when my world came crashing down the sound of that crash echoed across a distressingly empty desert of humanity. Things are lonely enough if you are the one who is left. The silence from friends and family can drive the isolation home in ways that cut deeply into the soul. If you are the perpetrator, it's easy for friends and family to choose to ostracize and isolate you. Though they may think you deserve it, it is not helpful.

Why this tendency of family and friends to pull back? Why do people respond so quickly and compassionately to the death of a spouse, yet ignore and withdraw when a couple divorces? As I thought about this it occurred to me that though the death of a spouse and divorce both create enormous losses, only death is recognized by our society as a true grief event worthy of a compassionate and healing response. The reasons for this are outlined in the table on the next page. This table compares reactions among friends and family between the death of a spouse and the divorce of a couple.

The reasons for bringing this up are two-fold:

(1) To give you some understanding as to why most friends and family will not respond as you might expect during the pain and suffering you are enduring as a divorced man.

(2) To raise awareness among all of us that divorce is as traumatic as the death of a spouse and as such needs a similar response.

Following are reasons people respond with sympathy and compassion to grief from the death of a spouse but not so much to the losses incurred in divorce:

The Death of a Spouse is Final, but the Death of a Marriage is Not.

When a spouse dies, the finality of death allows people to do the culturally acceptable and expected things for those left behind and then move on with their lives. When friends and family have expressed their condolences to the grieving spouse through calls, cards, visits, memorial service attendance and in some American sub-cultures, delivering food, they have met expectations and can move on. Add to this the uniquely American perspective that grieving for a dead spouse should be short-lived, and you get the idea that the entire grief response of friends and family to the death of one's spouse is well-defined and brief.

In contrast, the death of a marriage is anything but final. Though divorce incurs most of the same losses of the death of a spouse (and in some ways, greater losses), the two partners keep living. A death has occurred (the death of a marriage) but the partners still live. When a couple divorces there is not a body to view. A thing has died—a marriage—but that dead thing has no substance such as a corpse.

Whereas in the case of a the death of a spouse, friends and family know that their obligation to help is limited in scope and time. In the case of divorce, friends and family know that if they show compassion or sympathy toward one or both partners in the divorce, they could be entangled in 'grief' work for a long time.

The Death of a Spouse is Recognized as a Severe Loss.

When a spouse dies it is usually assumed that the couple loved each other and so the grieving spouse is heartbroken. The love presumed between a couple when a spouse dies is obviously not present in

DEATH Compared	With DIVORCE
Death is final	Divorce has an end, but it doesn't really. Divorce is a death that keeps on living.
Death is recognized as a loss and is acknowledged as painful.	The losses of divorce are not as evident as the losses of death, therefore people are slow to recognize these losses though some of these mosses may be significantly greater than loss incurred through the death of a loved one.
Everyone knows what to do—call, send flowers, go to funeral, call again, then we're done.	People are unsure of how to help the divorced. Friends and family are wary of personal, long-term, entanglement. People may assume the divorced person doesn't want their involvement. Divorce appears more personal and private than death.
Death is unavoidable. Usually no one is blaming the one who died.	Divorce is a choice and choice implies blame. When personal responsibility is involved, sympathy of outsiders diminishes.
The people left behind assume the person who died loved them.	The person who is left deals with the loss of the loved one *and* his/her rejection.
People experience the death of someone in their lives only rarely.	Divorce is common today, so people assume it is not as painful as it once was.
Death leaves only the grieving to deal with. Sympathy toward the person left does not require choosing sides.	Divorce results in two people in pain. Friends are hesitant to take sides.
Summary: The death of a partner solicits immediate empathy, sympathy and support.	Summary: Divorce leaves deeply wounded people with friends and family unsure what to do and how to help, increasing the loneliness and frustration of the divorcee.

divorce, so it may be assumed by friends and family that for the people getting divorced, the divorce is a good thing, perhaps something even to be celebrated! In the minds of some, there is nothing really to grieve, giving an excuse for friends and family not to step in to offer much needed sympathy and support.

And yet the losses incurred in divorce can be worse than death. If my wife had died I could at least presumed she loved me. In divorce, the marriage partner left is suffering the loss of his/her spouse and the tremendous pain of rejection.

Financially, in some cases death provides a financial boost in the form of life insurance. In divorce, tremendous financial losses are always incurred.

The Death of a Spouse sometimes causes the one left to struggle with his/her identity, but divorce always strips away identity on multiple levels.

These losses compound to make divorce as traumatic or sometimes more traumatic than death, but it is seldom recognized as such by family and friends which compounds the pain of divorce.

People are Unsure how to Help the Divorced.

When a husband or wife dies, everyone knows what to do. Even then, helping the grieving is awkward for some people. But when a couple divorces, people don't know what to do. Do you console the one left? Do you berate the leaver? Do you commiserate with how terrible the ex-spouse is, or grieve his/her loss? Do you encourage the couple to try to reconcile or congratulate them for their divorce? The complex and multiple variables in the dissolution of a marriage relationship greatly complicate our response to those experiencing divorce.

Death is usually not a choice but divorce is always a choice at least for one of the partners. Choice implies blame. When pain comes from the choices people make, sympathy of outsiders diminishes. This is especially true in American culture where stoic grit is highly valued as a coping mechanism for suffering.

One of the reasons I wrote this book is that friends of men who are in the middle of a divorce will be able to offer quality help (in the form of this book) and yet be involved with that man at a level they are comfortable with. Friends may understandably not want to get entangled in a couple's divorce. But with this book a friend can offer help and choose their level of involvement.

Divorce is Considered Private and Shameful.

While death is public, divorce is considered a private matter. In fact, with no-fault divorce laws and little societal pressure to remain married, divorce is considered strictly a choice between two people.

Death is just a tragedy. Divorce is considered a failure as much or more than it is a tragedy. Seldom do we blame the one who died for the grief his/her death brought about. Divorce is different. We know someone (usually both) are to blame. Blame and shame go hand in glove with divorce. Neither fit death.

Blame and shame also complicate people's reaction to divorce since sympathizing and/or showing compassion to one partner necessarily implies taking sides against the other. This puts everyone in an awkward position. The idea that divorce is a private affair combined with the awkwardness people feel in trying to help, conspire to keep family and friends out of the divorcing couple's lives leading to tremendous (and sometimes deadly) isolation.

Death has Predefined Rituals that Mark Stages of Progression through the Grief Process and Allow the Community to Participate in Grief thus Sharing the Burden.

Upon the death of a spouse the news is disseminated, friends and family respond with sympathy, a memorial service is planned, people attend, a card is sent. At this point well-defined societal obligations have been met and people can move on.

We have these rituals surrounding death because they invite the community to come together to share the burden of grief. When friends and family gather at a memorial service they are collectively acknowledging that a painful thing has happened, and in that acknowledgement they take some of the weight of the tragedy upon themselves.

For the reasons listed above, divorce has no rituals except mediation and a court appearance. Friends and family don't show up at mediation or court to acknowledge that a tragedy has taken place. No one is there to share the burden. When the now divorced couple go to their respective homes, they go to an empty house or, more likely, an empty apartment.

In summary, when a husband or wife dies, the loss is immediately recognized and friends and family respond with compassion and sympathy. In contrast, though divorce leaves at least one partner deeply wounded (perhaps more wounded than if they partner had died), friends and family are unsure what to do and how to help. In fact, friends and family often withdraw, leaving the wounded divorcee even more isolated and floundering in pain. Pauline Boss is correct when she writes, *The loss associated with divorce is often more difficult than the loss that results from death because the former remains inherently unclear.*[161]

When that happens, don't despair. Don't rage. Try to understand why the people in your life are not responding with effective help. Ask God to place a few people into your life who can really help you (see Day 23).

As you seek out people to help you, follow a few simple guidelines:

Get connected to the right people: a therapist/counselor, a pastor, a counselor, a lawyer. I can't emphasize enough your need for professionals to guide you through your divorce. We go to professionals for work on our bodies (dentists, cardiologists, barbers). Why do we hesitate to go to professionals to help heal our souls?

[161]Pauline Boss, *Ambiguous Loss: Learning to Live with Unresolved Grief* (Boston: Harvard University Press, 2000), Kindle Locations 301-302.

Find one or two friends who will listen to you and to whom you can be accountable. As you seek one or two friends, hold the people in your life loosely. The people you most thought would go deep with you might not, for whatever reason. Let them go and let God lead you to the one or two people who will walk the journey with you.

The purpose of friends is not to build a hate group against your ex but to form a support network for you. Part of the conversation with your friends will be your frustration with your spouse, but the primary purpose is to gain support for you, not build the case against your spouse.

Release those people who you thought should be more supportive of you but weren't. God will bring to your side those few people who will really help you. It's helpful to remember the wisdom of John Gardner: *Most people are neither for you nor against you; they are thinking of themselves.*[162] We really want to believe people will be strong, loyal, honest and true to us. Most people will fail us this side of heaven. The flip side of this is for us to determine to be there for others when they go through their crises.

We were not meant to go this journey alone. God will bring some people into your life to hang in there with you.

[162] "*John Gardner's Writings,*" accessed August 06, 2017, http://www.pbs.org/johngardner/sections/writings_speech_1.html.

Appendix D: Balancing Fault and Responsibility

Two things have become glaringly obvious to me these past four years of heartbreak and loss: (1) men are not supposed to feel pain and (2) men are not to expect any empathy, sympathy, comfort or consolation during their hard times.

Whenever I would express any sort of pain or complaint about my situation I would be shut down by either being ignored or given the pat answers of *You must learn to forgive* or *Things will get better.* Dealing with the pain of loss is not taught by our culture in any significant, meaningful, deep or lasting way.[163]

People in our culture are uncomfortable being with hurting people. People don't want to hear about your troubles. But just because friends and family are uncomfortable with a man's raw pain doesn't mean the man doesn't feel the pain.

Divorced men are mired in troubles and heartache. Divorce causes losses on a scale most people don't know unless they, too, have been divorced. These losses can push us to consider suicide and/or homicide as viable options especially when appropriate avenues and methods of expressing grief and anger are shut down by our culture.

I lost my family, my career, my reputation, my income. These losses hurt so much because they were real. Millions of men experience this pain, but it goes unspoken and unaddressed because our culture says that men cannot feel that way. But I did. I felt an-

[163]Tim Keller notes that *Sociologists and anthropologists have analyzed and compared the various ways that cultures train its members for grief, pain, and loss. And when this comparison is done, it is often noted that our own contemporary secular, Western culture is one of the weakest and worst in history at doing so.... Our own contemporary Western society gives its members no explanation for suffering and very little guidance as to how to deal with it.* Timothy Keller, *Walking with God through Pain and Suffering*, 18.

gry, lonely, exhausted, shamed, embarrassed, sadness and deep grief. Whatever culture said I was supposed to feel (which is *nothing*) I felt deep and powerful emotions. You can't will away emotions. You can't decide not to feel.

When you're in pain, being told to 'man-up' is not going to get it done. Being ignored only adds to the suffering and drives men into further isolation where they find comfort in a bottle or porn or some other addiction. What this means for us is that when we hurt, we may not be able to find folks to listen to us and simply be with us.[164]

But we *must* express our suffering. Or, put another way, suffering *will be expressed.* As someone said *Talk it out or you will take it out.* No human can endure profoundly damaging events and go unscathed. Wounds to the soul find expression. Untransformed pain will flare outward or inward or both, torching ourselves and others in the process.

The Bible doesn't share our culture's discomfort with pain and suffering. In fact, Jesus always recognized pain and moved toward it, not away from it whether the bearer of the pain was male or female, perpetrator or victim. This is a huge comfort because it means that God is moving toward you, not away from you.

Nowhere does the Bible indicate that to be a real man means you never express anger, sadness, heartache or heartbreak or that you

---

[164] The story of Job in the Bible is a perfect illustration of this. Job suffered incredible losses, and his friends were not much help. Job complains about them in the verses that follow:

When desperate people give up on God Almighty, their friends, at least, should stick with them. But my brothers are fickle as a gulch in the desert—one day they're gushing with water from melting ice and snow cascading out of the mountains, but by midsummer they're dry gullies baked dry in the sun. Travelers who spot them and go out of their way for a drink end up in a waterless gulch and die of thirst. Merchant caravans from Tema see them and expect water, tourists from Sheba hope for a cool drink. They arrive so confident—but what a disappointment! They get there, and their faces fall! ***And you, my so-called friends, are no better—there's nothing to you! One look at a hard scene and you shrink in fear.*** *It's not as though I asked you for anything— I didn't ask you for one red cent— Nor did I beg you to go out on a limb for me.* ***So why all this dodging and shuffling?*** Job 6:14–23 (MSG, emphasis mine)

never seek comfort and consolation. Nowhere in the Bible is it stated that the amazing comfort God offers the suffering is for women only. Quite the opposite. Men, it is more than OK to say out loud what is happening in your head and heart. If the mighty prophet Elijah could tell God, *Take my life; I am no better than my ancestors* (see 1 Kings19.4), you and I have permission to verbally express our pain.

King David was as manly a man as there ever ways. But he wrote: *How long must I wrestle with my thoughts and every day have sorrow in my heart? How long will my enemy triumph over me?* (Psalm 13:2) If I posted that on Facebook I would be slammed! (See Day 34.)

I cannot emphasize enough how our culture shuts down, explains away and radically ignores real suffering. When you are suffering deeply, to be shut down and/or ignored amplifies and exacerbates suffering.

I believe that if friends and family would allow grieving people to really grieve, hurting people to really hurt, angry people to really be angry, sad people to really be sad, much of the transmitted pain would be transformed in our society, making us stronger, not weaker.

And therein lies the most significant myth about pain: that pain is weakness. Weakness is perceived as vulnerability, and vulnerability is defined as failure and failure is exactly the opposite of everything American. To express pain—to reveal your suffering—is to express everything un-American. Americans are not weak, we are strong. Americans aren't vulnerable, we are impenetrable. Americans don't suffer, we conquer. To acknowledge our suffering is to fail, and failure is un-American.[165]

But Americans also take tons of anti-depressants, drink ourselves under the table, view untold hours of pornography. We do everything possible to deny, avoid or medicate our pain. It's not working.

---

[165] Megan Divine notes that *Our culture sees grief as a kind of malady: a terrifying, messy emotion that needs to be cleaned up and put behind us as soon as possible. As a result, we have outdated beliefs around how long grief should last and what it should look like. We see it as something to overcome, something to fix, rather than something to tend or support. Even our clinicians are trained to see grief as a disorder rather than a natural response to deep loss... those outdated ideas add unnecessary suffering on top of natural, normal pain.* Megan Devine and Mark Nepo, *It's OK That You're Not OK: Meeting Grief and Loss in a Culture That Doesn't Understand* (Boulder: Sounds True, 2017), Kindle Locations 134-140.

I'm convinced that uncountable numbers of men take their own lives or end up bitter and weak because no one wants to hear their pain and shepherd them through it. Men, this ought not be.

How is our Pain Transformed so it is not Transmitted?

Look at the graphic on the next page. In the upper left corner notice that our culture's 'discomfort with discomfort' leads people to disrespect you if you express your pain. You are regarded as 'playing the victim' if you state any negative emotion regarding your situation.

On the far right of the graphic, we find that people expect you to only take responsibility for how you handle it. And there's truth to this notion that how we handle our pain is our responsibility. You may be the victim in this thing, but how you and I respond is our responsibility. But our culture makes the false assumption that a man who expresses his hurt is not handling the situation responsibly and is, therefore, defaulting to the 'victim mentality.' The two appear to be mutually exclusive but they are not. This is a critical distinction.

If we express our pain, a second false assumption is made: that we are not moving forward, we are not 'accepting' our situation, we are not working on it. People assume we are 'stuck' and that we like it that way. They assume that we feel good when we feel bad. If we would just shut our complaining mouths and shut down our raging emotions, we could get on with our lives (and quit bothering everybody with our heartache).

Is it possible to express your hurt, anger, grief and mount a defense of yourself (if you are not the primary perpetrator) without being labeled a victim, or, worse yet, actually falling into the victim role?

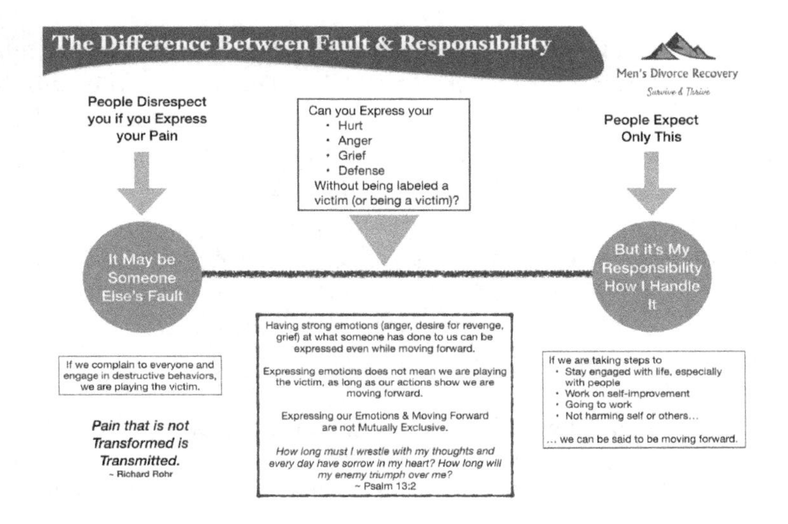

The Difference Between Fault & Responsibility
Men's Divorce Recovery
People Disrespect you if you Express your Pain
Can you Express your
• Hurt
• Anger
• Grief
• Defense
Without being labeled a victim (or being a victim)?
People Expect Only This
It May be Someone Else's Fault
But it's My Responsibility How I Handle It
Having strong emotions (anger, desire for revenge, grief) at what someone has done to us can be expressed even while moving forward.
Expressing emotions does not mean we are playing the victim, as long as our actions show we are moving forward.
Expressing our Emotions & Moving Forward are not Mutually Exclusive.
How long must I wrestle with my thoughts and every day have sorrow in my heart? How long will my enemy triumph over me?
~ Psalm 13:2
If we complain to everyone and engage in destructive behaviors, we are playing the victim.
Pain that is not Transformed is Transmitted.
~ Richard Rohr
If we are taking steps to
• Stay engaged with life, especially with people
• Work on self-improvement
• Going to work
• Not harming self or others...
... we can be said to be moving forward.

Society is right in pushing us away from a victim mentality. If we complain to everyone and engage in destructive behaviors, we are playing the victim. If we define ourselves by our wounds and let everyone know it, we are playing the victim. If we wallow in our despair, paralyzed by our pain, we are playing the victim. But I'm convinced that if a hurting man has just one or two people who really seek to understand his hurt and pain, the need to verbally vomit on everybody diminishes and eventually goes away.[166]

If we find one or two people who really understand our heartache but care enough not to leave us there, we can move forward into healing and recovery. Those few who get it understand that having strong emotions (anger, desire for revenge, grief) at what someone has done to us can be expressed even while moving forward. Expressing emotions does not mean we are playing the victim, as long as our actions show we are moving forward. Expressing our emotions and moving forward are not mutually exclusive.

[166]McKay et al, state: *There is only one requirement for listening with empathy: simply know that everyone is trying to survive. You don't have to like everyone or agree with everyone, but recognize that you do share the same struggles.* Matthew McKay, Martha Davis and Patrick Fanning, *Messages: The Communication Skills Book* (Oakland: 2009), Kindle Locations 364-366.

The Bible commands us to *Carry each other's burdens, and in this way you will fulfill the law of Christ.* (Galatians 6.2).[167] The church must bear one another's burdens. The church must not make burdens more unbearable by denying the burden or telling the one suffering that the burden is not as heavy as they think it is.

Once we find someone who can absorb some of our pain we are free to move forward toward responding responsibly to our situation. What does moving forward look like?

If we are taking steps to

- Stay engaged with life, especially with people...
- Work on self-improvement by acknowledging the parts of our lives that need to change...
- Resist addictions such as alcohol/drugs, pornography, materialism...

[167]John McArthur writes, *It is our duty as believers to help bear one another's burdens. When someone staggers, we help steady the load. If he is straining, we help bear the burden. And if he stumbles, we lift him up. Helping fellow believers carry the weight of their worldly troubles is one of the chief practical duties that ought to consume every Christian.... When Paul suggests that burden-bearing "fulfill[s] the law of Christ," he makes it clear that he has the whole moral law in view. Every act of compassion and self-sacrifice on behalf of our brethren is a practical means of displaying the love of Christ and thereby fulfilling the moral demands of His law.*

But the apostle clearly has in mind spiritual, emotional, and temperamental encumbrances — not physical freight only. The burdens we need to help carry for one another include guilt, worry, sorrow, anxiety, and all other similar loads.

Do you want to fulfill the moral requirements of the Law? Love your neighbor. How do you love him? By bearing his burdens.

It's interesting that Paul would emphasize this theme in an epistle written to confront people who were falling into legalism. It's as if he were saying, "You want to observe a law? Let it be the law of Christ. If you have to impose burdens on yourselves, let it be through acts of love toward your neighbor." If you will do that faithfully, your own burden won't seem so heavy. Best of all, you will find it easier to keep your focus heavenward, regardless of the trials you suffer in this life. John McArthur, *Bearing One Another's Burdens,* last updated January 1, 2010, https://www.ligonier.org/learn/articles/bearing-one-anothers-burdens/ accessed May 6, 2018.

- Go to work and fulfill other daily obligations...
- Not harm ourselves or others... we can be said to be moving forward.

Unfortunately finding people in our lives who can walk this journey with us in a balanced and helpful way is difficult. Most people are not capable or trained to do it. That's why a therapist or counselor should be engaged as soon as possible.

It is possible and necessary to express our pain without falling into victimhood. We are successful in doing this if we are taking active steps to get better, be healed, and move forward along the path God has for us.

Appendix E: For Men Who Are Primarily Responsible for the Divorce

Much of this book has been written from the perspective of the husband having been the victim of a wife who left. This was my experience and my experience is naturally reflected in this book. I was not unfaithful to my wife and in fact, she did not have biblical grounds to divorce me.[168]

Eighty percent of divorces are filed by women. This fact leaves us to assume that many a man facing divorce was surprised at his wife's decision to leave him. In my practice as a pastor over 35+ years of ministry, I would say that about half of the divorcing men I have worked with brought it on themselves and about half were the victims of wives who decided to divorce for reasons that were not biblical.

But the fact remains that those 80% of women who filed divorce had some reason to file for divorce whether their reason was biblical or not, or justified or not. Clearly a woman who files divorce is unhappy with her husband. Sometimes her reasons are trivial and don't rise to the level justifying abandonment. But many times husbands engage in behavior that is unacceptable, putting a woman into the painful place of having to decide to endure a hard and possibly abusive situation, or get out of the marriage.

If your wife divorced you because of your adultery, dishonesty, alcohol or drug addiction, sexual addictions or other bad behavior, you need to deal with it. You need to deal with it for your sake, for your children's sake and for the sake of the women you will possibly date and the woman you will possibly marry.

---

[168]Biblical grounds for divorce include adultery, abandonment and abuse. See Matthew 5.32, 1 Corinthians 7:15. See David Instone-Brewer, *Divorce and Remarriage in the Church: Biblical Solutions for Pastoral Realities* (Downers Grove: InterVarsity Press, 2003).

If you are one of these men, you face the challenges of reconciling your attitudes and actions with God, with yourself and with your children and others you have harmed. How do you do this? How do you own the damage caused by your waywardness? How do you gain forgiveness from God, your children, even your ex?

REALIZE THE DAMAGE, EMBRACE HUMILITY

Whatever your situation, I can assure you that you and I have caused damage to others because of our prideful, unyielding, stubborn spirit. The first part of recovery is to realize the damage you have caused by your behavior. You must shake off your stubborn spirit and humble yourself before God. This begins with taking a brutally honest look at yourself.

If you honestly believe that your behavior has not caused damage to others, ask God to show you who he really is and who you really are. That's a daring request. I dare you. When God reveals to you who you really are, you will be stunned. You will get a glimpse of God as he is—*holy, perfect, all-knowing, all-seeing, all-powerful.* And you will see yourself as you really are—*tiny, insignificant, dirty, selfish, puny.* In that moment, *don't despair.*

Even though what God reveals to you is true, the larger truth is that the very same holy, perfect, powerful God who could crush you in a split-second is the same God who willingly went to the cross and died the most humiliating death so you could be raised to new life.

Jesus shows us the way: the way up is down. The way for you to really stand tall on sure and steady legs is to bend low on your wobbly and shaky knees.

The Apostle James was tougher than any man you know. He rallied the church in Jerusalem when Christians were being hunted down and killed. This wasn't a movie—his people really were being killed and his own life was in peril. Later, James boldly and courageously led the church through a huge church squabble (Acts 15) that would have enormous implications for at least the next 2,000 years. Clint Eastwood nor any other man we think strong could hold a candle to James. James' advice? *Humble yourselves before the Lord, and he will lift you up.* (James 4.10)

To humble ourselves means to go down on the knee before God and admit that he is God and we are not. It's to confess our sins to him. It is to acknowledge the damage our sins have done to others. It's to bend low before God so he can lift us up.

This is tough for men. We absolutely hate to admit fault and have carefully honed our ability to rationalize bad behavior to a stunning degree. Through the years I've heard amazing excuses for bad behavior, like the man who claimed he was on mission for Jesus every time he went to the strip club and the man who assured me it was God's will for him to leave his wife to have an affair with his administrative assistant. That's not God's will. Not even close.

Destructive rationalization is not limited to men. When I was a young pastor a mother of three in my church left her husband and children (one of whom was severely handicapped) to run off with a guy to Africa to be missionaries! If you talked to her you would think she was the most godly woman in the world. If you talked to her husband, you would know the truth: she was a master manipulator, liar and rationalizer.

When things go poorly we naturally try to discover the reasons. People in pain want to know why they are hurting. As mentioned earlier, our culture has done a terrible job of helping us understand the origin and nature of pain and suffering. Without a cohesive 'theology of pain,' people in our society tend to blame God or others. If others blame us, we push back through defense mechanisms. On the other hand, we really may not be at fault. The Bible is full of stories of men who made bad choices and didn't take responsibility for their choices. Plenty of Bible stories are about men and women who were falsely accused.[169]

When we make excuses, minimize, rationalize, and blame others we may be denying responsibility for our part in the divorce. Are you making excuses for your behavior? Are you blaming someone else for consequences you need to own? Are you minimizing the impact of your behavior on others? To get on the road to healing and

---

[169]Joseph, Jeremiah, King David, the Apostle Paul and, of course, Jesus all come to mind.

recovery you and I need to tackle this issue whether we see ourselves as primarily the victim or acknowledge that we are the perpetrator or, most likely, a combination of the two. Brennan Manning speaks truth when he writes: *The alternative to confronting the truth is always some form of self-destruction.*[170]

Take an honest look at yourself. List below the things you have done that you believe led to your divorce:

____

____

____

____

____

____

Now list the people you have harmed either by your behaviors that led to the divorce or your actions during and after the divorce:

____

____

____

____

____

____

Now ask yourself, *Have I lied about anything I just wrote?*

At this point you should be feeling low. It's not an easy thing to face ourselves and own who we really are. But the only way to healing is through a true view of ourselves. You may feel low but you are also due some congratulations for doing the hard thing: being real and being humble.

Bob Sorge bluntly states: *Here's some excellent counsel: Become a good repenter. The only way to move forward in God is through repentance. If*

[170]Brennan Manning, *The Ragamuffin Gospel: Good News for the Bedraggled, Beat-Up, and Burnt Out* (Colorado Springs: Multnomah Press, 2005), 134.

your pride hinders you from repenting, get over it. You're a wretch. You need mercy so badly it's scary. Wise up and master the art of repentance. Call your sin in its worst possible terms. Grovel. Eat dust.[171] Strong but true words.

The great news is that God does not leave us in the dirt, even if we put ourselves there. He welcomes us to himself. Which leads us to...

RECEIVING FORGIVENESS FROM GOD

Each of us desperately needs God's welcome embrace and his forgiveness. God welcomes us home when we humble ourselves enough to come to him, admit our sin to him and receive forgiveness from him.

Forgiveness is not free. Our forgiveness from God came at a price. He paid the price. What God did for us in securing for us our salvation is the greatest story of all time. To find out how to embrace God's forgiveness, go to Appendix F. There I explain what God did for us and how Jesus saves us from ourselves.

> *Let the wicked forsake his way and the evil man his thoughts. Let him turn to the Lord, and he will have mercy on him, and to our God, for he will freely pardon.* (Isaiah 55.7)

ADDICTIONS

Thomas Moore wrote,

> *The great malady of the twentieth century, implicated in all of our troubles and affecting us individually and socially, is "loss of soul." When soul is neglected, it doesn't just go away; it appears symptomatically in obsessions, addictions, violence, and loss of meaning.*[172]

---

[171]Bob Sorge, *Secrets of the Secret Place* (Grandview, MO: Oasis House, 2010), Kindle Location 341.

[172]Thomas Moore, *Care of the Soul: Guide for Cultivating Depth and Sacredness* (New York: HarperCollins, 1994), Kindle Location 43.

The heart of addiction is that we try to get horizontally what can only be gained vertically. We look to the world to fulfill desires that can only be filled with God.

This is well-stated by the inventor of the computer nearly 500 years ago, Blaise Pascal. Pascal, among other things, proved that nature has a vacuum. What he proved of nature as a scientist he applied to the soul as a Christian. The soul, without God, is a vacuum. Only God can fill the vacuum:

> *What else does this craving, and this helplessness, proclaim but that there was once in man a true happiness, of which all that now remains is the empty print and trace? This he tries in vain to fill with everything around him, seeking in things that are not there the help he cannot find in those that are, though none can help, since this abyss can be filled only with an infinite and immutable object; in other words by God himself.*
>
> *God alone is man's true good, and since man abandoned him it is a strange fact that nothing in nature has been found to take his place: stars, sky, earth, elements, plants, cabbages, leeks, animals, insects, calves, serpents, fever, plague, war, famine, vice, adultery, incest. Since losing his true good, man is capable of seeing it in anything, even his own destruction, although it is so contrary at once to God, to reason and to nature.*[173]

I doubt if you have tried to fill the vacuum in your soul with cabbages or leeks, but you get the point! When we find a measure of satisfaction and relief of our pain in doing something like taking drugs, drinking alcohol or watching porn, a cycle starts that leads to us depending on these things for relief.

Craig Nakken in his book *The Addictive Personality*, writes,

> *Addiction is an emotional relationship with an object or event, through which addicts try to meet their needs for intimacy. When looked at in this way, the logic of addiction starts to become clear.*

[173]Blaise Pascal, *Pensées* (Harmondsworth: Penguin Books, 1966), 125.

> *When compulsive eaters feel sad, they eat to feel better. When alcoholics start to feel out of control with anger, they have a couple of drinks to get back in control. My definition of addiction is as follows:* ***addiction is a pathological love and trust relationship with an object or event****. Because addiction is an illness in which the addict's primary relationship is with objects or events and not with people, the addict's relationships with people change to reflect this. Normally, we manipulate objects for our own pleasure, to make life easier. Addicts slowly transfer this style of relating to objects to their interactions with people, treating them as one-dimensional objects to manipulate as well.*[174]

The heart of addiction is that we build a relationship with an object (drugs, alcohol, stuff, work, etc.) and make people objects. To break psychological, emotional and physical cycles requires hard work that begins with the strong desire to stop the behavior. The best way to do this is through the help of a counselor. I strongly urge you to go to a competent counselor/therapist/psychologist, honestly explain your situation, and then follow their recommendations for help. This may include time at a rehabilitation facility. It may cost a lot of money. Your healing is worth whatever the cost in time and/or money. It is worth it for yourself, for your kids, for your future spouse. Healing from and victory over your addictions is essential if you want to finish well. Do it!

ADULTERY

I am continually astounded at the rampant cheating that takes place in our world. It's simply stunning. My former father-in-law was a successful physician, an obstetrician/gynecologist. He had everything a man could want—a great job, money, a plane, boat and other toys. He had a beautiful wife and three daughters. He ran in the highest social circles of our city. But it wasn't enough. He had affairs with patients and nurses. Eventually he was caught. He never expressed

[174]Craig Nakken, *The Addictive Personality: Roots, Rituals, and Recovery* (Center City, MN: Hazelden, 1988), 26.

any remorse for his philandering. He ended up divorcing his wife and marrying one of his lovers. He lost tons of money but worse, he lost the respect of friends and family. Back then he was able to continue to practice medicine, but he would probably not be able to continue under today's rules. He never seemed to begrudge all the hurt, heartache and loss he brought upon himself and others. He died at the age of 59 of a rare bone disorder.

Just over half of men and women admit to having been unfaithful in any relationship they have ever had and two of ten men and one out of ten women had confessed to cheating while married. What is more stunning is that almost 75% of men say they would have an affair if they knew they would never get caught.[175] People who have cheated are 350% more likely to cheat again.

The heartbeat of any relationship is fidelity. To break sacred bonds promised in marriage is a serious offense before God and family. Jesus strengthened the importance of marriage (See Matthew 19 and Matthew 5), but said that the one thing that would crack the foundation of marriage to the point of sanctioned dissolution was adultery.

> *It has been said, 'Anyone who divorces his wife must give her a certificate of divorce.' But I tell you that anyone who divorces his wife, except for marital unfaithfulness, causes her to become an adulteress, and anyone who marries the divorced woman commits adultery.* (Matthew 5:31–32)

King Solomon wrote a lot of proverbs (wise sayings) that he failed to follow himself, but are nonetheless true:

> *The woman Folly is loud;*
> *she is undisciplined and without knowledge.*
> *She sits at the door of her house,*
> *on a seat at the highest point of the city,*

[175] Statistics for 2016. *Infidelity Statistics*, Statistic Brain Research Institute, accessed May 9, 2018, https://www.statisticbrain.com/infidelity-statistics/. See also *Infidelity Statistics 2017L Why, When and How People Stray,* last updated February 1, 2017, accessed June 4, 2018, https://www.trustify.info/blog/infidelity-statistics-2017.

calling out to those who pass by,
who go straight on their way.
"Let all who are simple come in here!"
she says to those who lack judgment.
"Stolen water is sweet;
food eaten in secret is delicious!"
But little do they know that the dead are there,
that her guests are in the depths of the grave.
(Proverbs 9:13–18)

God is crystal clear when he speaks through the prophet Malachi:

> *Another thing you do: You flood the Lord's altar with tears. You weep and wail because he no longer pays attention to your offerings or accepts them with pleasure from your hands. You ask, "Why?" It is because the Lord is acting as the witness between you and the wife of your youth, because you have broken faith with her, though she is your partner, the wife of your marriage covenant.*
>
> *Has not the Lord made them one? In flesh and spirit they are his. And why one? Because he was seeking godly offspring. So guard yourself in your spirit, and do not break faith with the wife of your youth.*
>
> *"I hate divorce," says the Lord God of Israel, "and I hate a man's covering himself with violence as well as with his garment," says the Lord Almighty.*
>
> *So guard yourself in your spirit, and do not break faith.* (Malachi 2:13–16)

That adultery is ubiquitous does not make it right. In fact, adultery is never justified. It doesn't matter how ugly your ex-wife was, or how naggy or gripey. We never have an excuse to cheat.

Adultery feels good. But just because it feels good does not mean it will lead to life. Cheating of any kinds always takes life away. Cheating always leads to death: *But little do they know that the dead are there, that her guests are in the depths of the grave.* (Proverbs 9.18)

If you are divorced because of adultery, hopefully you do know that adultery leads to death and you are experiencing godly conviction because of your unfaithfulness.

The good news is that adultery is not the unforgivable sin. Jesus clearly indicated that even adultery can be forgiven provided that the one who commits adultery confesses and moves toward healing that results in a lifestyle true to God (see John 8.1-11).

There is never biblical justification for adultery. It is always wrong and always wreaks havoc not just upon the spouse who was cheated on but children, extended family and friends. If you are divorced because of adultery, know that Jesus allows your ex to divorce you. She is not commanded in the Bible to divorce but she can. She has permission from Jesus because Jesus knows that adultery fractures the covenant of marriage to an almost irreparable degree.

This should cause you great conviction. If you are feeling the weight of guilt, know that through Christ you can be forgiven. To know about and experience God's forgiveness, see Appendix F. Then seek to discover what led you to cheat in the first place and fix it before you enter a new relationship. This is best done with a competent counselor/therapist. Determine now that you will never do to another woman what you just did to your ex-wife.

I once had a middle-aged man in my office who had been married and divorced multiple times. The cause was always his infidelity. I told him, *Brother, you need Jesus and you need to be healed of your addiction to sex. You can actually live your life without thinking of sex all the time.* He looked at me in disbelief! But he hung in there with me. He came to know Jesus as his friend and savior, and through a period of discipleship, God healed his addiction.

About a year later he brought a beautiful young woman to meet me. They wanted to get married. I put him through the wringer, determined to test the genuineness of his faith in order to protect this young woman from potential heartbreak. He passed the tests, I did the wedding, and they have been happily married for over a decade now, proof enough that Jesus can heal us and move us to a better place in life.

Appendix F: You Need Jesus

Many a man has sat in my office (as a pastor) heartbroken that his wife left him. They cry and pray, asking God to bring her back. It is a classic attempt of bargaining: *God, I will change my ways, I will go to church, I will give money, if you only make my wife come back to me.*

I tell these men the same thing: *I don't know if your wife will come back to you. But I do know that God loves you and that your relationship to him is what we need to work on first. And I know that if you are tight with God, no matter what happens regarding your wife, the second half of your life can be far better than the first half.*

Why We Feel Far from God

When I was a kid my friends and I would get into rock fights, that is, we would throw rocks at each other. We also had a tendency to try to shoot each other with BB guns. That's what boys do. Boys like to shoot things, burn things, and blow things up. And I define 'boys' here loosely!

One day my friend and I got into rock fight at my house. My friend threw a rock at me and missed. That was the good news. The bad news was that the rock hit my dad's car and put a significant dent just below back window on the passenger side.

Oh, this was very very bad. My dad was definitely *not* the kind of dad who you just walked up to and said, *Father, I have failed you. My friend just threw a rock at me and instead of hitting me it hit your car. Please forgive us.* To say such a thing to my dad was to sign your death warrant.

But here's the thing. Even though my dad had no clue what we had done, my guilt and fear of him drove me to avoid him. My fear of what he would do to me if he found out made me not want to be in his presence.

That's the way we are with God. God made us and then gave us rules to live by. Those rules are for our own good but they are also a test of our love for God. If we love God we obey his rules, just like a husband who loves his wife doesn't cheat on her but instead, remains faithful to her, not out of begrudging obligation but from a heart of joyful love.

Ever since Adam and Eve turned against God, however, we've been rebels. We are like my daughter, who at the age of seven decided she could do better without us. So she packed her little suitcase and walked right out the front door *at night.* I think all of us would agree that had we not rescued her, a night alone for a 7-year-old would not have ended well.

What we see around us is the result of humanity trying to live without God. The daily cable news channels bear 24/7 witness to the folly of this strategy. We may not consciously be aware of it, but deep inside we know we have done what God has told us not to do, and we have failed to do what God requires of us. The Biblical word for rebellion and rule-breaking is *sin.* The Bible is clear: *For all have sinned and fall short of the glory of God.* (Romans 3.23)

So, just like I tried to avoid my dad out of fear of what he would do to me, we avoid God out of fear of what he will do to us. Unlike my dad, however, God is all-knowing *and* he is all-powerful. As much as I feared my dad, my dad didn't know everything (though he acted at times as if he did!) and he wasn't all-powerful (though he felt very powerful in my life).

Sin separates us from God. Our rebellion against God has put a very real gap between God and us. We avoid God because we fear his punishment. When we sin we are rebelling against a perfect and holy God. Our sin separates us from God. Our sin is our running away from God in a hopeless bid for autonomy rather than living in dependence upon him and submission to him. Because of our sin we are far from him.

Our sin causes unspeakable damage to ourselves, to the people around us and to our world. The cost of sin is immeasurable. When my friend threw the rock that put the dent in my dad's car, damage was done and repairing the car would be costly. Someone would have to pay to have the car fixed. Our sin puts us in debt to God because of the damage it causes to his creation. Because we have turned away from God, we are far from him and the cost to repair the damage is far beyond us.

The great news is this: God loves us too much to leave us in our lost, separated and miserable state. Since we couldn't go to him he came to us. He sent his son Jesus, fully God and fully human, to be the bridge between him and us.

When Jesus hung on the cross he was taking upon himself all the hell you and I rightfully deserve for the damage we have caused by our rebelling against God. When Jesus hung on the cross he not only suffered terribly physically (as portrayed in the movie *The Passion*) but he suffered far, far more spiritually as he paid the price to repair the damage we have caused. That's why out of the billions of people who have died, only Jesus' death can affect your life on earth and your life after you die.

A really manly man wrote this about Jesus: *[Jesus] himself bore our sins in his body on the tree, so that we might die to sins and live for righteousness.* (1 Peter 2.24)

And Jesus said this about himself: *For even the Son of Man did not come to be served, but to serve, and to give his life as a ransom for many.* (Mark 10.44–45)

Jesus paid this unspeakably high price so our debt to God would be paid and we would be forgiven of every sin we have committed and all the sins we will commit.

When Jesus hung on the cross he took upon himself your sin, and when he died, your sin was killed on that cross. In exchange for our sin, Jesus gives us his righteousness. He exchanged our black for his white, our infection for his healing, our damage for his restoration.

What we see on banners in end zones of countless football games is the most important truth the world could ever know: *For God so loved the world that he gave his one and only Son, that whoever believes in him shall not perish but have eternal life. For God did not send his Son into the world to condemn the world, but to save the world through him.* (John 3.16–17)

Or as the Apostle Paul wrote: *[God] made [Jesus] who knew no sin to be sin for us, that we might become the righteousness of God in*

Him. (2 Corinthians 5.21)

Tim Keller is right when he says, *Jesus lived the life we should have lived and died the death we should have died.*

When Jesus died on the cross *all your sins were put upon him and he paid for every one of your sins on that terrible and amazing day.* It's a done deal. It's not something that *might* happen. *It happened.* It's not something that could be, *it is.* You don't have to hope Jesus paid for your sins. He did. You don't have to plead with him to forgive you. He has.

It's a done deal. God won. Your sins are paid for, your debt erased. You are forgiven.

What is our part in receiving God's forgiveness through Jesus's sacrifice on the cross?

Ray Pritchard says there are three elements to receiving God's gift of salvation: *True saving faith involves the* ***intellect****, the* ***emotions****, and the* ***will*** *. . . Faith starts with* ***knowledge****, moves to* ***conviction****, and ends with* ***commitment****.*[176]

To receive forgiveness now and heaven forever, you need to **know some facts**, be **convinced they are true**, and then **make a decision**.

What you need to **KNOW**:

Here are the basics:

- We don't get to heaven based on our goodness. Instead, we get there only by God's grace because **no one is good enough. Our rebellion against God, expressed as sin, separates us from God**.

- Since we can't go to God, he came to us. God sent his Son, Jesus, to take the punishment we deserve for our sin. **On the cross Jesus took upon himself your sin**, and when he died,

[176]Ray Pritchard, *An Anchor for the Soul: Help for the Present, Hope for the Future* (Chicago: Moody Publishers, 2011), 123. Emphasis mine.

your sin was killed on that cross. In exchange for our sin, Jesus gives us his righteousness.

- After Jesus died on the cross **he rose again**, proving he is who he said he is, and proving his power over our greatest enemy which is death.

To solve any problem you have to understand it and then map out the solution. You and I have a problem: we are separated from God because of our sin. God provided the solution by sending his own Son to die in our place. These are the basics of what you need to know about your problem and its solution.

Do you know these facts and are you convinced they are true? If you need more convincing, ask! Ask a pastor or a friend who is close to God. Find answers to your questions. Many smart people for hundreds of years have thought about the answers to questions regarding Jesus and God's plan of salvation for us. The website *Christianity Explored* (URL below) has answers to your questions about the Bible, Christianity, etc.[177]

Once you are convinced these facts are true, you must **make a decision**.

John 3.16 says, *For God so loved the world that he gave his one and only Son, that whoever **believes** in him shall not perish but have eternal life.*

The best way I can describe what believing looks like in today's world is the airplane.

Suppose someone gave you a free ticket to Hawaii. You didn't earn this ticket. It's a free gift. But to get to Hawaii, you have to exercise tremendous faith in an airplane, which, I might remind you, is an aluminum tube hurtling through the air at 600 mph seven miles above the earth!

---

[177] https://www.christianityexplored.org/Groups/276317/CE_ORG/Tough_Questions/Tough\Questions.aspx

The reality is that you probably wouldn't hesitate to get on that plane because at some point in your life you had learned about airplanes and modern flying. You had deemed your knowledge about airplanes is trustworthy and true. You came to believe that airplanes are remarkably safe and that if you choose to fly, there is a very high probability you will safely arrive at your destination.

But no matter how much you know about flying or how much you believe in the safety of modern air travel, *You won't get to your destination unless you actually get on the airplane.*

The same is true of getting to heaven. Faith starts with **knowledge**, moves to **conviction**, and ends with **commitment**.[178]

To receive forgiveness now and heaven forever, you need to **know some things**, be **convinced they are true**, and then **make a decision.**

We have talked about some facts as revealed in the Bible about our problem (sin) and God's solution (Jesus). Do you believe those facts? Do you trust they are true?

If so, now is the time to make a decision. To be right with God you must get on the plane. To get to heaven, you have to walk down the jetway, step into the airplane and take your seat. Your trip is bought and paid for by Jesus Christ. But to get to your final destination, you have to trust the ride.

What does this look like when it comes to placing our trust in Jesus? My experience is that at some point a person's heart that has been leaning away from God *leans toward God.* When your heart leans toward God (and you will know when it does), you are saved. That moment is usually expressed with words spoken in your heart and/or verbally (see below).

Another way to think of what trusting Jesus looks like is to project your life forward to your deathbed. Think about who or what you will trust in that moment to get to you to the other side. The only right answer is Jesus.

Pritchard writes, *How much faith does it take to go to heaven? It depends. The answer is not much but all you've got. If you are willing*

[178]Ray Pritchard, *An Anchor for the Soul*, 123. Emphasis mine.

to trust Jesus Christ with as much faith as you happen to have, you can be saved.[179] I like that!

The good news is that though we are not good enough to get to heaven, Jesus is. Through his death on the cross he has taken our sins upon himself and given us his righteousness instead.

Is your heart leaning away from God or toward God?

Are you trusting your own good works to get you to heaven? Or perhaps you feel you have sinned so much God can never forgive you. You aren't good enough to get into heaven, but you have not done anything so horrendous to keep you out of heaven. Jesus paid the price for your sins (all your sins!) so you can be free and clear, forgiven and heaven-bound. (If you are struggling with God's acceptance of you, go back and re-read Days 58-63).

If you are ready to make this commitment to God, if you are ready to get on God's airplane, trusting him with your life, simply say that to him. Using your own words, express your need for his forgiveness because of your sin and your desire to accept this gift of salvation through Jesus and what he did for you.

Your prayer may be something like this:

> *Dear God, I know that I am a sinner and there is nothing that I can do to save myself. I confess my complete helplessness to forgive my own sin or to work my way to heaven. At this moment I trust Christ alone as the One who bore my sin when He died on the cross. I believe that He did all that will ever be necessary for me to stand in your holy presence. I thank you that Christ was raised from the dead as a guarantee of my own resurrection. As best as I can, I now transfer my trust to Him. I am grateful that He has promised to receive me despite my many sins and failures. Father, I take you at your word. I thank you that I can face death now that you are my Savior. Thank you for the assurance that you will walk with me through the deep valley. Thank you for hearing this prayer. In Jesus' Name. Amen.*[180]

[179]Ibid., 129.

[180]Prayer by John Barnett: https://www.crosswalk.com/faith/prayer/prayers/the-

When you come to Jesus your life changes!

Despite where you are today, God promises that when we come to him, *he will grow you into the man he always wanted you to be.* What looks to us like an ending becomes a new beginning. What looks like a funeral is a celebration of new birth. In fact, the Bible describes those who have come to him for salvation as being born again. Your spiritual birthday is today and your new life begins today! Now you will want to grow up in your faith.

Growing in your faith means that you will become more and more like Jesus. You will come to *love the things God loves and grieve the things he grieves.* You will react to the situations in your life as Jesus did—with *wisdom and peace, confidence and gentleness.*

You will come to see people as God sees them. You will live with an open hand and warm spirit. You will know what to fight and when to fight, what weapons to use and what constitutes a victory (See Day 76).

God will transform you from the inside out. He will change your desires. You will want to experience God's presence in your life through prayer, reading and consuming his Word (the Bible), being with other Christians, and serving God through your church. Following God will not be a burden but a natural outgrowth of your life as you experience more of God's love.

The best is yet to be for you. The second half of your life can be better than the first half. You have a hope and future. You will give yourself to something much bigger and far more lasting than anything you have sold out for up to now.

For specific teachings on growing in Christ, check out this website.[181]

---

sinners-prayer-4-examples.html, accessed May 12, 2018.

[181]https://www.cru.org/us/en/train-and-grow/10-basic-steps.html

To grow in Christ begin with the following steps:

1. Tell someone you have decided to follow Jesus.
2. Pray! Just talk to God. It is really simple. Don't make this complicated.
3. Read your Bible. Start with the Gospel of John in the New Testament. Start with Psalms in the Old Testament (sometimes called the Hebrew Bible).
4. Find a local church. Jump in! This is tough but you will be rewarded.
5. Be baptized. When you are ready follow Christ's command to be baptized. This happens in the local church.
6. Give. Live with an open hand and heart. Nothing will grow you like giving.

These are just beginning steps. God is so happy to have you in his kingdom!

Brennan Manning wrote, *My deepest awareness of myself is that I am deeply loved by Jesus Christ and I have done nothing to earn it or deserve it.*[182] Amen!

To see an excellent video presentation of this good news, visit the link below.[183]

[182]Brennan Manning, *The Ragamuffin Gospel*, 25.
[183]https://vimeo.com/14035242

Works Cited

Anderson, Neil T., and Joanne Anderson. 1993. *Daily in Christ: A Devotional.* Eugene, Oregon: Harvest House.

Armstrong, Kristin. 2008. *Happily Ever After: Walking with Peace and Courage Through a Year of Divorce.* New York: Faith Words.

Berry, Wendell. 1998. *The Selected Poems of Wendell Berry.* Berkeley: Counterpoint.

Blackaby, Henry, and Richard Blackaby. 2006. *Experiencing God Day by Day.* Nashville: B&H Publishing.

Bly, Robert. 2015. *Iron John: A Book About Men.* Boston, MA: Da Capo Press.

Boss, Pauline. 2000. *Ambiguous Loss: Learning to Live with Unresolved Grief.* Boston: Harvard University Press.

Briggs, J. R. 2014. *Fail: Finding Hope and Grace in The Midst of Ministry Failure.* Downers Grove: InterVarsity Press.

Brown, Brené. 2017. *Rising Strong: How the Ability to Reset Transforms the Way We Live, Love, Parent, and Lead.* New York: Random House.

Chambers, Oswald. 1992. *My Utmost for His Highest: Selections for The Year.* Uhrichsville, OH: Barbour & Co.

Clapp, Genevieve. 2000. *Divorce and New Beginnings: A Complete Guide to Recovery, Solo Parenting, Co-Parenting, and Stepfamilies.* 2nd ed. Hoboken, NJ: Wiley.

Cloud, Henry. 2008. *9 Things You Simply Must Do to Succeed in Love and Life: A Psychologist Probes the Mystery of Why Some Lives Really Work and Others Don't.* Detroit: Gale, Cengage Learning.

Cordeiro, Wayne. 2009. *Leading on Empty: Refilling Your Tank and Renewing Your Passion.* Minneapolis: Bethany House.

Cowman, L. B. 2008. *Streams in the Desert: 366 Daily Devotional Readings.* Grand Rapids: Zondervan.

Darwin, Charles. 2016. *Life and Letters of Charles Darwin.* Rare Books Club.

Descartes, René. 2015. *The Passions of The Soul: And Other Late Philosophical Writings.* Oxford: Oxford University Press.

Devine, Megan, and Mark Nepo. 2017. *It's OK That You're Not OK: Meeting Grief and Loss in a Culture That Doesn't Understand.* Boulder: Sounds True.

Donahue, Bill. 2012. *Leading Life-Changing Small Groups: Groups that Grow.* Zondervan.

Driscoll, Mark. 2013. *Who Do You Think You Are? Finding Your True Identity in Christ.* Nashville: Thomas Nelson.

Dungy, Tony, and Nathan Whitaker. 2011. *The One Year Uncommon Life Daily Challenge.* Carol Stream, IL: Tyndale House Publishers.

Eisenhower, William. 1986. ""Fearing God,"" *Christianity Today* (March).

Fisher, Bruce, and Robert Alberti. 2016. *Rebuilding: When Your Relationship Ends.* 4th ed. Oakland: New Harbinger Publications.

Foster, Richard J. 2009. *Celebration of Discipline.* New York: Harper Collins.

Greenspan, Miriam. 2011. *Healing through the Dark Emotions: the Wisdom of Grief, Fear, and Despair.* Boston: Shambhala.

Grissom, Steve, and Kathy Leonard. 2005. *Divorce Care: Hope, Help, and Healing During and After Your Divorce.* Nashville: Thomas Nelson.

Grylls, Bear. 2014. *A Survival Guide for Life: How to Achieve Your Goals, Thrive in Adversity, and Grow in Character.* New York: William Morrow.

Hecht, Jennifer Michael. 2015. *Stay: A History of Suicide and the Philosophies Against It.* New Haven: Yale University Press.

Hines, Kevin. 2013. *Cracked, Not Broken: Surviving and Thriving After a Suicide Attempt.* Lanham, MD: Rowman & Littlefield Publishers.

Instone-Brewer, David. 2003. *Divorce and Remarriage in the Church: Biblical Solutions for Pastoral Realities.* Downers Grove: InterVarsity Press.

James, John W., and Russell Friedman. 2001. *When Children Grieve: For Adults to Help Children Deal with Death, Divorce, Pet Loss, Moving, and Other Losses.* New York, NY: HarperCollins.

James, Violet. 2017. *God Restores: Prayers & Promises for Restoration.* Maximum Potential.

Keating, Thomas. 1999. *The Human Condition: Contemplation and Transformation.* New York: Paulist Press.

Keller, Tim. 2013. *Walking with God through Pain and Suffering.* New York: Penguin.

Lewis, C. S. 1992. *Poems.* San Diego: Harcourt Brace & Co.

———. 2013. *Selected Literary Essays.* New York: Cambridge University Press.

Lewis, C. S., and Walter Hooper. 1999. *The Business of Heaven: Daily Readings from the Writings of C. S. Lewis.* London: Fount.

Manning, Brennan. 2005. *The Ragamuffin Gospel: Good News for the Bedraggled, Beat-Up, and Burnt Out.* Colorado Springs: Multnomah Press.

Manning, Brennan, John Blase, and Jonathan Foreman. 2015. *Abba's Child: The Cry of the Heart for Intimate Belonging.* Colorado Springs: NavPress.

Martin, Keturah C. 2014. *Jesus Never Wastes Pain but Can Bring Eternal Gain.* Bloomington, IN: Xlibris Corp.

Martindale, Wayne, and Jerry Root, eds. 1990. *The Quotable Lewis Carol.* Stream, IL: Tyndale House Publishers.

Maxwell, John C. 2000. *Failing Forward: Turning Mistakes into Stepping-Stones for Success.* Nashville: Thomas Nelson Publishers.

———. 2007. *The Maxwell Daily Reader: 365 Days of Insight to Develop the Leader Within You and Influence Those Around You.* Nashville: Thomas Nelson.

McBride, Jean. 2016. *Talking to Children About Divorce: A Parent's Guide to Healthy Communication at Each Stage of Divorce: Expert Advice for Kids' Emotional Recovery.* San Antonio: Althea Press.

McKay, Martha Davis, Matthew, and Patrick Fannin. 2009. *Messages: The Communication Skills Book.* Oakland: New Harbinger Publications.

Moore, Thomas. 1994. *Care of the Soul: Guide for Cultivating Depth and Sacredness.* New York: HarperCollins.

Morley, Patrick. 2015. *Devotions for The Man in The Mirror.* Grand Rapids: Zondervan.

Nakken, Craig. 1988. *The Addictive Personality: Roots, Rituals, and Recovery.* Center City, MN: Hazelden.

O'Donohue, John. 2004. *Anam Ċara: A Book of Celtic Wisdom.* New York: Harper Perennial.

Pascal, Blaise. 1966. *Pensées.* Harmondsworth: Penguin Books.

Peterson, Eugene. 2006. *God's Message for Each Day: Wisdom from the Word of God.* Nashville: Thomas Nelson.

Peterson, Eugene H., Dale Larsen, and Sandy Larsen. 1996. *A Long Obedience in The Same Direction: 6 Studies for Individuals or Groups. With Guidelines for Leaders & Study Notes.* Downers Grove: InterVarsity Press.

Pritchard, Ray. 2011. *An Anchor for the Soul: Help for the Present, Hope for the Future.* Chicago: Moody Publishers.

Rees, Erik. 2006. *S.H.A.P.E.: Finding and Fulfilling Your Unique Purpose for Life.* Grand Rapids: Zondervan.

Reich, Alex J. Zautra, John W., and John Stuart Hall, eds. 2012. *Handbook of Adult Resilience.* New York: Guilford Publications.

Reivich, Karen. 2003. *The Resilience Factor: Seven Essential Skills For Overcoming Life's Inevitable Obstacles.* New York: Random House.

Rohr, Richard, Joseph Durepos, and Tom McGrath. 2010. *On the Threshold of Transformation: Daily Meditations for Men.* Chicago: Loyola Press.

Shneidman, Edwin. 1995. *The Suicidal Mind.* Oxford: Oxford University Press.

Sorge, Bob. 2010. *Secrets of the Secret Place.* Grandview, MO: Oasis House.

Stephenson, Bret. 2006. *From Boys to Men: Spiritual Rites of Passage in an Indulgent Age.* Rochester, VT: Park Street Press.

Stiles, Wayne. 2015. *Waiting on God: What to Do When God Does Nothing.* Grand Rapids: Baker Books.

Stoltz, Paul Gordon. 2014. *Grit: The New Science of What It Takes to Persevere, Flourish, Succeed.* Climb Strong Press.

Thomas, Gary. 2009. *Holy Available: What If Holiness Is About More Than What We Don't Do?* Grand Rapids: Zondervan.

Thoreau, Henry David. 2010. *Works of Henry David Thoreau.* Hustonville, KY: Golgotha Press.

Tozer, A. W. 1961. *The Knowledge of The Holy: The Attributes of God, Their Meaning in The Christian Life.* New York: Harper & Row.

Tripp, Paul David. 2014. *New Morning Mercies: A Daily Gospel Devotional.* Wheaton, IL: Crossway.

Victorious Christian Living International. 2017. "Seven Areas of Life Training." Accessed February 3. http://www.vcli.org/salt/.

Wallerstein, Judith, Julia Lewis, and Sandra Blakeslee. 2000. *The Unexpected Legacy of Divorce: A 25 Year Landmark Study.* New York: Hachette Books.

Walton, John H. 2009. *The Lost World of Genesis One: Ancient Cosmology and the Origins Debate.* Downers Grove: IVP Academic.

———. 2015. *The Lost World of Adam And Eve: Genesis 2-3 and the Human Origins Debate.* Downers Grove: IVP Academic.

Warren, Rick. 2005. *The Purpose Driven Life.* Cleveland: Findaway World.

Wicks, Robert J. 2015. *Spiritual Resilience: 30 Days to Refresh Your Soul.* Cincinnati: Franciscan Media.

Willard, Dallas. 1998. *The Divine Conspiracy: Rediscovering Our Hidden Life in God.* San Francisco: HarperSanFrancisco.

———. 1999. *Hearing God: Developing A Conversational Relationship with God.* Downers Grove: IVP Academic.

Witwer, Sean. 2016. *Divorce Recovery 101: A Step by Step Guide to Reinvent Yourself in 30 Days.* Amazon Digital Services.

Worthington, Everett L. 2003. *Forgiving and Reconciling: Bridges to Wholeness and Hope.* Downers Grove: IVP Academic.

Wright, H. Norman. 2003a. *Experiencing Divorce.* Downers Grove: InterVarsity Press.

———. 2003b. *The New Guide to Crisis and Trauma Counseling.* Ventura: Regal Books.

About the Author

Dale Brown, Ph.D., has pastored six churches in Texas and New England, lived, traveled and taught overseas and led Men's Retreats and Conferences. He has served as a chaplain with hospice, several hospitals and volunteer Fire Departments. He has taught and ministered in various prisons and has worked with sex offenders and victims. He holds a B.S. degree from the University of Texas and the M.Div. and Ph.D. degrees from Southwestern Baptist Theological Seminary. Dale has a passion to see men make a lasting impact on the world and finish well. Dale is husband to Kelly and dad to Lindsey, Davis and Aaron. Dale enjoys hiking, hunting, backpacking, guitar, swing and two-step.

Sooner or later, a beat dog bites.

Beat Dog Press

CPSIA information can be obtained
at www.ICGtesting.com
Printed in the USA
BVHW081255290719
554568BV00022B/2118/P